T0337452

Public Policy

Vast literature on public policy has emerged in recent years. However, it has been developed primarily in context of the Global North and there remains a question of whether this literature is relevant in the Southern context. Against this backdrop, this book engages with the literature on public policy in light of the experience of policy processes in India.

Policy choices in India have been shaped by the dominant narratives of their time, while being located in global discourses. These choices have been made in an overall context of the globalisation of governance and the spread of the good governance agenda. Different sectors of policy-making differ from each other in the extent to which actors have been able to influence the policy process. Policy researchers should pay attention to the dominant narratives and paradigms that influence the framing of the issue. At the same time, policy outcomes on the ground have deviated from the intended outcomes. This book presents a repertoire of concepts and theoretical frameworks that can be employed to explain the 'implementation gap'.

The literature presented in the book cuts across the disciplines of economics, political science, sociology, anthropology and management. It presents and reviews concepts, theories and theoretical frameworks that explain policy choice as well as the processes of policy-making and implementation. It studies five broad themes: basic concepts in the analysis of public policy and institutions, theories and models of policy choice and change, the drivers of policy change, processes of policy implementation and policy monitoring and evaluation.

Vishal Narain is Professor of Public Policy and Governance at the Management Development Institute Gurgaon, India. His teaching and academic interests are in the inter-disciplinary analyses of public policy processes and institutions, water governance, gender, rights and equity analyses in water management, peri-urban issues and vulnerability and adaptation to environmental change.

Public Policy

A View from the South

Vishal Narain

CAMBRIDGE
UNIVERSITY PRESS

CAMBRIDGE
UNIVERSITY PRESS

University Printing House, Cambridge cb2 8bs, United Kingdom

One Liberty Plaza, 20th Floor, New York, ny 10006, USA

477 Williamstown Road, Port Melbourne, vic 3207, Australia

314 to 321, 3rd Floor, Plot No.3, Splendor Forum, Jasola District Centre, New Delhi 110025, India

79 Anson Road, #06–04/06, Singapore 079906

Cambridge University Press is part of the University of Cambridge.

It furthers the University's mission by disseminating knowledge in the pursuit of education, learning and research at the highest international levels of excellence.

www.cambridge.org
Information on this title: www.cambridge.org/9781108429580

© Vishal Narain 2018

This publication is in copyright. Subject to statutory exception and to the provisions of relevant collective licensing agreements, no reproduction of any part may take place without the written permission of Cambridge University Press.

First published 2018

Printed in India by Rajkamal Electric Press, Kundli, Haryana.

A catalogue record for this publication is available from the British Library

ISBN 978-1-108-42958-0 Hardback
        978-1-108-45449-0 Paperback

Cambridge University Press has no responsibility for the persistence or accuracy of URLs for external or third-party internet websites referred to in this publication, and does not guarantee that any content on such websites is, or will remain, accurate or appropriate.

Contents

List of Tables

Acknowledgments

Writing a book is a good opportunity to acknowledge many debts, intellectual and personal. This book is a culmination of several years of my engagement with the subject of public policy and represents the imprint of many ideas, influences and experiences.

First of all, I owe enormous gratitude to Cambridge University Press. I thank Aditya Majumdar, Anwesha Rana and Qudsiya Ahmed for their support. I complement them for their very professional handling of the manuscript. In particular, I benefited enormously from the feedback of two anonymous reviewers on earlier drafts of chapters in this book.

I thank MDI Gurgaon for giving me the space and opportunity to engage with the subject. In 2006, when I joined the institute, I started teaching the course on Public Policy Analysis in MDI's Post-Graduate Programme in Public Policy and Management. I thank all the participants of the programme who contributed to the process of refining many of the ideas in the book.

However, my engagement with the public policy literature goes back to well before that, to my doctoral research days at Wageningen University. Linden Vincent introduced me to the Policy Sciences literature. My ideas around legal pluralism are indebted to Franz von Benda-Beckmann. Peter Mollinga introduced me to ideas around the social construction of technology. All these bodies of literature have since influenced my approach to research and teaching.

I benefited immensely from my former association with TERI and the TERI School of Advanced Studies. Interactions with Masters and Doctoral level students there provided new perspectives on the subject, and opened up new avenues for engaging with it. I thank Vikram Dayal for stimulating discussions on research and for being a friend and mentor through the years, especially the early years of my career.

The collaboration with Pranay Ranjan, SumitVij, Aman Dewan, Pratik Mishra and Aditya Kumar Singh in my research projects was instrumental in further shaping my thinking. In particular, I thank Pranay, Sumit and Aditya for lively discussions on institutions, politics and power and exchanges of relevant literature (and to Aditya also for help in generating keywords for this book!)

It is not possible to name the many farmers, bureaucrats and NGOs that I have interacted with in the course of my fieldwork and research. It is in the field and in the day-to-day experiences of people that public policy is experienced, and that is where knowledge about public policy processes is created.

My wife, Shilpa, deserves gratitude for consistent support at home and in my career. I thank my son, Gautam, for being an inspiration in his own way; for asking me questions that I do not have answers to, for pushing me out of my comfort zone. I derive great personal strength from other family bonds, especially with my sister Nishu and her husband Arvind; my nieces Shyla and Atreya are a source of great joy. Finally, I thank my parents for consistently standing by my side and encouraging me in my efforts and endeavours. Theirs is a silent support that I always cherish.

1

What is public policy?
Concepts, trends and issues

In recent years, three distinct fields of enquiry have developed that contribute
to our understanding of public policy. The first of these is the field of policy
sciences that grew in response to a call by Harold Lasswell in the 1950s, to
overcome the weaknesses of conventional disciplines in understanding the
poor record of development policy. This evolved as an inter-disciplinary field,
drawing on several disciplines. Contributions to this field came to be organised
around the journal *Policy Sciences*. The second was the field of policy studies,
that emerged as a sub-field of political science; contributions to this field of
enquiry were organised around the journals *Policy Studies Review* and *Policy
Studies Journal*. The third was the field of policy analysis, further developed by
a Ford Foundation grant in the 1990s, which began as a group of institutions
doing applied micro-economics, later broadening under the *Journal of Policy
Analysis and Management*. Policy analysis was an applied extension of micro-
economics to the study of public policy.

Each of these fields retains a distinct approach to the study of public policy.
However, they suffer from several weaknesses in terms of their applicability
to a context beyond the one in which they developed. Policy sciences, in
particular, emerged as a very inter-disciplinary field, drawing on several
concepts across disciplines. However, the large bulk of this literature is rooted
in western contexts and has been developed by western scholars. There remains
a question of whether these terms and concepts can be used to understand
public policy processes in the global South. Within the international public
policy scholarship, there is a burning question of whether tools, theories and
concepts that explain policy change developed in the north can be used to
understand policy processes in the South.

In general, efforts to understand the relevance and application of these
concepts and theories to a Third World context are lacking. There remains a
critical challenge of integrating public policy literature developed in the global

North with the policy experience of the global South. The large number of books on public policy available to Indian students are written by western authors and cater to a western context; they use examples and cases from Britain and the USA. This is of little relevance to Indian students, who need something tailored to or drawing upon an Indian context.

This gap is glaring as over the last decade, many Indian institutes, such as TERI School of Advanced Studies, New Delhi, IIM Ahmedabad, and IIM Bangalore, have launched programmes on public policy. These programmes have been targeted at mid-career civil servants. Participants are exposed to theories of the policy process that have developed in the west, but are unable to contextualise them in a Third World or Indian context. At the same time, though there are books on the public policy process in India, they predominantly describe the processes empirically. This is a valuable insight and contribution; however, the practice and theory of public policy remain disconnected.

This book seeks to bridge this gap in public policy literature; we draw upon concepts, theories and tools of public policy literature and use them to analyse the public policy experience in India. The approach is inter-disciplinary, drawing on various disciplines in the social sciences. The book does not necessarily or completely belong to any one or more of the above cited three intellectual traditions, but draws on them (and other literature that has not so far been integrated with the literature on public policy) to explain different approaches, tools, concepts and theories that are relevant to the study of public policy. These include approaches to explaining policy choice, the processes of policy formulation, implementation and evaluation.

In my experience with teaching mid-career civil servants at Management Development Institute (MDI) Gurgaon, I found that they have rich experience with public policy formulation and implementation, but need analytic or conceptual frameworks to integrate their understanding. This book is intended to give them the necessary analytic skills to accomplish this. Besides, the vast majority of participants in these programmes has a background in engineering and the natural sciences and feels uneasy with social science jargon. With no prior orientation or exposure to the social sciences, they need a reference book that can demystify the study of public policy. Public policy literature needs to be presented in a way that participants get comfortable with and enthused to learn the subject. This book is inspired by that larger objective. In the book, I also draw upon the experience of mid-career civil servants as shared in class over the last ten years of my course delivery.

Personally, this book is a reflection of my own journey and engagement with the subject of public policy. Several years of immersion in public policy literature, interface with Masters and Doctoral level students and my own experience with policy processes in the field have shaped the contents of this book. It is enriched by nuances that were brought out through my efforts at teaching this course at MDI Gurgaon, and the stimulating, and sometimes controversial, insights and debates generated in the class room; finally, it is shaped by my own research and field experiences around this fascinating subject especially in the area of water resource governance and access.

With this backdrop, this chapter provides the conceptual groundwork for the analysis of public policy and institutions. In essence, it unpacks the language of public policy and provides a review of the terms and concepts to which we revert in subsequent chapters of this book.

1.1 What is policy?

We start by asking ourselves a fundamental question: what is policy? The word 'policy' can be quite confusing since it is used loosely by different segments of society, such as academicians, practitioners, NGOs, students and policy-makers themselves, to mean different things. When we use the word 'policy', it is important to define explicitly what we mean by it and to state in what context the term is being used. A very practical implication of this is at the stage when students of public policy choose a subject for their assignments or dissertations. An understanding of what all could be taken to constitute policy is essential to understand what all might make a potential subject of research. An understanding of the various dimensions of public policy and the types of policy studies can enable students better to define the scope of their study. A discussion of the various models and theoretical frameworks for the study of policy processes can help structure such studies as well. There seems to be a (mis) understanding that all kinds of policy research should culminate in some policy prescription. It is of value for students of public policy to be aware that prescription is only one of the goals of such studies; these studies can also be policy relevant in many other ways.

Anderson (1975) defines policy as a purposive course of action followed by an actor or set of actors in dealing with a problem or matter of concern. Policy comprises decisions taken by those with responsibility for a given policy arena, and these decisions usually take the form of statements or formal positions on an issue, which are then executed by the bureaucracy (Keely and Scoones 2003).

The term 'policy' is indeed a confusing one. As noted by Hogwood and Gunn (1984), the word is used rather loosely in many different ways. First, the word 'policy' is used as a label for a field of activity. This is perhaps the broadest sense in which this word is used. This is the case when we refer to a country's health policy, foreign policy, or economic policy. The reference here is not to any specific policy statement or course of action, but to a broad field of activity. Likewise, when we refer to India's policy towards Pakistan, the reference is not necessarily to any specific statement, law, or resolution, but to a broad area or field of activity. Within this broad area or field of activity, there might be several initiatives, thrusts or changes from time to time. When we talk of a policy shift, we refer to changes in the manner in which a specific issue is approached by policy-makers over time.

The second use of the term 'policy' is as an expression of general purpose. This use occurs when we refer to a desired state of being projected in the future. Examples are party manifestos and speeches inundated with such rhetoric as 'we shall endeavour to…' or 'we shall see to it that…' or 'our policy will be to…'. This use of the word becomes very common, for instance, at election time, when political parties try to appease voters with their professed statements of intent.

A third use of 'policy' is with reference to a specific proposal, or means to achieving an end. When a Chief Minister asserts '…we shall provide subsidised rations in order to promote food security,' the reference is to a specific means to achieving an end. This use of the word 'policy' is different from the previous one, in that it is more specific. A fourth use of the term may be in reference to a specific programme. This often appears as a package of legislation, organisation and resources committed to a particular activity. If we go to a village, we may find the inhabitants referring to as 'policy' what is actually a new programme initiated by the government. Examples include a mid-day meals' scheme or a primary education programme. The words 'policy' and 'programme' are sometimes used interchangeably. In the Indian context, interventions such as the *Sarva Shiksha Abhiyaan* or *Indira Awas Yojana* would fall in this category.

A fifth use of the term is when referring to an authorisation. This is the case, for instance, when we refer to legislation – a specific act of parliament or a statutory instrument. Law is a form of policy.[1] It is a form of policy with certain characteristics that define its legitimacy.

---

1 More specifically, it could be seen as a policy instrument. We revert to this later in the chapter when we define the various types of policy instruments.

Finally, policy could refer to specific decisions of a government encapsulated in specific statements, such as, in the Indian context, the National Water Policy of 2002 or the National Forest Policy of 1988. These are not necessarily decisions in the sense that they are binding legally or otherwise, but may simply provide guidelines or directives. In a federal structure like India's, they provide a framework for state governments to make their own plans and policies modelled on them. They are specific statements of intent, describing desired states of being. These policy statements or resolutions are intended to be directives or wish-lists of what policy-makers would like to see on the ground. In essence, they are prescriptive in nature, and typically use finely crafted language and words. These words and phrases express desired states of being. Often, they are an embodiment of certain development narratives and discourses on which policy interventions are based.[2] They tend to be overly prescriptive to the point of sounding utopian and idealistic. They may often also be developed to appease the international or donor community or to attract financial resources on the strength of the state's apparent intention to implement certain reforms promoted or deemed appropriate by them.

Schneider and Ingram (1992) provide a seemingly comprehensive definition of policy, when they state policies are revealed through texts, practices, symbols and discourses; these discourses define and deliver values including goods and services as well as regulations, income, status and other positively or negatively valued attributes. This definition means that policies are not only contained in laws and regulations; once a rule or law is made, policies continue to be made as the people who implement the policy (that is, those who put those policies into effect) make decisions about who will benefit from those policies and who will shoulder burdens as a result. In studying policy, therefore, we look at the broader sweep of politics, not simply the written rules and laws themselves (Birkland 2005). This point will become clearer in subsequent chapters of this book as we look at the role that various actors play in the policy process, that is, in the processes of public policy formulation, as well as implementation. Policies are moulded and remoulded in the course of their implementation as different actors bring to them their own perceptions, interests and agenda.[3]

---

2 A discussion of narratives and discourses and how they shape public policy is provided in Chapter 3.

3 See, in particular, the discussion on the interactive model of the policy process in Chapter 2.

1.2 What is public policy?

A policy becomes a public policy when it is adopted, implemented and enforced by the institutions of the State (Dye 2002). Essentially, public policy is policy that gets its legitimacy from the State. A public policy must to some degree have been generated or at least processed within the framework of governmental procedures, influences and organisations (Hogwood and Gunn 1984). It comprises a series of patterns of related decisions to which, nevertheless, many circumstances and personal, group and organisational influences may have contributed.

It is important to note that the institutions of the State essentially provide a source of legitimacy to public policy. That is, public policy has the backing of the institutions of the State. In practice, however, many actors outside the State may have contributed to its formulation. Many more, of course, as we shall see in subsequent chapters of this book, will contribute to its implementation.

Perhaps it is from this perspective that Birkland (2005) defines public policy as an expression by the government of what it intends to do or not to do, such as a law, regulation, ruling, decision or order or a combination of these. Fischer (1995) defines public policy as a political agreement on a course of action (or inaction) designed to resolve or mitigate problems on the political agenda—economic, social, environmental, and so on. Whether public policies are arrived at through political deliberation or formal vote, they involve a specification of ends or goals to be pursued and the means (or instruments) for achieving them.

Dye (2002) expands the scope of the term 'public policy' to refer to the description and explanation of the causes and consequences of government activity. Public policy is about what governments choose to do or not to do. As Dye puts it, public policy '...is concerned with what governments do, why they do it, and what difference it makes (Dye 2002: 1).' The analysis of public policy, therefore, involves a description of the content of public policy; an analysis of the impact of social, economic and political forces on the content of public policy; an inquiry into the effect of various institutional arrangements and political processes on public policy; and, an evaluation of the consequences of public policies on society, both expected and unexpected.

A consensus definition of public policy: what makes policy 'public'?
'...There is no standard definition of public policy (Fischer 1995: 2).' Birkland (2005), however, asserts that while reaching a consensus on a definition of public policy may be difficult, the many variants of a definition of public

policy suggest that public policy-making is *public;* that is, it affects a greater variety of people and interests than do private decisions and this is what makes government decisions sometimes so controversial and frustrating, but nevertheless important. However, since it is 'public' that is the source of political authority – that is, the authority to act on the public's behalf – it is clear that the government is at the centre of efforts to make public policy.

Reviewing various definitions of public policy, Birkland (2005) identifies certain attributes that make a policy 'public', namely, that

1. The policy is made in the public's name
2. Policy is generally made or initiated by the government
3. Policy is implemented and interpreted by public and private actors
4. Policy is what the government intends to do
5. Policy is what the government chooses not to do

Public policy gets three distinctive characteristics from the government (Dye 2002). First, the government lends legitimacy to policies. Government policies are generally regarded as legal obligations that command the loyalty of citizens. People may regard the policies of other groups and associations in society, but only government policies involve legal obligations. Second, only government policies involve universality, in that only government policies may extend to all people in society. Finally, government policies monopolise coercion in society: only government can legitimately imprison violators of its policies. It is for these reasons that individuals are encouraged to work for enactment of their preferences into policy. This explains why different groups lobby with the government to formulate policies to serve their interests and to translate their intentions into specific statements of public policy. This is an activity that assumes prominence, for instance, at budget time when many interest groups lobby with the government in order to translate their preferences into public policy through the budget; the budget is an important tool of public policy that seeks to allocate financial resources in specific directions and give incentives and signals to producers and consumers to act in specific ways to pursue development goals deemed appropriate by the government.

For a policy to be meaningful, acceptable and enforced, it must have a source of legitimacy. *Legitimacy* refers to a system or basis of sanction or authority. It is a measure of political acceptability or perceived fairness. As noted above, public policy is authoritatively determined, enforced and implemented by the institutions of the State. Public policy has its legitimacy in the State; this could be contrasted, for instance, with customary law and practices that work on a system of social sanction. They derive their legitimacy from a system of social organisation and relationships. This discussion will assume greater significance in Chapter 4 of this book, when we examine the relationship of statutory and non-statutory institutions. Statutory institutions draw their legitimacy from the state while non-statutory institutions could have their legitimacy outside the institutions of the state, for instance, in social practices, norms, customs or religion. Often, this may lead to a situation of conflict; at other times, they may be mutually supportive and strengthen each other. Very often, non-statutory institutions may take precedence over statutory institutions on account of their greater social acceptance and legitimacy.

Public policy, can, of course, be implemented through different kinds of policy instruments – law, economic instruments (pricing, taxes and subsidies) as well as specific policy statements or resolutions. Each of these could be called the *tools* of public policy. They are specific, more concrete, forms through which the intentions of the government are expressed. They provide a more concrete operationalisation of government intent. State intent manifests itself through these tools. Policy choice concerns itself both with choosing among a menu of policy options as well as deciding what the most appropriate tools would be. The goals of public policy can be attained using one of these tools or a combination.

To conclude this discussion, public policy emanates from the corridors of the government, even though many actors outside the government may have a role in its shaping or coming into being, and most certainly in its implementation. In fact, a hallmark of contemporary public policy is the increasing role of non-state actors, both in the formulation as well as in the implementation of public policy. In the Indian context, this corresponds both to the pluralisation of the state (Shylendra 2004) and the rise of what is called network governance (Mathur 2008). This is an important theme discussed in Chapters 3 and 4 of this book.

Policy space

The term *policy space* can be taken to be an area or space within which governments have the freedom or autonomy to choose among a number of policy options. It could be seen as representing a menu of options from which policy choices can be made. The concept of policy space serves as an analytic construct that helps us examine the menu of options that policy-makers have to choose from and the factors that influence these choices. The concept assumes relevance when global or international commitments and pressure compel governments to make certain policy choices, curtailing their autonomy. In this case, we say that the policy space has been constrained. For instance, in Chapter 3, we demonstrate how the globalisation of governance, manifest for instance, in the rising role of international institutions, has led to an erosion of policy space in the developing world (see also Chang 2006). When nation-states lose autonomy of policy choice, we say that their policy space has been constrained. Likewise, development narratives and discourses impact upon the policy space by focusing the attention of policy-makers on specific options for action to the exclusion of others, and influence the choices for action. By presenting certain ways of intervening as superior to others, narratives and discourses eliminate certain policy options and narrow down the policy space. This concept assumes greater relevance in Chapters 2 and 3, when we explain the process of policy choice.

The expression 'crowding of policy space' on the other hand could be used to denote the existence of several policy options in a particular area of public policy formation. If we find the emergence of several policy options within an area of public policy formation, we say that the policy space has become 'crowded'. Why certain policy spaces get more crowded than others is an important issue for researchers and students of public policy.

Mainstreaming policy

Mainstreaming policy can be taken to mean making one area of public policy-making an integral part of another. Mainstreaming the environment into development policy-making, for instance, means that environmental considerations are considered in the design of policies for development. This has indeed been the major thrust of several international meetings and conferences on the environment, such as the UNCED (United Nations Conference on Environment and Development) at Rio in 1992 and the many others that have followed in its wake.

The word mainstream represents a 'dominant' mode of thought. Thus the word 'mainstreaming' is used in the public policy literature to make an issue more central to public policy and to align it with the dominant mode of thinking about the issue. Perhaps the most widespread use of the term 'mainstream' is in the context of mainstreaming gender into public policy. This means that we make a conscious effort to look at how men and women are impacted differently by public policies. Lately we have been talking about mainstreaming environmental education into school curricula. Likewise, the National Aids Control Organization (NACO), works at mainstreaming AIDS awareness into various state level programmes.[4] The rationale behind mainstreaming initiatives is that initiatives that are of a standalone nature are much less effective than when part of larger initiatives. The effectiveness of certain initiatives can be increased if they are made part of larger initiatives. But of course, what should be mainstreamed into what is a question of perspective and value judgement!

1.3 Why study public policy?

This brings us, then, to an important question, namely, why should we study public policy? The reasons for this are many, and obvious. Policies are seen as central to the development effort, particularly in the context of developing countries.[5] They are seen as crucial for directing the pace and direction of economic development and improving human well-being as well as for mobilising and allocating resources. Further, they involve and affect several actors in different capacities; this is an important reason for the wide level of interest in them. Public policies, as noted above, tend to be very wide in their reach and sweep. Besides, new laws and policies seem to serve as a 'magic charm' that provide a way out of society's ills; while existing policies serve as 'scapegoats' for poor development (von Benda-Beckmann 1989). We elaborate on each of these points below.

Steering development

Policies are seen as essential to the development effort. In particular, public policy has been seen as central to development in the context of developing economies. In the economics literature, the case for public policy is built on several grounds; for correcting market failure, protecting and enforcing property rights, maintaining law and order and mobilising and securing equitable distribution of resources (material, financial and natural) in the pursuit of economic development.

In the Indian context, especially in the earlier phases of planned economic development, State intervention was seen as being crucial for sectors having large resource requirements or long gestation periods, or for strategic and security reasons. The State was seen as an agency that would attain

---

4 I thank Ritu Shukla, participant of the third batch of the Post-Graduate Diploma Programme in Public Policy and Management at MDI Gurgaon, for bringing this observation to my notice.

5 This explains the important role assigned to the State in India and other developing countries that began their course of development after attaining independence from colonial rule. See also Narayanan (2008).

'commanding heights' in the Indian economy. Further, several of the ideals enshrined in the notions of a welfare state as well as the Directive Principles of State Policy provide a context in which public policies are understood to be formulated and which could be seen to provide a source of justification for the genesis and formulation of certain public policies.

Starting with a phase of economic reforms in 1991, that was influenced by a neo-liberal paradigm emphasising fewer controls and restrictions and a greater integration of India with the global economy, the role of the State has been subjected to both debate as well as transformation. There has been what is called in popular parlance 'a rolling back of the boundaries of the State'. However, few would question the important role of public policy itself in the changing political, social and economic environment. It is often stated that after the phase of economic reforms was initiated in 1991, the role of the State has changed from being a controller of development to its facilitator. While some of this may be little more than jargon and rhetoric, the point that needs appreciation in this context is that, in essence, the role of the State is being redefined. The contours of State involvement in economic and political activity are being reconstituted. This means that the thrust of public policy in India is gradually undergoing a change (or at least, seemingly so!)[6]

Scapegoat and magic charm

Law and policy are seen as both a 'scapegoat' and as a 'magic charm' (von Benda-Beckmann 1989). Policies are seen as a way of correcting social and economic evils–a law or policy is perceived as a 'magic charm' with that potential. At the same time, an undesirable situation in society is blamed on poor laws and policies. Thus, policy serves as a 'scapegoat' for social ills. Undesirable situations are blamed on poor policies, till a new policy or law – a new 'magic charm' – comes along. The tendency to treat law and policy as both scapegoat and magic charm lends a great prominence to, and interest in, thinking about policy. This can be seen quite commonly in the way we articulate our interest in public policy; when things go badly, we blame them on 'poor policy', and reinforce our faith in 'new policies' that are needed to correct the situation, as if the mere announcement of new policies would do much to take us closer to where we desire to be. The 'magic charm' potential of public policy can also be seen at election time when incumbent

---

6 For a more detailed and recent exposition of the changing role of the Indian State in the context of globalisation and liberalisation, see Nayar (2009).

governments draw attention to new policies that were launched, or new initiatives undertaken during the period of their tenure, that (they claim to have!) produced miraculous results. When new governments come into power, they often blame the previous government's policies for the current state of affairs, once again seeing them as 'a scapegoat'.

Affect several actors

Another reason why there is considerable interest in public policy, and perhaps the most important, is that policies involve (and affect) several actors. This includes bureaucrats, non-government organisations (NGOs), multilateral organisations, politicians, civil society, corporations and governments. Each of these actors has strong, and often divergent, interests in the policy process. As we shall see in subsequent chapters of this book, the divergence of these interests is an important factor in shaping the outcomes of public policy.

In fact, the policy process is seen as a complex political process in which there are many actors (Hill 2005). Keely and Scoones (2003) go to the extent of describing the policy process as a 'policy drama' that unfolds through a cast of characters. Each of these has a different role in the policy process and has the potential of affecting policy processes both in terms of their formulation and implementation as well as outcomes. These actors influence policies through their varying roles and capacities: as people who influence the direction and pace of policy change in processes of policy formulation, as people who are involved with policy implementation or as people who are affected by these policies (the so-called 'beneficiaries'). As we shall see in subsequent chapters of this book, several theories and models of the policy process seek to explain the interface of policy with various actors, both in the processes of public policy formulation and implementation. This, in particular, is the focus of Chapters 3 and 4. In Chapter 2, when we examine the interactive model of the policy process, we will see how policy outcomes can be extremely variable, depending upon the motivations, intentions and actions of those involved in their implementation.

Essential in a democracy

It could be argued that an understanding of policy is essential for the exercise of informed discretion by citizens in a democracy. An understanding of what the current range of public interventions is, and what its impacts are likely to be, is an essential characteristic of a vibrant democracy. Informed choices about the nature of polity and political processes can only be made in an environment where awareness and understanding of public policy is strong.

1.4 Understanding public policy processes

India is considered by many to be a policy rich country. In the over six decades of planning, we have seen policy developments in several sectors—health, education, food security, the environment and natural resources, and many others. As a matter of fact, there seems to be no dearth of policy prescription. Society, at least seemingly, knows solutions to a wide range of societal, environmental and economic problems. Much of this policy prescription takes the form of rhetoric – 'encourage civil society participation', 'price goods and services to reflect their scarcity value', 'empower citizens', 'institute accountability', 'promote decentralisation', and so on. These policy prescriptions are advocated by a wide range of actors (academics, NGOs, multilateral organisations and the media). But why then are the commonly understood solutions to problems not implemented? In other words, why do we continue to see some disenchantment with the state of affairs as regards public policy implementation?

Answering this question requires an understanding of the processes through which policies are implemented. There is often a gap between the intended and actual outcomes of policy. Models and concepts developed in the public policy literature, and discussed in subsequent chapters of this book, particularly in Chapters 2 and 3, provide a set of tools through which policy change can be analysed, and when possible, processes improved.

The analysis of policy processes acquires a new dimension in the context of emerging trends worldwide. In particular, we notice parallel trends towards internationalisation and localisation. Along a continuum between the local and global, a wide range of coalitions, networks, alliances, and connections exist, that are created by knowledge and power relationships (Keely and Scoones 2003). Policy is seen as being co-constructed across space through such particular networks and connections linking global and local sites. Policy processes are understood as being located in certain contexts shaped, for instance, by the interactions between bureaucrats and farmers. Certain forms of knowledge become embedded within organisational and institutional contexts. Understanding policy processes requires an understanding of these dimensions.

At the same time, there is a need for a critical understanding of what drives policy change. Where does policy change come from? Whose interests and agenda does it represent? Why is it that some areas see more policy developments than others? Why do some policy spaces get more 'crowded' than others? It is important for students of policy to ask not only how policies are framed, but also to examine who is included and who is excluded in the process, which actors and interests dominate, and how policy changes over time (Keely and Scoones 2003).[7]

In the Indian context, despite the presence of prominent economists to guide policy-making, a well functioning democracy that was ruled by single party governments almost uninterruptedly for about five decades and an established governance structure at the central, state and local levels, the results on the ground in terms of social and economic development have been rather disappointing (Jalan 2006). One explanation for the below expectation performance of the Indian economy has been that political priorities have tended to be distinct from those laid down by economists and experts. The reasons for this are that economic plans have not reflected political realities and aspirations. The political decision-making in our country, according to Jalan, has been driven more by special interests than by the common interests of the general public. These special interests tend to be more diverse in India than in other more developed and mature economies.

Jalan (2006) notes the existence of special regional interests not only among states but also within states, depending upon the electoral strength of the party in different parts of the state. Economic policy-making at the political level is further affected by occupational divide (e.g., farm vs. non-farm), the size of enterprise (e.g. large vs. small), caste, religion, political affiliations and other divisive factors. Thus, most of the economic benefits of specific government decisions have tended to flow to a special interest group or to distributional coalitions. These coalitions have been more interested in influencing the distribution of wealth and income in their favour rather than in the generation of additional output which has to be shared with the rest of society. These special interest groups are much more united in their approach for the protection of their interests, though they are in a minority compared to the majority who are fractured along lines of caste, class, religion, location or occupation. This, according to Jalan, is why policy development has been skewed in favour of the elite minority which has been able to influence policy development to further their interests. This makes a case for a deeper understanding of the politics of policy. Models and theories of the policy process, described in Chapters 2 and 3 of this book, give us a set of tools or conceptual lenses to understand these dynamics.

---

7 For a discussion of these issues in the water sector across the globe, see Huitema and Meijerink (2009). See also Mollinga (2008).

While this may be an important factor explaining the course and trajectory of public policy formulation in India, many failures of public policy can actually be seen to be located in the manner in which policies are implemented. Understanding policy processes, therefore, is crucial for improving the effectiveness of policy implementation. This builds a strong case for the analysis of policy processes, which is one of the key areas of focus in this book.

1.5 The policy sciences

Policy sciences is an umbrella concept and includes both knowledge *of* the policy process as well as knowledge *in* the policy process; in other words, it includes studies of both the *descriptive* and *prescriptive* dimensions of policy, respectively.

Laswell (1970) stated that policy sciences include both knowledge *of* the policy process as well as knowledge *in* the policy process. When we refer to knowledge *of* the policy process, we refer to knowledge about how policies are formulated and implemented. Knowledge *in* the policy process refers to knowledge that leads to the formulation of policies. In other words, knowledge *of* the policy process conforms to the descriptive dimensions of public policy, while knowledge *in* the policy process conforms to the prescriptive dimensions of public policy.

Knowledge in the policy process

Knowledge in the policy process refers to studies that focus on the prescriptive dimensions of policy. These studies typically take the form of research projects that culminate in some kind of policy prescriptions for governments and policy-makers to act upon. These studies are normally carried out by think-tanks that provide services in the form of advisory support to governments and policy-makers in terms of the kinds of interventions they should initiate to accomplish societal or developmental goals. They take place before the formulation of a policy so as to provide inputs into the formulation of public policy.

Placed in this category could be the research done by a number of research institutes and think-tanks in the country such as TERI (The Energy and Resources Institute, New Delhi), IGIDR (Indira Gandhi Institute for Development Research, Mumbai) and IEG (Institute of Economic Growth, New Delhi). At the international level, falling in this category is research being done by a host of institutes constituted under the CGIAR (Consultative Group on International Agricultural

Research), such as IWMI (The International Water Management Institute, Colombo) and IFPRI (The International Food Policy Research Institute, Washington, D.C.). In much of this research, the focus is on studies that give some kind of policy recommendations. This is, in fact, the usual understanding of policy analysis, namely, that it must result in some kind of policy advice or recommendations.[8] One weakness of this kind of research is that it does not unpack the process dimensions of policy, that is, the processes through which policies are formulated and implemented. Processes, so to say, remain a black box.[9] Thus, these policy prescriptions remain little more than wish-lists, in the absence of a realistic assessment of the social and political realities in which they will be implemented or the government machinery through which they will reach the intended beneficiaries.

Knowledge of the policy process

Knowledge *of* the policy process refers to studies of public policy that describe how policies are made and implemented. Such studies capture the *process* dimensions of policy. These studies can be methodologically quite challenging since they require an insiders' perspective on what drives policy change and implementation. These studies are predominantly descriptive (or qualitative) in nature, as against the prescriptive studies mentioned above. Methodologically, they may require ethnographic approaches to be employed to obtain an analysis of the processes through which policies are formulated and/or implemented.

Gordon, Lewis and Young (1997) argue that in every government, there are deep structures of policy: the implicit collection of beliefs about the aims and intentions of the departments and about the relevant actors who influence or benefit from the policy. Policy analysts are in the position of either having to accept the deep structures and the assumptions made about the problem definition and the range of possible solutions or trying to stand outside the organisational consensus and policy-makers themselves, but the

---

8 Among students of public policy, this may lead to an unhealthy obsession with making some (hurried) policy recommendations from their study. This may also lead, unfortunately, to a tendency among students as well as researchers and faculty to discount other types of studies of a policy orientation as not being policy studies, unless they result in some kind of policy prescription. This is precisely the reason why a complete understanding of the different types of studies of public policy is needed.

9 See also Mollinga (2008).

major potential contribution of social scientists lies in challenging the deep structures of policy-making. In order to realise this potential, they argue, it is important that policy studies engage in the analysis of policy processes, systems and content; a narrowly utilitarian approach to funding policy research will in itself, in the long run, be self-defeating.

It must be noted that the literature on understanding policy processes is relatively underdeveloped in the Indian context and provides an opportunity for further research, investigation and analysis. In fact, Mooij (2003) notes that interest in the study of policy processes is relatively recent. She notes that the study of policy processes in developing countries has been generated largely by interest among donors and by research institutions linked with development agencies and donors. The literature on policy processes happens to be dominated by work produced in the US and Britain, and less so by work produced in developing countries. The Overseas Development Institute (ODI), London and the Institute of Development Studies (IDS), Sussex, UK, are two academic institutes that have been engaged in producing literature on policy processes.[10] This sub-discipline draws upon several disciplines such as sociology, anthropology and political science.

As noted above, perhaps the most obvious distinction in varieties of policy analysis is in terms of explicit purpose and/or client, separating analysis 'of' policy from analysis 'for' policy (Gordon, Lewis and Young 1997). Analysis 'for' policy leans towards the prescriptive dimensions of policy; analysis that is carried out to inform policy-making. Such analysis, as we have noted above, is directed at policy-makers and governments. This type of analysis usually seeks to answer the 'what' question. What should governments do in order to address a certain issue or social problem? This type of analysis is carried out before a policy has been formulated and is intended to serve as an input in the policy-making process.

Analysis 'of' policy, on the other hand, refers to analyses of policy processes, impacts and outputs. It is typically carried out after a policy has been formulated and/or implemented. It answers the 'how' question: how has a certain policy been received by the concerned stakeholders? While analysis for policy is prescriptive in nature, telling governments what they should do, analysis of policy tends to be descriptive in nature, describing what has actually happened on the ground.

---

10 This is borne out by the large number of working papers produced by these two institutes on different dimensions of public policy processes. As examples of this output, see Mooij (2003) and Sutton (1999).

Hogwood and Gunn (1984) emphasise that the distinction between *description* (how policies are made) and *prescription* (how policies should be made) is necessary, but should not be taken too far. The defining characteristics of policy analysis as well as its novelty and value lie in its prescriptive aspect: it was the applied, socially relevant, multi-disciplinary, integrative and problem-directed nature of policy analysis that attracted many social scientists in the US and Britain in the 1960s and 1970s.

The distinction between the two is relevant, however, as a starting point for the design and conduct of studies of public policy. Thus, when we wish to carry out a study of public policy, it helps to ask ourselves this fundamental question: are we interested in the prescriptive dimensions of public policy or are we interested in the process dimensions? That is, what is our approach to engaging with the study of public policy? Conventional researchers and academics would tend to dismiss studies of policy processes as 'narrative', 'qualitative' or 'descriptive', and with limited generalizability. However, these studies are necessary to understand why policies that may be based on sound logic and theoretical foundations could be so difficult to implement. It is also worthwhile to note that these studies are likely to be engaged with by researchers of different intellectual inclinations. Economists and political scientists tend to be more interested in the prescriptive dimensions of policy while sociologists and anthropologists tend to engage more with the process dimensions.[11] Both these types of studies can usefully complement each other. The 'prescriptive' type studies are needed to understand what needs to be done while the 'process' studies help us understand why it may be so difficult to do that. The 'process' studies can give us useful insights into how the prescriptions advocated by policy scientists can be more effectively implemented, and sometimes, why they can never be so! They can also help us understand why policies fail on the ground even though they may be based on sound prescription!

Hill (2005) notes that often it may not be possible or perhaps desirable to distinguish between both of them and the two are more closely related than is conventionally thought. Besides, one may feed into another; the important issue perhaps is only to bear in mind that the two are conceptually different. This distinction, further, is useful since it may help a policy researcher or analyst to identify his own orientation and interest in or towards a particular kind of engagement with the subject of public policy. As noted above, it helps researchers and students of

---

11 For an interesting discussion of how economists and anthropologists approach policy and development issues from different perspectives, see also Bardhan (1989).

public policy to identify what kinds of studies of public policy they seek to engage with: the prescriptive dimensions of policy or the process dimensions of policy? Are we interested in analysis for policy? Or, are we interested in analysis of policy? Finally, how can the two analyses complement each other?

1.6 Types of studies of public policy

Within this broad framework of the types of policy studies, there can be different sub-types of policy studies. That is, we can further categorise the different types of policy studies as follows:

Studies of policy content

Policy content focuses on the origins, intentions and operation of policies. Analysis of policy content includes studies that have been carried out within the policy and social administration fields, of the origins, intentions and operations of specific policies (Gordon, Lewis and Young 1997). They are usually conducted for academic advancement rather than for public impact. Their goal is not usually to inform policy-makers.

Studies of policy content help us understand what the basic thrusts and contents of a policy are: what are the basic provisions, what does a law or policy postulate and what does it allow citizens and governments to do, or not to do. Note that one reason for poor implementation of a policy may simply be that it is flawed in its content, when actually the blame may be put on its implementation. There is little that can be accomplished by implementing a policy that is poorly drafted, or ambiguous. A good example of this is represented by the model groundwater bills that have been in circulation in India for over four decades. These bills essentially focus on creating a technocratic authority for imparting clearances for the installation of tubewells. Critics of this approach argue that not only is this approach difficult to implement but also fundamentally flawed in that in the absence of a property rights structure for limiting groundwater withdrawals, such an approach would not succeed in arresting the problem of groundwater depletion (Narain 1998; Saleth 1996; T. Shah 1993). [12] Given the nature of the development of groundwater, which has been mainly through the autonomous efforts of millions of individual groundwater users geographically spread over lakhs of hectares, law may not be a very potent tool

---

12 For a critique of the model groundwater bills and the general approach to limiting groundwater withdrawals in India, see Vani (2009). See also Narain (1998).

to regulate groundwater extraction. That is, even if the model groundwater bills were enacted and implemented, they would attain little in terms of addressing the problem at hand. Content analysis can give us insights into what certain policies seek to do and whether they are appropriately designed to accomplish the task at hand.

Policy monitoring and evaluation

Another form of analysis of policy is policy monitoring and evaluation that frequently takes the form of post hoc analysis of policies and programmes (Gordon, Lewis and Young 1997). Monitoring and evaluation can be aimed at providing direct results to policy-makers about the impact and effectiveness of a specific policy. Post hoc review of policy impact may be used for feasibility analysis in future policy design, via the specification of a feasible set of actions. Within this broad category, there could be studies of *policy outputs* and *outcomes*. Policy outputs refer to the physical results of a public policy delivery process while outcomes refers to the impacts of the policy in question. While monitoring policy outputs is the easier and more common practice, this means little in the absence of efforts at monitoring policy outcomes. We come back to this point in Chapter 5 of this book, where issues surrounding the monitoring and evaluation of public policy are discussed at greater length.

Policy processes

As noted above, studies of policy processes focus on the processes through which policies are formed and implemented and involve a study of the politics of policy, envisaging the balance of power among the concerned actors, in terms of who drives processes of policy change and implementation or whose interests a particular policy represents. Such studies could be useful in throwing light on why policies fail in their objectives. These kinds of studies are methodologically far more challenging and complex to undertake, and that is perhaps one reason that they are relatively underdeveloped. As noted above, studies of policy processes in India provide a fertile ground for further research and enquiry not only because such studies are needed to enhance the effectiveness of public policy implementation but also because they can be methodologically challenging and interesting. Studies of policy formulation processes can help distil who the dominant actors in the policy process are, and what strategies they employ to pursue their interests in the policy process. Studies of policy implementation can throw light on the challenges and constraints to policy implementation, and hence give direction to improving the effectiveness of public service delivery.

Policy advocacy

Policy advocacy refers to any research that terminates in the direct advocacy of a single policy, or of a group of related policies, identified as serving some end taken as valued by the researchers (Gordon, Lewis and Young 1997). Such research may be aimed at policy-makers, or may serve to challenge existing policies and appeal to rival groups or public opinion at large. This style of policy analysis is carried out by reformist pressure groups.[13]

Essentially, policy advocacy refers to a process wherein individuals or organisations lobby for certain kinds of policy change. Those engaged in policy advocacy draw the attention of governments to certain social, economic or environmental issues and press governments for action. Policy advocacy requires the skills of rhetoric, persuasion, organisation and activism (Dye 2002). It can be carried out at different levels (local, national and international). Many civil society organisations (CSOs) in India and abroad are engaged in policy advocacy. As we shall see in Chapter 3, in recent years there has been an increase in the role of large transnational NGOs that engage with policy advocacy around a large number of humanitarian and environmental issues. This constitutes an important aspect of the trend corresponding to the globalisation of governance, altering the balance of power among the State, markets and civil society at a global level.

In India, particularly over the recent years, we notice a growing role of NGOs lobbying for policy change with the government, especially around natural resource and environmental management. The kind of work done by NGOs such as Centre for Science and Environment (CSE), New Delhi under the leadership of Anil Agarwal earlier, and now Sunita Narain, would stand out as illustrations in this regard. At one stage during the writing of this book, a group of activists comprising eminent academics, environmentalists, journalists and authors had been lobbying for several months to prevent the use of the Yamuna flood-plains near Delhi for the development of the Commonwealth Village for the Commonwealth Games, scheduled to be held in the year 2010, on the grounds that it would harm the ecological health of

---

13 Individuals or organisations that engage in policy advocacy and through their efforts seek to bring about policy transitions are called change agents or policy entrepreneurs. See the discussion in Chapter 3. See also Huitema and Meijerink (2009).

the region. [14] Medha Patkar, Anna Hazare and Aruna Roy are other names that stand out in the Indian context of people who have engaged in policy advocacy around certain societal issues.

Process advocacy

Process advocacy refers to lobbying for the adoption of certain processes of policy formulation. There is an implied assumption within policy analysis that developing policy scientific knowledge about the forces shaping public policy is itself a socially relevant activity and that such analysis is a prerequisite to prescription, advocacy and activism. In India, for instance, NGOs have lobbied to make processes for policy formulation for Participatory Irrigation Management more participatory (Narain 2003a; Mollinga 2001). This resulted in the creation of platforms for dialogue between the farmers on the one hand and state governments on the other, such as *Sahayog*, founded in the state of Karnataka.

Information for policy

In this mode, the researcher's task is to provide policy-makers with information and perhaps advice (Gordon, Lewis and Young 1997). It assumes a case for action, either in terms of the introduction of a new policy or review of an existing one. It may be carried out within the research branch of a government department; by outside researchers funded by that department; or, by independently funded researchers who may choose to address their research to policy issues. As noted above, this corresponds to the prescriptive dimensions of policy and the role of the policy researcher here is akin to that of a think-tank, in terms of offering policy advice.

Studies of these different dimensions of policy are all relevant. Besides, these different categories are not necessarily water-tight compartments. They are closely related and one could precede or form a basis for the other. In fact, each of these may become relevant at a certain stage of the policy process. In a chronological sequence, for instance, process and/or policy advocacy may precede information for policy. Studies of policy content may precede studies

---

14 An important issue here is the difference between policy advocacy and lobbying. The difference is conceptually a bit thin; however, the word lobbying is generally used when certain groups try to protect their own interest by pressing governments for action. Advocacy is usually used to refer to a context when the urge is to push for policy change to further a larger societal goal. But, of course, one can question the motivation of those who engage in policy advocacy and if that serves to further their own interest or ideologies in some way, but that is how the two can be understood to be conceptually different.

of policy processes, policy impacts and evaluation studies. Each of these analyses could, further, serve as an input into another. [15]

1.7 Types of policies

In 1964, Theodore Lowi developed the classic policy types that were updated later by Ripley and Franklin (Birkland 2005). Lowi divided policies into three categories: *distributive, redistributive* and *regulatory*. Ripley and Franklin updated the typologies by further dividing regulatory policies into two categories: *protective regulatory* and *competitive regulatory*. Again, these typologies are not necessarily watertight; however, they serve as useful analytic tools in talking about the intentions of public policy. They facilitate thinking about policy in terms of the overall motivation behind it; the motivation behind these policies is the basis of their classification.

Distributive policies

Distributive policies involve the granting of some sort of benefit to a particular interest group or other well-defined, relatively small group of beneficiaries. Examples of distributive policies include agricultural subsidies and state spending on local infrastructure projects like dams, flood control systems, aviation and highways and schools. They often become a subject of debate with regard to whether their benefits reach the target beneficiaries. This has been a subject of great interest, for instance, with regard to irrigation and fertiliser subsidies in India.[16]

Regulatory policies

Regulatory policies are in general terms policies that are intended to govern the conduct of business. *Competitive* regulatory policies involve policies designed to limit the provision of goods and services to one or a few designated deliverers, chosen from a larger number of potential deliverers. These include the grants of licenses or franchises to operators in specific sectors. *Protective* regulatory policy, on the other hand, is intended to protect the public at large from the negative effects of private activity, such as consumer protection, environmental protection and public interest litigation. The telecommunication and electricity sectors, have, for several years now, been witnessing important changes with

---

15 For a further detailed analysis of the types of public policy studies, see Hogwood and Gunn (1984).

16 For a review of subsidy issues in Indian agriculture, see Gulati and Narayanan (2003).

regard to the regulatory policy environment in India, and have been the subject of much interest and debate.

Redistributive policies

Redistributive policies seek to reallocate or manipulate the allocation of wealth, resources and opportunities. Examples include welfare, civil rights for racial, religious or social minorities, aid to poor cities or schools, and the like. Redistributive policies could involve the transfer of goods and resources from the less well-off to the better-off. For this very reason, many redistributive policies tend to be controversial, since they involve a redistribution of resources. They raise important issues as well, such as those pertaining to their targeting.

Substantive and procedural policies

An alternative typology of policy is developed by James Anderson (1990) in terms of *substantive* and *procedural* policies. He defines the distinction between *substantive* and *procedural* policies in terms of what the government does vis-a-vis how it does it. *Substantive* policies refer to specific actions or policy statements by the government while *procedural* policies refer to policies that set the rules for policy-making.

Material and symbolic policies

Finally, one could distinguish between *material policies*, that provide a material or tangible benefit to people, and *symbolic policies*, which simply appeal to people's values without any resources or actual effort behind them though they do not deliver any tangible good or service. A very good example of this is provided in the work of Arora (2008) who studied the problem of groundwater depletion in the Kurukshetra belt of the state of Haryana.[17] Farmers in this region had taken to the cultivation of *saathi*, a variety of paddy that matures in 60 days. In the absence of any successful effort at limiting groundwater withdrawals, the Agriculture Department simply intervened by burning the *saathi* crop on a large scale. Apart from the destruction of the paddy crop, this intervention had some symbolic meaning for the farmers as well; namely, it was meant to give a strong signal to them that the State would not tolerate further cultivation of this crop.

---

17 Kurukshetra saw a massive groundwater boom to support the Green Revolution that took off in the mid-1960s. The stress on groundwater was further aggravated when farmers started cultivating *saathi* between the *rabi* harvest (usually around April) and the sowing of the *kharif* paddy crop that starts in July. This aggravated the stress on groundwater and accentuated the fall in the water table.

1.8 Institutions

Institutions refer to regularised patterns of interaction by which society organises itself: the rules, practices and conventions that structure human interaction. The term is wide and encompassing, and could be taken to include law, social relationships, property rights and tenurial systems, norms, beliefs, customs and codes of conduct as much as multilateral environmental agreements, international conventions and financing mechanisms. When certain practices, or patterns of interaction among individuals get regularised, we refer to it as the institutionalisation of those practices. For instance, in each culture, there are specific practices for greeting people when they meet and specific practices at the time of birth, death and marriage. These provide a stability to social interaction and some measure of certainty about what needs to be done on specific occasions. These practices are said to be institutions.

Institutions could be formal (explicit, written, often having the sanction of the State) or informal (unwritten, implied, tacit, mutually agreed upon and accepted). Formal institutions include law, international environmental agreements, bye-laws and memorandum of understanding. Informal institutions include unwritten rules, codes of conduct, beliefs and value systems.[18]

This understanding of institutions may be applied in specific contexts to denote or to refer to the principles of social organisation in that context. For instance, when this understanding of institutions is applied in the context of natural resources, the reference is to conventions and practices that structure human interaction with nature. Agarwal (1999) defines institutions as sets of formal and informal rules and norms that shape interaction of humans with each other and with nature; without them, social interaction would not be possible. Institutional arrangements could thus be defined as rules and conventions, which establish people's relationships to resources, translating interests into claims and claims into property rights.

Similarly, in the context of access to global resources such as financial resources, global technology, oceans or the atmosphere, institutions could be seen as referring to the rules, regulations and mutually accepted and understood conventions among nations that regulate access to and the use of such resources. Institutions for the management of global commons refer to rules and regulations

---

18 An alternative classification might simply be in terms of statutory and non-statutory institutions, to avoid a debate on what is 'formal' and 'informal'. See the discussion on legal pluralism in Chapter 4.

that regulate and guide access to global commons or transboundary resources such as marine and fishery resources, transboundary rivers and atmosphere (as in the context of climate change).[19] Institutions for the management of local common property resources refer to institutions that guide and regulate access to such resources as village tanks, grazing lands and pastures.

Rules and *norms* could both be considered to be part of the umbrella concept of institutions. While the distinction between rules and norms is a bit thin, rules could be considered to be directions for behaviour, which can be explicit or implicit. A norm, on the other hand, is an accepted standard or a way of behaving or doing things that most people agree with. Rules tend, more often than not, to be written or explicit while norms tend to be implied or unwritten.

An interesting aspect of the use of the term 'institutions' is that it is used across different disciplines, though the usage and meaning tend to converge. We briefly review these below.

Institutions in the New Institutional Economics

New Institutional Economics developed as a body of work to integrate a theory of institutions with neo-classical economic theory. As against the old institutional economics that emphasised the role of institutions in economic development while failing to provide a coherent theory to this effect, the new institutional economics emphasises the institutional context in which economic decisions and choices are made.

In the New Institutional Economics, institutions are defined as rules of the game in society that structure human interaction (North 1990); they could be formal as well as informal. Institutions include law, property rights, social relationships (social capital), values and belief systems. Institutions are seen as a mechanism for structuring human interaction of a repeated nature. They provide a measure of predictability to human interaction. Without institutions, social settings would be fraught with unpredictability and uncertainty.

From a new institutionalist perspective, institutions are seen as a way of reducing transaction costs inherent in human exchange. Transaction costs are the costs of information, contracting and enforcement; in other words, they are the costs of dealing with the market (North 1990). By providing a structure and predictability to human interaction of a repeated nature, institutions reduce the transaction costs inherent in such interaction.

---

19 A detailed discussion of institutions for the governance of the global commons is reserved for Chapter 3, when we talk of the context of the globalisation of governance.

Several examples of this can be found in our day-to-day lives. For instance, the reason one may want to enter into a contract with a taxi agency to drive to the office daily is to avoid the costs of having to deal with the market recurrently, in terms of searching for vehicle hire agencies (seeking information), negotiating recurrently on the terms (contracting) and making sure that the terms are honoured (enforcement). Likewise, we often hire contractors to build houses for us, or to organise parties, or approach travel and tour operators to arrange holidays for us. The basic rationale is that it saves us the hassle of organising the many activities that each of these may comprise. In other words, we lower transaction costs (the costs of dealing with the market) that we would have to incur if we were to organise these activities on our own. From a new institutionalist perspective, therefore, institutions emerge to bring stability to human interaction of a repeated nature. From this perspective, efficient institutions are those that keep transaction costs low.

Another good example of transaction costs is brokerage in real estate. At any point of time, there is a market for real estate; there are buyers and sellers. However, it can be difficult for individual buyers to look for a property on their own; this entails enormous effort in locating potential sellers, negotiating a good price, entering into a deal and then making sure that the deal is honoured. Potential sellers also face the same challenges. That is why we enter into real estate dealings through a broker. There is a market for real estate but there is a cost of dealing with the market. This cost represents the transaction cost. And the brokerage paid to property dealers and real estate agents is a measure of this transaction cost.

For a public resource agency or management organisation, transactions costs are related to its coordinating function: data collection, analysis, design and implementation of regulations, communications and conflict resolution (Hanna 1995). For individual resource users, the transaction costs of resource management may be related to participation in group activity: the cost of work time lost to meetings; time required to acquire information and communicate to other users; and, direct monetary expenditures for information, travel and communication.

The relevance of this concept to the analysis of public policy is that some policies may become less attractive once we consider the transaction costs inherent in their implementation. For instance, policies for collection of irrigation fees may not be justifiable if the costs incurred in their collection are higher than the collections themselves.[20] The challenge, then, is to find

---

20 This, in fact, turned out to be an important reason for the discontinuation of collecting irrigation fees in states such as Bihar and Odisha (Saleth 1996).

ways of lowering or subsidising the transaction costs. Alternatively, some policies may have to be abandoned when the transaction costs do not justify the gains from those policies. To what extent the transaction costs of implementing certain policies are considered in the design of public policies is, of course, an empirical question. To what extent such costs *should* guide the framing of public policies is a question of value judgement, and one that has no clear-cut answer(s).

This literature further uses concepts of marginal analysis used in traditional micro-economic theory to explain whether individuals will contribute to a collective good. The other focus in this literature, thus, is on the costs and benefits of participation and the resulting incentives for participation. It is argued that individuals make decisions with subjective assessment of the benefits they are likely to receive and the costs they are likely to bear over a reasonable period of time (Brewer et al. 1999). Benefits come through improved access to services or reduced costs of organising supplies. Organisational costs are comprised of consensus building, organising and maintaining costs. Consensus building is necessary to make members agree that an improvement in the current situation is possible and desirable, and the means to achieve it are appropriate.

In moving to a new institutional arrangement, or in forming a collective institution, transaction costs are incurred in terms of evolving consensus, convincing potential users of the benefits of participation, negotiating with the bureaucracy and establishing norms, rules and rights and obligations. Leadership, community organisers and external agents can subsidise transaction costs of collective action (Meinzen-Dick 1996). The involvement of a charismatic or trusted individual reduces the transaction costs of organising and provides assurances that make people more willing to participate in collective action (Gulati, Meinzen-Dick and Raju 1999). In reviewing some experiences from farmer participation in Indonesia, Thailand and the Philippines, for instance, Bruns (1993) views the reliance on community mobilisers to organise farmers as a state subsidy for the transaction costs of collective action. When leaders or community mobilisers bear this role, we say that the transaction costs get subsidised and participation in collective action institutions becomes more attractive.

There is a direct relationship between group size and transaction costs. Often larger groups may become financially viable; however, the transaction costs of monitoring group behaviour tend to increase as size advances (Meinzen-Dick 1996). As the size of user groups increases, the transaction costs within the group increase but transaction costs in dealing with the bureaucracy tend to diminish (Gulati, Meinzen-Dick and Raju 1999). Finding the appropriate balance between the two may often be an important issue.

New institutional economists have devoted much of their intellectual energies towards studying the relationship between institutions and economic growth. The focus of their research and contributions is on how such factors as institutional frameworks (law, property rights and systems of rules and regulations) influence the pace and pattern of economic development. Property rights and transaction costs are understood to be fundamental determinants of economic growth (North 1990). Institutional frameworks characterised by complexity have high transaction costs and retard economic growth.

According to North, economic change depends largely on 'adaptive efficiency', a society's effectiveness in creating institutions that are productive, stable, fair, and broadly accepted and, importantly, flexible enough to be changed or replaced in response to political and economic feedback. Understanding the process of economic change accounts not only for past institutional change but also for the diverse performance of present-day economies. These propositions are summarised as follows (North 2005):

1. there is a continuous interaction between institutions and organisations in the economic setting of scarcity; hence, competition is the key to institutional change
2. competition forces organisations to continually invest in new skills and knowledge to survive
3. the institutional framework provides the incentive structure that dictates the kinds of skills and knowledge perceived to have the maximum pay-off
4. perceptions are derived from the mental constructs of the players
5. the economies of scope, complementarities and network externalities of an institutional matrix make institutional change overwhelmingly incremental and path dependent

North (2006) has argued that humans have a ubiquitous drive to make their environment more predictable. Understanding economic welfare requires that we cast a net much broader than purely economic change because it is a result of changes in the quantity and quality of human beings, the stock of human knowledge particularly applied to the human command over nature and the institutional framework that defines the deliberate incentive structure of a society. A complete theory of institutional change, would, therefore, integrate theories of demographic change, stock of knowledge and institutional change.

Management of common pool resources

The New Institutional Economics explains behavioural and economic outcomes in terms of incentives generated by institutions as 'rules in use'. These institutions generate incentives for individual and group behaviour, which affect behavioural outcomes. Thus, the key to moving to an alternative set of outcomes is to alter the incentive structure facing individuals and groups. Poor outcomes are thus explained in terms of 'perverse incentives'.

These premises of new institutional economics have found wide application in the analysis of the governance and management of common pool resources, wherein institutions as 'rules in use' are seen as necessary for averting the 'tragedy of the commons (Hardin 1968).' It is argued that rational self-seeking individuals will try to maximise their gains from the use of a common pool resource (Ostrom and Gardner 1993). Given the subtractability of the resource and the difficulty of exclusion, common pool resources will be overexploited in the absence of effective rules that regulate the use of the common pool resource. Thus, the crucial determinant of a community's success in managing a resource is its ability to build institutions that internalise the externalities and the consequences of individual actions.

This idea is expressed most clearly by Ostrom and Gardner (1993) when they note that '...if exclusion is not accomplished by the design of appropriate institutional arrangements, free-riding related to the provision of the common-pool resource can be expected. After all, what rational actor would help to provide the maintenance of a resource system, if non-contributors can gain the benefits as well as contributors (Ostrom and Gardner 1993: 93).' Further, '...the resource units...that one person appropriates from a common-pool resource are not available to others. Unless institutions change the incentives facing appropriators, one can expect substantial over appropriation (Ostrom and Gardner 1993: 94).'

Ostrom and Gardner (1993) note, for instance, that maintaining an irrigation system over the long term requires immediate and costly contributions of labour or fees while benefits are hard to measure and dispersed over time and space. Whatever allocation rules that officials and/or farmers establish for an irrigation system, there is the temptation to cheat by taking more water than authorised, by taking water at an unauthorised time or by contributing less inputs than required for provision of one's given water allocation.

Under these circumstances, the case of the provision of the collective good is likened to the classic 'Prisoners Dilemma' in game theory; each user of the common-pool resource is likely to benefit as much as the other from the provision of the good. However, not being sure of whether the other user will cooperate by contributing labour and/or funds, each user feels better off not contributing and the collective good ends up being not provided, or being over appropriated. This gives rise to what is called the 'tragedy of the commons (Hardin 1968).'

Thus, the New Institutional Economists maintain that institutions or rules structuring human interaction are needed to curb opportunistic behaviour. Such behaviour may take the form of rent seeking, corruption or free riding (Ostrom 1992). In particular, there could be a strong temptation to free ride (Ostrom 2000; Tang 1991).

Ostrom (1992) identifies three levels of rule making. These include (1) Operational rules that serve as a guide to day-to-day activities; (2) Collective choice rules that regulate decision-making and conflict resolution processes; and, (3) Constitutional rules that regulate membership and define user rights. The emphasis on rules is used to explain the crafting of effective institutions. Ostrom (2000, 1996, 1990) applies these design principles to the governance of common pool resources in general, while Ostrom (1992) focuses more specifically on crafting irrigation institutions.

Further, it is argued that rule setting should be the domain of users and not just the government alone (Cernea and Meinzen-Dick 1994). When users of a common-pool resource organise themselves to devise and enforce some of their own basic rules, they tend to manage local resources more sustainably than when rules are externally imposed on them (Ostrom 2000). It is, therefore, important to involve farmers in crafting their own operational and collective choice rules. Without considerable confidence about the ability to affect outcomes, farmers will have little incentive to participate in collective efforts.

The concepts of incentives and rules are used further to explain accountability and the appropriateness of community managed irrigation systems over bureaucratically managed ones. Ostrom (1996) explains the poor performance of government-managed irrigation systems in Nepal in terms of the absence of correct incentives among bureaucrats and the staff at donor agencies. In the same setup, farmer-managed irrigation systems were found to perform better because they built in better accountability mechanisms. The results in Taiwan and Korea have been found to be different largely because the system of operations and maintenance reward engineers for drawing on local knowledge and working directly with farmers.

Tang (1991) argues that the reliance on bureaucratic systems is less effective than community managed irrigation systems that are more sensitive to local conditions. In a sample of 36 irrigation systems, it was found that rule conformance and maintenance were better in community systems than in bureaucratic systems. Similarly, they were higher, within bureaucratic systems, in those that had local farmers' organisations than those that did not. Tang's explanation of this phenomenon is that bureaucrats do not face direct accountability to the users and do not have direct access or proximity to local information. Besides, bureaucratic systems tend to impose a uniform set of operational rules on different irrigated areas regardless of specific circumstances. Community organisations, on the other hand, are characterised by a wider diversity of operational rules; furthermore, the collective choice rules in community organisations are more conducive to rule formulation, rule enforcement and official accountability than bureaucratic organisations.

Tang (1992, 1991) takes this analysis further and argues that collective outcomes depend on the physical attributes of the resource, attributes of the community and institutional arrangements. Together, these generate incentives for collective action and influence the management of common pool resources. By changing the set of rules, we change the incentive structures facing the resource users. By doing so, we influence their ability to manage the common pool resource. Also used widely in this body of work are game theoretic approaches that focus on the conditions under which cooperation is likely to take place (Bac 1998; Ostrom 2000; Seabright 1993).

A major achievement of this body of work, that grew in understanding and recognition in the 1990s, was in its emphasis on a shift from participation in natural resource management that became an important paradigm in natural resource management during the 1970s and 1980s to self-governance (Narain 2004). This literature becomes more meaningful in the broader context of the debate surrounding Hardin's 'tragedy of the commons' (Hardin 1968). While most prescriptions advocated privatisation of natural resources or their nationalisation (for a review, see Singh 1997) as a way of averting the tragedy, the New Institutional Economists emphasised the distinct possibility of effective self-governance. 'Considerable empirical evidence from field and experimental settings holds that appropriators frequently do constitute and enforce their own rules, and that these rules work (Ostrom and Gardner 1993: 96).' Through the study of community-based natural resource systems in several parts of the world, Ostrom and her colleagues furnished evidence that communities were indeed capable of crafting appropriate institutions or 'rules in use' to avert the tragedy of the commons. Other than the state and the market, there was an effective third possibility, that of community-based self-governance. This became the basis for policy prescriptions to build community-based natural resource management institutions.

Elinor Ostrom was awarded the Nobel Prize in Economics in recognition of her contribution to studies of economic governance, i.e. application of the tools and concepts of micro-economic analysis to the study of institutions for governance. Throughout the 1990s, the IAD framework (the Institutional Analysis and Development) framework dominated thinking on institutions and provided the basis for policy prescriptions for institutional reforms (getting the 'incentives' right by correcting the institutional structure). The new institutionalist school of thought, namely, that institutions affect incentives and outcomes, led to efforts at institutional (re)design and development, on the assumption that institutions could be (re)designed to affect outcomes and performance in favourable ways.

Post-institutionalism

In more recent years, however, a view has emerged that viewing institutions as a cure for poor performance can be simplistic. These criticisms come from a school of thought that has come to be called Post-institutionalism. Post-institutionalism argues that the process of institutional design has limitations because its assumptions are inadequately informed of social and political complexities. Consequently, the real outcomes of these designs do not coincide with designers' anticipations.

Essentially, Post-institutionalists argue that in assuming that institutions or 'rules in use' can correct development failures, New Institutional Economics neglects the socio-cultural and political embeddedness of institutions and the relevant actors. In other words, it ignores the social and political context in which the institutions are embedded, the wider political dynamics within the system and the social and power relations that influence institutional outcomes (Cleaver 2002; Mehta et al. 2001).

Simplistic design principles of common pool resources, for instance, often overlook ecological uncertainties, social heterogeneities and unbalanced power equations (Agrawal and Gibson 1999; Leach et al. 1999). A number of more specific criticisms of this approach to the management of common pool resources came to be noted. These include the limited view of human agency, the treatment of technology as a black box and the bracketing of social relationships of which collective action is an expression.[21]

The design school assumes the instrumentality of actors, i.e., that they 'construct' or 'design' institutions to achieve specific outcomes. Pierson

---

21 See Narain (2004).

(2000), on the other hand, notes that in practice, actors seeking conscious design of institutions may get more influenced by the conceptions of 'appropriateness' than those of 'effectiveness'. This is because actors are not only the 'resource users' but have multiple social-political identities, which influences their knowledge-base, decisions and actions (Cleaver 2002; Robbins 2000). That is, they simultaneously belong to different social and normative orders, each of which places some demand on them and their behaviour. Institutions specifically designed for a particular resource management purpose, for instance, do not remain aloof from other social norms, markets and other institutions, and this may seriously influence institutional outcomes (Kant and Berry 2005; Meinzen-Dick and Pradhan 2001).

Institutional interplay

Some insights into a critique of new institutionalist approaches come from the concept of institutional interplay.[22] Institutional interplay can be described as interaction between institutions. The concept is founded upon the premise that institutions do not work in isolation with their environment and their environment often includes other institutions.

King (1997) and Young (2000) define institutional interplay as the interactions occurring between institutions operating at the same or at different levels. Oberthür and Gehring (2003) insist that such interaction must influence the performance of at least one of the participants to differentiate it from mere co-existence of multiple institutions. They argue that institutional interaction is a cause–effect relationship between a *source institution* and *target institution*/s. Accordingly, further analysis of an interplay case must involve identification of source institution, target institutions and the causal pathways between the two through which these actions (and interactions) takes place.

Institutional or legal pluralism

Sociological and anthropological approaches to institutions focus on the regularisation of practices and codes of conduct. Giddens (1984) defines institutions as regularised practices performed over time. Institutions are seen

---

22 I thank Vrishali Ramakrishna Chaudhary, doctoral candidate at TERI School of Advanced Studies, New Delhi for bringing this concept to my notice and for directing me to this literature.

as regularised patterns of behaviour between individuals and groups in society (Leach, Mearns and Scoones 1999; Mearns 1995). Radcliff-Brown (1940) defined institutions as standardised modes of behaviour.

It is interesting to note that more than one set of rules, regulations and institutions pertaining to a field of activity may exist at the same time. This is referred to as legal pluralism (von Benda-Beckman, 1989). Legal (or institutional) pluralism is a term used to denote the co-existence of more than one legal or institutional system with regard to the same set of activities. For instance, state law may co-exist with customary law and practices, social relationships and local systems of property rights and tenurial systems. It is important to note that different institutions can co-exist at the same time with regard to the same set of activities. However, they have different bases of legitimacy. Statutory institutions draw their legitimacy from the institutions of the state while non-statutory institutions draw their legitimacy from systems of social sanction, customs or religion. To characterise a situation as being one of legal pluralism requires us to understand the different institutions, norms and practices associated with that activity as well as their bases of legitimacy. Legal pluralism is thus about the plurality of legality or the co-existence of different bases of authority or sanction.

Legal pluralism provides an analytical framework for the analysis of the interface of statutory and non-statutory institutions. A common example is the case of such natural resources as water or fisheries where customary rights may co-exist with statutory rights. Often this may lead to situations of conflict and ambiguity. Likewise, state law may come into conflict with religious laws.

Legal pluralism is pervasive and at any point of time, we can find the existence of more than one set of laws or institutions with regard to the same activity. We shall return to the subject of legal pluralism in greater detail in Chapter 4 of this book, when we examine its relevance in studying processes of policy implementation. In that chapter, we will look at how policies engendered by the institutions of the State may get diluted as they come into an interface with non-statutory institutions that may have greater force in day-to-day life. One way to understand the implementation gap is to see how statutory laws and policies interface with non-statutory institutions and get remoulded in the course of implementation. Non-statutory institutions can be socially embedded and hard to penetrate; this can come in the way of implementing statutory law and public policy.

Comparing new institutionalist and legal pluralistic perspectives on institutions

An essential point of comparison between new institutionalist and legal pluralist perspectives on institutions is the basic point of focus. New institutionalist perspectives focus on institutions or rules in use, and how they generate incentives for individual and group behaviour. That is, the focus is on an institutional framework that is understood to provide incentives for individual and group behaviour; the premise is that by changing the institutional framework, we can alter human behaviour. This premise is put to question from a legal pluralistic perspective, however, where the focus is not on the institutional framework per se, but rather on the individual who is confronted with different sets of rules, institutions and normative practices with regard to the same activity. From this perspective, then, to assume that we can change human behaviour by changing a set of rules seems somewhat simplistic. In a new institutionalist economics framework, we focus on the institutional framework per se and how it generates incentives for individual and group behaviour, whereas in legal pluralistic analysis, we focus on an individual or set of activities and the norms, practices and codes of conduct surrounding that activity or individual, the relative significance of these, as well as their relationship with each other.

In the New Institutional Economics approach to institutions, we see institutions or rules in use as a source of incentives that guide human behaviour. In legal pluralistic perspectives, institutions are seen as resources that people mobilise in the pursuit of their goals and objectives. In terms of the conceptions of human agency, the New Institutional Economics approach works with the rational, utility maximising postulate while legal pluralistic perspectives focus more on the concept of power (c.f. Giddens 1984), in terms of the capacity of individuals to act.

In terms of the relevance of these conceptual lenses for the study of public policy, New Institutional Economics has been instrumental in the prescriptive dimensions of public policy. The assumption that institutions generate incentives that influence outcomes has been the basis of policy prescriptions for institutional design and reform. A legal pluralistic analysis is more relevant while studying the descriptive dimensions of public policy, i.e., in terms of how the processes of policy implementation are shaped. When public policy or state law come to the ground, how do they interface with non-statutory institutions and how does this interface shape the policy implementation process as well as the policy outcomes ? The key differences between these two approaches to institutional analyses are summarised in Table 1.1.

Table 1.1 Comparing new institutional economics and legal pluralistic
perspectives on institutions

	New Institutional Economics	Legal Pluralism
Disciplinary affiliation of proponents	Economists, political scientists	Legal anthropologists, sociologists, lawyers, development practitioners
Perspective on institutions	Rules of the game, source of incentives for individual and group behaviour	The multiple nature of institutions, norms and practices and their relationship with each other
Focus	Institutional structure as source of incentives	The individual as confronted with different normative systems
View of human agency	Rational, utility maximisation	Concepts of action and power: the capacity to act
Role of institutions	Minimise transaction costs	Institutions are resources that individuals mobilise in the pursuit of their objectives
Key concepts and application	Free riding, opportunistic behaviour, rent-seeking, marginal costs and benefits, transaction costs	Plurality, normative orders, legitimacy, forum shopping, power, legality, extra-legality
	Sustainability of resource use, efficiency of institutions, links between institutional structure and economic development or outcomes	Conflicts over natural resources, relationship between different institutional structures, resolution of conflicts

source: compiled by author

Socio-technical perspectives on institutions

When we look at institutions from a socio-technical perspective, we essentially look at the interface of technology with institutions. This approach looks at the different ways in which institutions and technology are related. Ideas in this stream of thought point to the social shaping or construction of technology. Kloezen and Mollinga (1992) provide three ways in which this relationship manifests itself: namely, that technology has social requirements for use; technology is socially constructed; and, technology has social effects. Within studies of water governance, for instance, this approach has been applied to, among other subjects, situations of irrigation management transfer (Khanal 2003; Narain 2003a); analysis of market-oriented reforms in irrigation (Kloezen 2002); the social construction of tank irrigation technologies (Shah 2003) and of canal irrigation technology (Mollinga 2003).

This approach questions the premise that technology is socially neutral or value free; rather that it is an embodiment of societal values and belief systems. Further, that technologies are moulded and remoulded in the course of social interaction. It also provides an entry point for inter-disciplinary analyses of institutions both for social scientists and engineers. For the former, it encourages them to consider the implications of technology for the design of institutions; for the latter, it is an invitation to consider the social implications of their professional training.

When we examine institutions from a socio technical perspective, we may be interested in such issues as

1. how does the design of institutions correspond to the technology ?
2. how does technology impact upon institutions? For instance, what are the social effects of certain technological interventions?
3. how can public policy interventions aiming at the introduction of new technologies be made more effective by ensuring a fit between the technologies and prevailing institutions?

This approach can be used to inform our analyses of institutions in terms of their relationship with the technology. An important reason for institutional failure can be its misfit with the technology. Likewise, technological failures can result when we find them not to gel with institutions. For instance, an important reason for the limited impact of solar cookers was that they needed sunlight for their operation, while women did most of their cooking during early morning. Likewise, studies have shown that one reason for the limited use of hand-pumps among women was that women had certain perceptions about it that prevented them for using it for their domestic purposes (Venkateshwaran 1995). Often when government operations are computerised, they fail to meet clients' needs unless the institutional framework–the system of rules, regulations and procedures–develops to respond to and to accommodate them. Technological change can improve processes of governance, for instance, by lowering transaction costs. This has been an important reason behind the thrust on e-governance in the country.

1.9 Why are institutions important?

We now look at why an understanding of institutions is necessary to understand development and governance processes in society. Once again, we notice that the importance of institutions is recognised across different disciplines.

Institutions in the economics literature

In development economics, there were two sets of views regarding the importance of institutions for development (Platteau 2000). The first of these, led by the likes of Rostow, Simon Kuznets and Gerald Meier, held that traditional systems, structures and institutions were inimical to development, that is, in the sense pursued by modern-day developed countries and that developing countries needed a strong, external, big thrust to push developing economies out of this trap. This view was contested by the likes of Hirschman and Arthur Lewis who maintained that there was a need to build on existing developing country institutions and structures to put them on the path to development. These would themselves evolve over a period of time as countries moved to higher levels of development.

Apart from development economics, institutions are dealt with in the economics literature in the old institutional economics and the new institutional economics. The old institutional economics took as its departure point neo-classical economics that it criticised for its lack of attention to institutions.[23] It emphasised a move from the *homo economicus* assumption of neo-classical economics to *homo culturalis*; the economy was to be seen in light of the political structures under which it functioned (namely, from a political economy perspective). That is, it was considered important to understand economic behaviour as shaped by cultural and political factors, rather than by the behaviour purely of rational, utility-maximising consumers and profit-maximising firms. However, the old institutional economics remained somewhat a loose body of work sustained by the contribution of such institutional thinkers as Veblen and Ayres, and failed to integrate a coherent theory of institutions with neo-classical economics. In essence, what we understand as the old institutional economics remained a set of ideas and views regarding the role of institutions in economic development developed and advocated by several scholars that could not be brought together as a coherent body of work, or a theory.

In contrast, the distinguishing feature of the new institutional economics is that it seeks to integrate a theory of institutions with neo-classical economic

---

23 For a review, see Hodgson (2004) and Platteau (2000).

theory. The New Institutional Economics is considered to be a milestone in the evolution of institutional thought in economics; this is largely on account of its inter-disciplinary character and its perceived triumph over the old institutionalism that is criticised for its lack of coherent theory (Eggertsson 1990; Lewis 1989; Nabli and Nugent 1989; North 1990, 1986). The basic tenets of the New Institutional Economics have been discussed above; namely, that institutions emerge to minimise transaction costs (that are positive, and on which neo-classical economics was silent) and to structure human interaction. Institutions generate incentives for individual and collective action (North 1990). As noted earlier, some economies are able to grow much better than others because they have institutional structures that are more conducive to economic growth and promote economic efficiency. From this perspective, therefore, institutions are important because they structure human interaction and minimise the transaction costs inherent therein.

When India embarked on a phase of economic reforms in the early 1990s, the underlying rationale was to simplify the institutional framework and to move towards one with fewer controls, regulations and procedures. Thus, the implicit assumption was that we would be able to move towards an institutional framework that would be characterised by lower transaction costs. When after almost three decades of such reforms, foreign investors still shy from India because of the institutional framework, it is a signal that they find the cost of doing business in India (the transaction costs) very high. These are the costs of dealing with the market, in terms of cumbersome rules, regulations and procedures.

Institutions as breaks on resource degradation

This view challenges the Malthusian view about the relationship between population and resources. According to this view, population growth itself is not a threat if institutions exist to contain the stress on natural resources. Natural resource systems collapse because the institutional supports that are required to keep them in place are not up to the task (Thompson 1998). Population growth per se may not be a problem, if the right institutions are in place. This view, therefore, challenges the notion of carrying capacity and presents the possibility of 'more people, less erosion (Tiffen et al. 1994).' In essence, this view suggests that appropriate institutions can help avert the 'tragedy of the commons (Hardin 1968).'

According to this view, therefore, resource degradation is not so much a problem of anthropogenic pressure, but occurs because of inappropriate institutions. Resource systems collapse because the institutional support systems are not up to the mark. Resource degradation occurs because institutions are either not in place or break down. This view is consistent with the narrative of the tragedy of the commons described above.

Institutions and the structuration of society

Sociologists like Anthony Giddens emphasise the role of institutions in providing stability and structure to society (Giddens, 1984). Routinised patterns of action among actors, situated in time and space, lead to the structuration of society. Thus, institutions like marriage, family and others provide a structure to society. These institutions provide the rules, norms and codes of conduct that structure human interaction and provide a measure of stability to society.

Institutions as resources: the concept of social capital

This view emphasises the importance of institutions in shaping the access of people to resources. That is, there is a need to look beyond the physical availability of resources to the institutions, such as property rights and gender relations, that shape access to them. In essence, this view holds that institutional scarcity might be more important than physical scarcity. A classic example of this is provided by Mearns (1994) who notes that woodfuel scarcity in Africa is not so much a question of physical availability, but the fact that women, who collect woodfuel for homes do not have access rights to planted trees. Therefore, according to this view, it is not the physical availability of resources per se that is important; instead, it is the existence of institutions that shape access to the resource in question. That is, access to resources in society is shaped by the prevailing institutions.[24] An understanding of poverty is, therefore, incomplete without an understanding of the institutions through which access to resources is mediated.

An important aspect of institutions that scholars have begun to pay increasing attention to in several disciplines in recent years is social capital. One specific way in which institutions shape access to resources is through the concept of social capital. Though there are varying interpretations of the term, in general, social capital attempts to describe features of populations such as levels of civic participation, social networks and trust (McKenzie and

---

24 For an exposition of how water scarcity is a manifestation of institutions much more than the physical availability of water, see Mehta (2005).

Harpham 2006); such forces are said to shape the quality and quantity of social interactions and the social institutions that underpin society.

Putnam (2003) lists five characteristics of social capital: 1) community networks, voluntary, state, personal networks and density; 2) civic engagement, participation and use of civic networks; 3) local civic identity, sense of belonging, solidarity and equality with local community members; 4) reciprocity and norms of cooperation, a sense of obligation to help others and confidence in return of assistance; and, 5) trust in the community.

The concept of social capital helps us understand the role that social relationships play in accessing resources. People mobilise social relationships in the pursuit of their livelihood objectives. Rights may be defined by the State, but actual access to resources may be shaped by social relationships: the social networks in which people are located. As noted by Bourdieu (1986), an individual's social relationships allow differential access to resources and these relationships define social capital.

The relevance of social capital comes out very often while researching the strategies that resource users employ in order to improve their access to resources. For instance, while researching irrigation practices among farmers in Northwest India, one often comes across the concept of 'bhaichara' – literally meaning brotherhood (Narain 2003b). In northwest Indian irrigation systems that are protective in nature, farmers receive water through a system known as *warabandi* that allots water to farmers only on a fixed day of the week; farmers are authorised to take water for a fixed time of the day. However, this fixed time of the day and period for taking water is very inadequate relative to the farmers' requirements for water; besides, a farmer may not need water on a day when his turn falls; conversely, he may need water on a day that his turn does not fall. Farmers, therefore, exchange their time slots to suit their convenience. Though these time exchanges are prohibited under law, they are quite common and are justified on the basis of their 'bhaichara', or social relationships. The word *bhaichara* denotes a feeling of brotherhood *(bhai* is the Hindi word for brother). Thus, the term symbolises a system of mutual cooperation based on social relations. Irrigators mobilise their social relationships in order to make their water rights more effective. The concept of social capital thus helps us understand the difference between the concretisation and the materialisation of rights (Gerbrandy and Hoogendam 1996); rights may be defined by state law, but get materialised through a number of other factors, and social capital plays an important role in the materialisation of rights.

It is interesting to note that individuals use a number of terms to describe their social capital; 'bhaichara' (meaning brotherhood), 'len-den' (literally meaning give and take), 'uth-baith' (literally referring to the practice of being together); in northeast Indian states, the term used is 'jur', literally meaning cohesion, and referring here to social cohesion.[25] In studies of irrigation in Pakistan, scholars note the role of *biradari* in shaping access to water (Merry 1986 a, b). In many societies, there is a tradition of families helping each other during times of harvest. In parts of northwest India, this system is called '*dangosra*'.[26]

It is important to note, however, that social capital is a complex concept and it is difficult to consider it a single continuous variable; areas and people cannot be simply categorised as having high or low social capital; further, some scholars see social capital as an ecological phenomenon embedded between individuals, groups, and between groups and abstract bodies such as the state (McKenzie and Harpham 2006). Many of us may find the concept of social capital somewhat reductionistic: are our relationships reducible to a form of capital, is a question that we may often feel prompted to ask of ourselves, and of others.

Several factors are understood to erode social capital over a period of time. For instance, the types of urbanisation that are a consequence of globalisation may be expected to decrease social capital (McKenzie and Harpham 2006). Migration can break the bonds between people that are the substrate of social capital. McKenzie (2008) notes that social capital is easy to break down but hard to generate; rapid unplanned urbanisation, particularly undermines the development of social capital; likewise, migration to cities undermines existing social capital as well. '…if countries are to take seriously the need to avoid the health impacts of rapid urbanisation that is the consequence of globalisation, they could start by considering how to promote the maintenance of existing social capital for migrants, how to develop bridging social capital between migrant groups and how to produce urban areas with structures that allow new city migrants to be involved in local governance; rapid urbanisation may have an impact on the level of structural social capital in an area. In areas where migration is prevalent there are fewer relationships networks, associations and institutions that link people and groups together (McKenzie 2008: 373).'

The concept of social capital acquires a renewed significance in the context of current research on adaptation to climate change. As climate change affects the availability of water and other natural resources and causes increasing stresses at various levels, what role will forms of social capital play in facilitating the

---

25 This observation was brought to my notice by Navarun Varma, and I thank him for this.
26 See, for instance, Narain (2003a).

adaptation of people to climate change? Will social capital continue to provide a social glue that binds people together, enabling them to cope with adverse circumstances and enabling people to tide over their tough times, or will social capital break down under situations of extreme stress ? How can we build and strengthen social capital? These are new issues for researchers of climate change to address and will assume greater significance in the times to come.

From a perspective of governance and public policy, social capital is significant in that one of its components is civic engagement. The extent to which citizens are integrated with governance processes and formal mechanisms of decision-making is an important constituent of their social capital. Building platforms for dialogue between the state and civil society and policies for decentralisation both build social capital in so far as they create a social glue as well as provide voice to citizens and promote civic engagement.

To conclude this section of the chapter, as can be seen from the above discussion on the role of institutions, they essentially provide some structure and stability to human interaction. Without institutions, there would be chaos and uncertainty. Thus, the importance of institutions could be summarised as follows; institutions perform several important functions in society, and most importantly, they serve to

- reduce transaction costs
- constrain, or facilitate, human interaction and the process of economic change
- shape access to resources
- provide a social glue
- mediate demographic environment relationships
- lead to the structuration of society

1.10 Organic and pragmatic institutions

In the sections above we spoke about the distinction between statutory and non-statutory institutions. This distinction is on the basis of legitimacy, i.e., state based legitimacy vis-a-vis non-state based legitimacy. Another classification of institutions is on the basis of their genesis, namely, that of organic and pragmatic institutions.

This distinction was introduced by Carl Menger (1883), an Austrian economist, to denote the nature of origin of institutions. Organic institutions are the product of spontaneous social processes and could be seen as unintended results of behaviour. They are spontaneous; that is, they evolve on their own as a result of social processes. Pragmatic institutions, on the other hand, are created through social will and planned intervention. In order to classify institutions as organic or pragmatic, we need to understand the source or genesis of these institutions.

From a public policy perspective, the relationship between organic and pragmatic institutions can be a stimulating subject of research, especially in the wake of recent efforts at institutional development in a large number of sectors. An important public policy challenge is in dealing with the interface between pragmatic and organic institutions. Pragmatic institutions, in settings where organic institutions are present, can lead to situations of conflict or ambiguity. An important challenge for policy-makers engaged with institutional development is how the effectiveness of pragmatic institutions can be increased by mobilising organic institutions; how can we create synergies between them and avoid conflicts and overlap? In essence, efforts at building pragmatic institutions need to start with an appreciation of pre-existing organic institutions, in order to create synergies and avoid redundancy and duplication.[27] Local organisational structures created as a result of State policies for decentralisation are rendered ineffective or redundant when they come into interface with pre-existing non-statutory institutions.

1.11 Organisations

The term *institutions* should be distinguished from *organisations* that could be defined as bodies of individuals with a specified common objective (North 1990). Organisations could be political (political parties, governments, ministries), economic (federations of industry), social (NGOs, self-help groups) or religious (church, religious trusts) (North 2006, 1990, 1986).

Uphoff (1993) argues that institutions are complexes of norms and behaviours that persist over time by serving collectively valued purposes while organisations, whether institutions or not, are structures of recognised and accepted roles. Institutionalisation is a process and organisations become institutional over time to the extent that they enjoy status and legitimacy and for having met their normative experiences.

The relationship between institutions and organisations is multi-faceted. All organisations are governed by institutions, that is, a system of rules, regulations and codes of conduct. These institutions, as noted above, could be

---

27 An important public policy issue, for instance, in debates on decentralised natural resource management has to do with the co-existence of several local level organisations for a wide variety of sectors. This can often lead to situations of conflict and ambiguity, more so when they deal with the same natural resources. See, for instance a paper with a very interesting title, called 'How Many Committees Do I Belong To?' (Vasavada et al. 2001).

written (explicit) or unwritten (implied). All organisations function within an institutional framework; institutions generate incentives for organisations to perform. At the same time, organisations are also capable of altering the institutional framework. For instance, farmers and industrial lobbies could pressurise governments to introduce new laws, rules and regulations. All organisations are supported by institutions; without institutions, organisations could collapse. However, institutions may exist in society regardless of organisational structures around them.

North (1990) describes the difference between institutions and organisations using an analogy of a football match. In a football match, a football team is an organisation. However, the rules of the match are the institutions. When we refer to G-8 as an organisation, we refer to it as a body with a certain membership and objective(s). When we refer to it as an institution, we refer to the rules and regulations surrounding its membership and practices of decision-making. The judiciary is an institution, while the Supreme Court, High Court and *nyaya panchayats* are organisations. Much of public policy analysis, as we shall see in Chapters 3 and 4, concerns itself with this interface of organisations and institutions; how various groups interface with the institutions of the state to bring about policy change. The relationship between institutions and organisations also provides a framework for the analysis of governance processes.[28]

1.12 Distinguishing governance from management

The term 'governance' is widely used, and in fact, loosely as well. As a matter of fact, it is a 'notoriously slippery term' (Pierre and Peters 2000). It has become an umbrella concept for a wide variety of phenomena, including policy networks, public management, coordination of sectors of the economy, public-private partnerships, corporate governance and good governance as reflected in the objectives of global regulatory authorities such as the World Trade Organization (WTO) and the World Bank.

We could define 'governance' to refer to the processes through which control and power are exercised over resources. 'Power', in turn, is defined in an absolute sense and in a relative sense (Giddens 1984). In an absolute sense, 'power' is defined as a capacity to act. In a relative sense, we speak of power relationships as regularised relationships of autonomy and dependence.

The terms 'governance' and 'management' are often used interchangeably. However, it is useful, both from an academic and practical perspective, to

---

28 See also Narain (2000).

make a conceptual distinction between the two. Governance refers to the manner in which power and authority are exercised over the allocation and use of resources. This should be distinguished from management, in terms of the handling of day-to-day affairs of a country, or for that matter any organisational unit. Thus, when we talk of governance, we refer more to the exercise of control, or authority; when we talk of management, we refer more to the handling of more routine matters or the nitty-gritty of different tasks.

Nevertheless, it is common for some writings to use these terms interchangeably. For instance, the Government of India (2002) defines governance as relating to the 'management' of all such processes that in any society define the environment which permits and enables individuals to raise their capability levels, on the one hand, and provide to realise their potential and enlarge the set of available choices on the other. It envisages a predictable, open and enlightened policy-making. The approach of the Government of India (GOI 2002) to governance emphasises three aspects: 1) institutions (formal and informal); (2) delivery mechanism; and, (3) legal framework.

A distinction is drawn between governance and governing by Kooiman (1993): where governing refers to the totality of interactions in which public and private actors participate and governance refers to theoretical conceptions of governing. Stoker (1998) develops five propositions that help us articulate thinking on the concept of governance. First, governance is defined as referring to a set of institutions and actors that are drawn from but also beyond the state. Second, governance identifies the blurring of boundaries and responsibilities for tackling social and economic issues. Third, governance identifies the power dependence in relationships between institutions involved in collective action. Fourth, governance could be seen as being about autonomous self-governing networks of actors. Fifth, it recognises the capacity to get things done which does not rest on the power of government to command or use its authority. These propositions emphasise the element of power relationships and the exercise of authority inherent in the concept of governance. They also point to the increasing role of actors outside the state, a point that becomes clearer as we distinguish governance from government in the following section.

1.13 Distinguishing governance from government

Governance needs to be distinguished from government in that government is only one of the institutions through which governance is exercised. There can be alternative mechanisms for governance: State, markets, local institutions and partnerships. Where an analysis of governance may have once focused purely on the formal mechanisms of government within the State, it is now considered increasingly necessary to look at actors and mechanisms beyond the State. Thus government is no longer as central to governing processes as it once was. The activity of governing is now shared between State-based institutions and agents that extend beyond the formal boundaries of government (Higgins and Lawrence 2005). Pierre (2000) notes that alongside the powerful changes in the State's external environment, the State itself has been restructuring in ways which seem to deprive it of many of its traditional sources of power, policy capacity, institutional capabilities and legitimacy.[29]

In much of the public and political debate, governance has come to refer to sustaining co-ordination and coherence among a wide variety of actors with different purposes and objectives as political actors and institutions, corporate interests, civil society and transnational organisations. What previously were roles of the government are now seen increasingly as more common, generic societal problems which can be resolved by political institutions but also by other actors; the main point here is that political institutions no longer exercise a monopoly of the orchestration of governance. What is happening is less a decline of the State and more a process of State transformation.

Drawing on the concept of network governance, Mathur (2008) notes that governance is concerned with networks of relationships of three actors: State, market and civil society. One institution depends on another; the monopoly of public institutions in providing essential services is diluted, and the blurring of boundaries between the public and the private sector is becoming more visible. Governance, in fact, is now coming to be perceived to be an alternative to the government, to control by the State (Hirst 2000). A more extreme position is taken by Pierre (2000) who notes that governance is more palatable a concept than government that has become a slightly pejorative concept.

Paradigm shifts in governance
Conventionally, governance has been understood to be carried out through the State, market or local institutions. These correspond to the classification of alternative systems of service delivery as proposed by Mollinga and Boulding (1996): threat systems, exchange systems and integrative systems (polyarchy and bargaining), respectively. Likewise, they could be seen as corresponding

---

29 For a more elaborate account of the changing emphasis from government to governance in the Indian context, see Mathur (2008). For a perspective on the changing role of the Indian State in the context of globalisation and liberalisation, see Nayar (2009).

to Hunter's threefold classification of approaches to rural development: administrative (state), economic (market) and political (local organisations) (Hunter 1996). Finally, they correspond to Amitav Etzioni's threefold classification of organisations: coercive (state), utilitarian (market) and normative (local organisations). Esman and Uphoff list a number of criteria along which we could distinguish between governance through the State, markets and local organisations. The three differ in terms of the principal mechanism through which they work, who the decision-makers are, the guides for behaviour, criteria for decisions, systems of sanctions and the mode of operation.

At the global level, there have been paradigm shifts in thinking on governance, emphasising the relative roles of the State, markets and local institutions. Till the 1980s, there was a predominant emphasis on the State.[30] This was followed by a thinking in favour of an enhanced role of markets, in wake of the neo-liberal agenda espoused by the World Bank in the 1980s.[31] In the 1990s, emphasis shifted to crafting local institutions as the New Institutional Economists argued that there is an alternative to the State and the market, namely in the form of local institutions (see, for instance, Ostrom 1992, 1990).

At the turn of the millennium, it came to be argued that neither the State, market nor local institutions is capable of delivering on their own. On the contrary, there is a strong need for partnerships across different actors. These partnerships could be seen as a mechanism for filling governance deficits that none of the State, market or local institutions could address on their own. At the global level, this has found emphasis in such developments as the emergence of type 2 partnerships that received a thrust particularly after the Johannesburg Summit of 2002.[32] At the national level, this finds emphasis in the creation of public-private partnerships that underline the strengths of the state and corporate actors, increasingly stemming from a realisation that

---

30 As noted earlier, the reason for this perhaps was that as several countries emerged from colonial rule in the middle of the twentieth century, the State was seen to have a predominant role in mobilising and allocating resources and in steering development in certain strategic areas. See also Narayanan (2008).

31 This shift emerged largely in response to the thinking that the State had certain weaknesses in its manner of functioning and can be seen to be associated with the espousal of the 'good governance agenda' by the World Bank. A detailed discussion of this is reserved for Chapter 4 of this book. See also Mathur (2008).

32 For a review, see Narain and Nischal (2005). A more detailed discussion of the role and potential of type 2 partnerships in the context of the globalisation of governance is provided in Chapter 3.

current infrastructure challenges are of a magnitude that cannot be addressed by either on its own.[33]

1.14 Public policy challenges and shifts in India

We conclude this chapter with a brief review and discussion of major public policy issues, challenges and shifts in India. Undoubtedly, in the phase of planned economic development, there have been several achievements of public policy. Dreze and Sen (1995) note some of these that can still be considered relevant: the elimination of substantial famine, the functioning of a multi-party democratic system, and the emergence of a large scientific community. However, as they aptly point out, the task identified by Pandit Jawaharlal Nehru, India's first Prime Minister, of the 'ending of poverty and ignorance and disease and inequality of opportunity' has been limited in its achievement. Elementary education, nutritional characteristics and status, protection from illness, social security and consumption levels have been important areas of public policy that have remained unaddressed or only inadequately so.

Despite a conducive environment for the formulation and implementation of public policy, achievements on the front of social and economic development have been below expectations (Jalan 2006). The recent spate of farmer suicides in the country could be seen as evidence of the failure of public policy, as much as the backlash against land acquisitions for the development of Special Economic Zones (SEZs). The latter, however, speaks more of the top-down, prescriptive nature of policy, devoid of participatory processes, that are necessary for policy proposals to find acceptance among those affected. In my own research on the implementation of policies for land acquisition in Gurugram, I have noticed the resentment amongst peri-urban residents against the manner in which policies for land acquisition have been implemented, through their complete exclusion from the policy process (Narain 2009). The growing resentment against policies for land acquisition has been voiced and is reported widely in the local media as well as in much of the rest of the country. As noted above, it speaks of the top-down manner in which policies for land acquisition have been implemented. It is a good example of policy-making processes in developing countries that are non-inclusive and devoid of public participation. Current research on urbanisation suggests that policies for urban expansion have also deepened social inequalities, pushing the marginalised further into the periphery (Narain 2014; Roy 2004).

---

33 For a review, see Baxi and Narain (2007).

Though the expansion of social opportunities was very much the central theme in the vision that India's first Prime Minister laid out for India at the onset of her independence, this has been perhaps the most important area of failure of public policy. In particular, adult education has been an important area of failure; particularly with regard to states such as Bihar, Uttar Pradesh, Arunachal Pradesh and Jammu and Kashmir where the adult literacy rate still remains well below the national average.

The eradication of poverty and unemployment has been another prominent area of concern (Natraj 2002). It is widely believed that the growth of employment has not kept pace with the growth of economic output. As a result of the globalisation- liberalisation paradigm embraced by India in the early 1990s, economic growth has occurred, but this has not been consistent. There are wide differences of opinion on whether the position of the poor has improved in the post-liberalisation era. Further, Dreze and Sen (1995) noted that in the field of basic education, India has been left behind by countries that have not done better than India in many other developmental achievements, such as Ghana, Indonesia, Kenya, Myanmar, and the Philippines. This, they point out, has to do with not only the nature of government intervention but also the nature of public discussion. In the era post 1991, much more energy has been spent debating the pros and cons of liberalisation than on the expansion of social opportunities that would enable the country's citizens to participate in the opportunities thrown up by the liberalisation of the Indian economy.

Public policy shifts in India

There have been several important public policy shifts in India over the last two decades. Of these perhaps the most important has been the adoption of the globalisation-liberalisation paradigm in the early 1990s that was made essential partly by internal economic circumstances and partly by external pressure and multilateral persuasion. Fiscal profligacy, populism, the lack of will to pursue policies which would through austere measures raise the domestic savings and a propensity to indulge the consumerist class and pampering the big farm lobby, all these factors are known to have culminated in the economic crisis of 1991 (Natraj 2002). The case for a *dirigiste* regime was further diluted by the collapse of the Soviet Union. To this added the anxiety of the West to ensure free trade to escape from the recession affecting those countries; besides, there was evidence in India of affluent sections advocating that the economy should be linked with the outside world.

Among the principal actors influencing public policy shifts today in India are the environmental movement, the rise of NGOs and the judiciary. An important change in terms of federal relationships has been that the locus of power has shifted towards states; in part this is due to the virtual disappearance of one-party, strong government at the centre, that prevailed till the first five decades of planning. Further, the institution of the State has contributed to discredit through corruption and inefficiency. Even the initial moves towards a more liberalised economy led to the argument that the State ought to step aside from the activities which it was not equipped to perform. The collapse of the Soviet Union and the dilution of State role in the wake of the neo-liberal agenda of the 1980s led to a weakening of faith in the potential role of the State. This period also saw in India the strengthening of the movement in favour of decentralisation through the institution of local government and a renewed faith in the potential of Panchayati Raj Institutions. Both these trends have been articulated since the 1980s. This has been paralleled by the emergence of a growing section of people who question 1) state initiation and sponsorship, 2) mega scale projects, and, 3) the primacy of science and technology. The confluence of these three has lead to the emergence of what is called by some as the Alternative Development Paradigm or ADP, that has questioned conventional approaches to development and public policy formulation.

Another issue with regard to the role of different actors in the policy process in India concerns the relative roles of the three arms of the State, namely, the judiciary, legislature and executive. In particular, there has been some interest in the role of the Supreme Court in policy formulation; recent years have seen a great deal of interest in the role of the judiciary in the public policy process. The debates have centred round how this role has tended to fill a void left in by a weak and ineffective executive arm of the government.

The common perception, in the case of air quality improvements, for instance, generated in large part by media coverage was that improvements happened through air quality practices that were prescribed by the Supreme Court and not by an institution with the mandate for making environmental policy. Research into the policy formulation processes by Narain and Bell (2006), however, shows that the government indeed was intimately involved in the policy process and the Supreme Court's role was mainly to force the government to implement previously announced policies. The policies ordered by the court were, as a matter of fact, suggested by the EPCA, a representative body of the central government. EPCA's policy recommendation, in turn, built directly on policies formulated and announced by the Delhi Government and the Ministry of Environment and Forests. This study made a convincing case for understanding policy processes, in that the Delhi air quality improvement case was cited for other State governments to follow as well.

Is public policy based on studies of public policy ?

An important issue for debate and consideration is the role that studies of public policy play in influencing policy development. The question is: Is public policy based on policy research? Does research on public policy play a role in the shaping of public policy?

In the Indian context, the Constitution of India and legislation make some policy pronouncements and our five-year plans have involved some analysis about resource allocation and investment decisions (Ganapathy 1985). Several committees and government statements in the form of white papers, resolutions, and other such statements are produced by the government from time to time that include some measure of the analysis of different policies. Nevertheless, Ganapathy (1985) notes that historically, some major policy issues such as exchange allocation, subsidies or prohibition have hardly been influenced by policy analysis. In fact, evidence seems to suggest that in practice, policy analysis has been only a minor determinant of policy-making. Other more important determinants have tended to be the context, leadership, the politics of the bureaucracy, legislature and interest groups, as well as the legislative and public image generated by the media about policy issues.

Mazoomdar (1996) notes the poor capacity for policy analysis to have been an important deficiency in India's planning machinery. Another, more academic but relevant concern about policy analysis is that it has tended to become a commodity, requiring specialised skill sets that only a few are trained to use, and who influence public policy. It has become a professionalised, technical activity that needs to be demystified. Thus, more policy analysis in the present context may not necessarily mean better policy-making.

The question of whether public policy formulation in India is based on policy analysis was posed to participants in the Post-Graduate Diploma Programme in Public Policy and Management offered by the School of Public Policy and Governance at the MDI Gurgaon. A strong sentiment expressed in response was that policy-making is increasingly coming to be based on policy analysis, though the experience varies across sectors and organisations. Participants representing organisations from such sectors as agriculture and railways as well as the Planning Commission seemed to voice more strongly that public policy was based on policy analysis. At the same time, it is important to keep in mind that some areas of public policy formulation have longer gestation periods than others and that affects the room for policy-making being based on research. In such areas as finance, for instance, pressures to act at the spur of the moment might be more acute and that may not allow enough time for conducting or commissioning research to influence public policy. However, there was also a strong sentiment that more often than not, policy research gets side-stepped by political considerations.[34]

It was felt among the participants that there is a strong inclination towards the 'prescriptive' dimensions of public policy, than the 'process' or descriptive dimensions. There is a leaning in favour of analysis 'for' policy, rather than analysis 'of' policy. Analysis 'of' policy seems to have been much more difficult, not only methodologically, since it requires getting behind the scenes to unpack underlying processes of policy formulation and implementation but also because it may not always be politically expedient, since it involves many stakeholders. It requires stronger political will to engage with segments of people that may be critical of government policies. Nevertheless, over time, one could notice a shift in favour of analysis 'of' policy.

It also seemed from the responses that there appears to be a greater concern with outlays, outputs and outcomes (in that order); this could, indeed, be cited as an important reason for the limited impact of public policy. Outlays and outputs are easier to map and monitor since they are tangible in the sense of being visible physically. Policy outcomes are much more difficult to assess, since, among other things, they have longer gestation periods. Besides, gauging policy outcomes requires interacting with diverse stakeholders that may be difficult or politically not expedient, with inbuilt risks of exposing failures and vulnerabilities.

An important issue raised among some of the participants was that in most government departments, there is a mechanism in place to capitalise on policy research, but it is not used effectively. To that extent, there is need for a greater interface between researchers and policy-makers, both at the individual level and the institutional level. This requires some forum where policy-makers and researchers can interact with each other on an institutionalised basis. In other words, there is need to institutionalise the relationship between studies of public policy and policy-making.

---

34 See also the discussion on incrementalism in Chapter 3, where we note that instead of basing policy choices on a systematic study of the available alternatives, policy-makers may simply choose options that are marginally different from the existing ones because it is politically expedient to do so.

1.15 Conclusion

In this chapter, we have reviewed some basic concepts that students of public policy need to be familiar with. We started the chapter by discussing the rationale for the analysis of public policy; in particular, the need for a deeper understanding of public policy processes. We examined the distinction between the process and prescriptive dimensions of public policy, while highlighting that both are relevant and essential. We also reviewed the various types of policy studies that scholars of public policy may engage with. An understanding of the various types of policy studies helps students of public policy define the scope of their work more clearly and also serves to make them more sympathetic to different types of policy studies that may be carried out.

We reviewed the paradigm shifts in thinking on appropriate forms of governance and the shifting emphasis from State to markets, local institutions and partnerships. These shifts provide a context for the analysis of public policy processes. In the latter part of the chapter, we reviewed some important shifts within the public policy context of India, as well as the drivers of those shifts in terms of the major actors that are influencing policy development. Finally, we examined an important question of whether policy formation is indeed based on policy analysis. This chapter has thus provided us with a foundation for the study of public policy. In subsequent chapters, we pay more attention to models, tools and concepts that help us theorise about and articulate the policy process.

References

Agrawal, A. and Gibson, C. C. 1999. 'Enchantment and Disenchantment. The Role of Community in Natural Resource Conservation.' *World Development* 27(4): 629–649.

Allison, G. T. 1971. *Essence of Decision*. Boston: Little, Brown.

Anderson, J. E. 1975. *Public Policy-making: Basic Concepts in Political Science*. New York: Praeger University Series.

Arora, R. K. 2008. 'Leadership and Collective Action – A Case Study in Common Property Resources Management in Haryana.' P. G. Diploma Dissertation, Management Development Institute, Gurgaon.

Bac, M. 1998. 'Property Rights Regimes and the Management of Resources.' *Natural Resources Forum* 22(4): 263–269.

Bardhan, P. 1989. *Conversations Between Economists and Anthropologists: Methodological Issues in Measuring Economic Change in Rural India*. New Delhi: Oxford University Press.

Baxi, C. V. and Narain, V. 2007. 'Public-private Partnerships: A Review of Literature and Evidence.' MDI Working Paper Series No. 003, Management Development Institute, Gurgaon.

Benda-Beckmann, F. von. 1989. 'Scape-goat and Magic Charm: Law in Development Theory and Practice.' *Journal of Legal Pluralism and Unofficial Law* 28: 129–149.

Birkland, T. A. 2005. *An Introduction to the Policy Process: Theories, Concepts and Models of Public Policy-Making.* Second edition. New York: M.E. Sharpe.

Bourdieu, P. 1986. *Forms of Social Capital.* New York: Free Press.

Brewer, J., Kolavalli, S., Kalro, A. H., Naik, G., Ramnarayan S., Raju, K. V., and Sakthivadivel, R. 1999. *Irrigation Management Transfer in India: Policies, Processes, and Performance.* New Delhi and Calcutta: Oxford and IBH Publishing Company.

Bruns, R. 1993. 'Promoting Participation in Irrigation: Reflections on Experience in South East Asia.' *World Development* 21(1): 1837–1849.

Cernea, M. M. and Meinzen-Dick, R. 1994. *Design for Water Users Associations: Organizational Characteristics.* ODI-Irrigation Management Network. Network Paper 30. Overseas Development Institute, U.K.

Cleaver, F. 2002. 'Reinventing Institutions: Bricolage and the Social Embeddedness of Natural Resource Management.' *The European Journal of Development* 14(2): 11–30.

Confederation of Indian Industry. 2005. 'PPPs in Infrastructure in Southern States- Issues and Concerns.' CII Policy Primer No.5, January.

De Janvry, A., Sadoulet, E. and Thorbecke, E. 1993. 'State, Market and Civil Society Organizations: New Theories, New Practices and Their Implications for Rural Development: Introduction.' *World Development* 21(4): 565–575.

Dreze, J. and Sen, A. 1995. *India: Economic Development and Social Opportunity.* New Delhi: Oxford University Press.

Dye, T. R. 2002. *Understanding Public Policy.* Tenth edition. Delhi: Pearson Education.

Eggertsson, T. 1990. *Economic Behavior and Institutions.* Cambridge: Cambridge University Press.

Esman, M. J. and Uphoff, N. T. 1984. *Local Organizations as Intermediaries in Rural Development.* Ithaca: Cornell University Press.

Fischer, F. 1995. *Evaluating Public Policy.* Wadsworth: Thomson.

Ganapathy, R. S. 1985. 'On Methodologies for Policy Analysis.' In *Public Policy and Policy Analysis in India,* edited by R. S. Ganapathy, S. R. Ganesh, R. M. Maru, S. Paul and R. M. Rao, 30–48. New Delhi: Sage Publications.

Geddes, M. 2005. *Making Public Private Partnerships Work. Building Relationships and Understanding Cultures*. Burlington: Gower.

Gerbrandy, G. and Hoogendam, P. 1996. 'The Materialization of Water Rights: Hydraulic Property in the Extension and Rehabilitation of Two Irrigation Systems in Bolivia. In *Crops, People and Irrigation*, edited by G. Diemer and F. P. Huibers, 53–72. London: Intermediate Technology Publications.

Giddens, A. 1984. *The Constitution of Society: Outline of the Theory of Structuration*. Cambridge: Polity Press.

Gordon, I., Lewis, J. and Young, K. 1997. 'Perspectives on Policy Analysis.' In *The Policy Process: A Reader*, edited by M. Hill, 5–9. New York and London: Routledge.

Government of India. 2002. *Tenth Five Year Plan 2002-2007: State Plans, Trends, Concerns, and Strategies*, Vol. 3. New Delhi: Planning Commission.

Grumm, John G. 1975. 'The Analysis of Policy Impact.' In *Policies and Policy: Making Handbook of Political Science*, Vol. 6, edited by Fred Greenstein and Nelson Polsby, 439–473. Reading, Mass.: Addison Wesley.

Gulati, A. and Narayanan, S. 2003. *The Subsidy Syndrome in Indian Agriculture*. New Delhi: Oxford University Press.

Gulati, A., Meinzen-Dick, R. and Raju, K. V. 1999. *From Top-down to Bottoms up: Institutional Reform in Indian Canal Irrigation*. Mimeo. National workshop on institutional reforms in canal irrigation. Delhi: Institute of Economic Growth.

Hanna, S. 1995. 'Efficiencies of User Participation in Natural Resource Management.' In *Property Rights and the Environment: Social and Ecological Issues*, edited by S. Hanna and M. Munasinghe, 60–67. The Beijer Institute of Ecological Economics and the World Bank. Washington, D.C. The World Bank.

Hardin, G. 1968. 'Tragedy of the Commons,' *Science* 162 (3589): 1243–1248.

Heiler, Terry. 2002. Public and Private Sector Partnerships- Review of International Models and Experiences. MAF Technical paper No: 2002/09. Prepared for MAF Policy.

Higgins, V. and Lawrence, G. 2005. 'Introduction. Globalization and Agricultural Governance.' In *Agricultural Governance: Globalization and the New Politics of Regulation*, edited by V. Higgins and G. Lawrence, 1–15. London & New York: Routledge.

Hill, M. 2005. *Public Policy Process*. Fourth edition. Harlow: Pearson Education.

Hirst, P. 2000. 'Democracy and Governance.' In *Debating Governance: Authority, Steering and Democracy*, edited by J. Pierre, 13–35. New York: Oxford University Press.

Hodgson, G. M. 2004. *The Evolution of Institutional Economics: Agency, Structure and Darwininism in American Institutionalism*. London and New York: Routledge.

Hogwood, B. A. and Gunn, L. A. 1984. *Policy Analysis for the Real World*. Oxford: Oxford University Press.

Huitema, D. and Meijerink, S. eds. 2009. *Water Policy Entrepreneurs: A Research Companion to Water Transitions Around the Globe*. Cheltenham: Edward Elgar.

Hunter, J. and Lewis, C. M. eds. 1989. *The New Institutional Economics and Third World Development*. London: Routledge.

Jalan, B. 2006. 'Economics, Politics and Governance.' In *India in a Globalizing World. Some Aspects of Macroeconomy, Agriculture and Poverty. Essays in Honor of C.H. Hanumantha Rao*, edited by R. Radhakrishna, S. K. Rao, S. M. Dev and K. Subbarao, 125–134. New Delhi: Academic Foundation.

Kant, S. and Berry, A. 2005. 'Organizations, Institutions, External Setting and Institutional Dynamics.' In *Institutions, Sustainability, and Natural Resources: Institutions for Sustainable Forest Management*, edited by S. Kant and A. Berry, 83–114. Dordrecht: Springer.

Keeley, J. and Scoones, I. 2003. *Understanding Environmental Policy Processes: Cases from Africa*. London: Earthscan.

Khanal, P. R. 2003. *Engineering Participation*. Hyderabad: Orient Longman.

King, L. 1997. 'Institutional interplay: Research Questions.' Background paper. Institutional Dimensions of Global Change, International Human Dimensions Programme (IHDP), Bonn, Germany.

Kloezen, W. and Mollinga, P. P. 1992. 'Opening Closed Gates: Recognizing the Social Nature of Irrigation Artifacts.' In *Irrigators and Engineers*, edited by G. Diemer and J. Slabbers 53–64. Amsterdam: Thesis Publishers.

Kloezen, W. M. 2002. 'Accounting for Water. Institutional Viability and Impacts of Market-oriented Irrigation Interventions in Central Mexico.' PhD dissertation, Wageningen University, The Netherlands.

Kolavalli, S. 1996. 'User Participation and Incentives to Perform in Indian Irrigation Systems.' Center for Management in Agriculture. Indian Institute of Management, Ahmedabad.

Kooiman, J. ed. 1993. *Modern Governance: Government-society Interactions*. London: Sage Publications.

Lasswell, H. 1970. 'The Emerging Conception of the Policy Sciences', *Policy Sciences* 1: 3–14.

Leach, M., Mearns, R. and Scoones, I. 1999. 'Environmental Entitlements: Dynamics and Institutions in Community-based Natural Resource Management.' *World Development* 27(2): 225–247.

Leitch, S. and Motion, J. 2003. 'Public-Private Partnerships: Consultation, Cooperation and Collusion.' *Journal of Public Affairs* 3(3): 273–278.

Lewis, C. M. 1989. 'Introduction: Development and Significance of NIE.' In *The New Institutional Economics and Third World Development*, edited by J. Harriss, J. Hunter and C. M. Lewis, 1–13. London: Routledge.

Linder, S. H. 1999. 'Coming to Terms with the Public-Private Partnership.' *American Behavioural Scientist* 43(1): 35–51.

McKenzie, K. and Harpham, T. 2006. *Social Capital and Mental Health*. London: Jessica Kingsley Publishers.

McKenzie, K. 2008. 'Urbanization, Social Capital and Mental Health.' *Global Social Policy* 8(3): 359–377.

Mathur, K. 2008. *From Government to Governance: A Brief Survey of the Indian Experience*. New Delhi: National Book Trust.

Mazoomdar, A. 1996. 'The Rise and Decline of Development Planning in India.' In *Development Policy and Administration: Readings in Indian Government and* Politics, edited by K. Mathur, 41–84. New Delhi: Sage Publications.

Mearns, R. 1995. 'Institutions in Natural Resource Management: Access To and Control Over Woodfuel in East Africa.' In *People and Environment in Africa*, edited by T. Binns, 103–114. Chichester: Jon Wiley and Sons.

Mehta, L. 2005. *The Politics and Poetics of Water. Naturalising Water Scarcity in Western India*. Hyderabad: Orient Longman.

Mehta, L., Leach, M. and Scoones, I. 2001. 'Environmental Governance in an Uncertain World.' *IDS Bulletin* 32(4): 1–9.

Meinzen-Dick, R. and Pradhan, R. 2001. 'Implications of Legal Pluralism for Natural Resource Management.' *IDS Bulletin* 32(4): 10–17.

Menger, C. 1883. *Problems of Economics and Sociology*. Translated by James Dingwell and F. Bert. New York: New York University Press.

Merry, D. J. 1986a. 'Reorganising Irrigation: Local Level Management in the Punjab (Pakistan).' In *Irrigation Management in Pakistan: Four Papers*, by D. J. Merry and J. Wolf, 26–43. Colombo: International Irrigation Management Institute.

Merry, D. J. 1986b. 'The Sociology of Warabandi: A Case Study from

Pakistan.' In *Irrigation Management in Pakistan: Four Papers*, by D. J. Merry and J. Wolf, 44–61, IIMI Research Paper No. 4. Colombo: International Irrigation Management Institute.

Mollinga, P. P. 2001. 'Power in Motion: A Critical Assessment of Canal Irrigation Reform, With a Focus on India.' IPIM Working Paper/ Monograph Series No. 1. New Delhi: Indian Network on Participatory Irrigation Management.

Mollinga, P. P. 2003. *On the Waterfront. Water Distribution, Technology and Agrarian Change in a South Indian Canal Irrigation System.* Hyderabad: Orient Longman.

Mollinga, P. P. 2008. 'The Water Resources Policy Process in India: Centralization, Polarization and New Demands on Governance.' In *Governance of Water: Institutional Alternatives and Political Economy*, edited by V. Ballabh, 339–370. New Delhi: Sage Publications.

Mollinga, P. P. and Bolding, A. 1996. 'Signposts of Struggle: Pipe Outlets as the Material Interface Between Water Users and the State in a Large-scale Irrigation System in South India.' In *Crops, People and Irrigation: Water Allocation Practices of Farmers and Engineers*, edited by G. Diemer and F. P. Huibers, 11–33. London: Intermediate Technology Publications.

Mooij, J. 2003. 'Smart Governance? Politics in the Policy Process in Andhra Pradesh, India.' Working Paper 228. Overseas Development Institute, U.K.

Nabli, M. K. and Nugent, J. B. 1989. 'The New Institutional Economics and Development: An Introduction.' In *Institutional Economics and Development: Theory and Application to Tunisia*, edited by M. K. Nabli and J. B. Nugent, 3–33. Amsterdam: North Holland.

Narain, U. and Bell, R. G. 2006. 'Who Changed Delhi's Air ?' *Economic and Political Weekly* 41(16): 1584–1588.

Narain, V. 1998. 'Towards a New Groundwater Institution for India.' *Water Policy* 1(3): 357–365.

Narain, V. 2000. 'India's Water Crisis: The Challenges of Governance.' *Water Policy* 2(6): 433–444.

Narain, V. 2003a. 'Water Scarcity and Institutional Adaptation: Lessons from Four Case Studies.' In *Environmental Threats, Vulnerability and adaptation: Case Studies from India*, 107–120. New Delhi: The Energy and Resources Institute.

Narain, V. 2003b. *Institutions, Technology and Water Control: Water Users Associations and Irrigation Management Reform in Two Large-scale Systems in India.* Hyderabad: Orient Longman.

Narain, V. 2004. 'Brackets and Black Boxes. Research on Water Users Associations.' *Water Policy* 6(3): 185–196.

Narain, V. 2014. 'Whose Land? Whose Water? Water Rights, Equity and Justice in a Periurban Context.' *Local Environment; the International Journal of Justice and Sustainability* 19(9): 974–989.

Narain, V. 2009. 'Growing City, Shrinking Hinterland: Land Acquisition, Transition and Conflict in Periurban Gurgaon, India.' *Environment & Urbanization* 21(2): 501–512.

Narayanan, N. C. 2008. 'State, Governance and Natural Resource Conflicts.' In *State, Natural Resource Conflicts and Challenges to Governance. Where Do We Go From Here?*, edited by N. C. Narayanan, 15–38. New Delhi: Academic Foundation.

Natraj, V. K. 2002. 'Industry Interests, Institutional Inertia and Activism. Late Liberalisation and the Environment In India.' In *Public Policy in the Age of Globalisation. Responses to Environmental and Economic Crises*, edited by H. Hveem and K. Nordhaug, 96–124. New York: Palgrave Macmillan.

Nayar, B. R. 2009. *The Myth of the Shrinking State. Globalization and the State in India.* New Delhi: Oxford University Press.

North, D. C. 1990. *Institutions, Institutional Change and Economic Performance.* Cambridge: Cambridge University Press.

North, D. C. 1986. 'The New Institutional Economics.' *Journal of Institutional and Theoretical Economics* (142): 230–237.

North, D. C. 2006. *Understanding the Process of Economic Change.* New Delhi: Academic Foundation.

North, D. C. 2005. 'Institutions and the Performance of Economies Over Time.' In *Handbook of New Institutional Economics*, edited by C. Menard and M. M. Shirley, 21–30. Netherlands: Springer.

Oberthür, S. and Gehring, T. 2003. 'Investigating Institutional Interaction: Toward a Systematic Analysis.' Paper presented at the 2003 International Studies Association Annual Convention, Portland, Oregon, 26 February–1 March.

Oberthür, S. and Gehring, T. 2006. 'Conceptual Foundations of Institutional Interaction.' In *Institutional Interaction in Global Environmental Governance: Synergy and Conflict among International and EU Policies*, edited by S. Oberthür and T. Gehring, 19–51. Cambridge, Massachusetts: MIT Press.

OECD. 2003. Public Private Partnerships in the Urban Water Sector. OECD Observer. 8.

Ostrom, E. 1990. *Governing the Commons. The Evolution of Institutions for Collective Action.* Cambridge: Cambridge University Press.

Ostrom, E. 1992. *Crafting Institutions for Self-governing Irrigation Systems.* San Francisco: Institute for Contemporary Studies.

Ostrom, E. 1996. 'Incentives, Rules of the Game and Development.' *Annual World Bank Conference on Development Economics,* 207–223. Washington, D.C.: The World Bank.

Ostrom, E. 2000. 'Collective Action and the Evolution of Social Norms.' *Journal of Economic Perspectives* 14(3): 137–158.

Ostrom, E. and Gardner, R. 1993. 'Coping with Asymmetries in the Commons: Self-governing Irrigation Systems Can Work.' *Journal of Economic Perspectives* 7(4): 93–112.

Partnerships British Columbia. 2003. An Introduction to Public Private Partnerships.

Pierre, J. 2000. 'Introduction: Understanding Governance.' In *Debating Governance. Authority, Steering and Democracy,* edited by J. Pierre, 1–10. New York: Oxford University Press.

Pierre, J. and Peters, B. G. 2000. *Governance, Politics and the State.* Basingstoke: Macmillan.

Pierson, P. 2000. 'The Limits of Design: Explaining Institutional Origin and Change.' *Governance: An International Journal of Policy and Administration* 13(4): 475–499.

Plateau, J. P. 2000. *Institutions, Social Norms and Economic Development.* Amsterdam: Harwood Academic Publishers.

Putnam, R. 2003. *Making Democracy Work: Civic Traditions in Modern Italy.* Princeton, NJ: Princeton University Press.

Radcliff-Brown, A. R. 1940. 'On Social Structure.' *The Journal of the Royal Anthropological Institute of Great Britain and Ireland* 70 (1): 1–12.

Richter, J. 2004. 'Public-Private Partnerships for Health: A Trend With No Alternatives?' *Development* 47(2): 43–48.

Robbins, P. 2000. 'The Practical Politics of Knowing: State Environmental Knowledge and Local Political Economy.' *Economic Geography* 76(2): 126–144.

Roy, D. 2004. 'From Home to Estate.' *Seminar,* January 2002. New Delhi.

Saleth, R. M. 1996. *Water Institutions in India: Economics, Law and Policy.* Institute of Economic Growth. New Delhi: Commonwealth Publishers.

Schneider, A. and Ingram, H. 1992. 'The Social Construction of Target Populations: Implications for Politics and Policy.' *American Political Science*

Review 87(2): 334–348.

Scott, W. R. 2008. *Institutions and Organizations. Ideas and Interests.* Third edition. California: Sage Publications.

Seabright, P. 1993. 'Managing Local Commons: Theoretical Issues in Incentive Design.' *The Journal of Economic Perspectives* 7(4): 113–134.

Shah, E. 2003. *Social Designs: Tank Irrigation Technology and Agrarian Transformation in Karnataka, South India.* Hyderabad: Orient Longman.

Shah, T. 1993. *Groundwater Market and Irrigation Development. Political Economy and Public Policy.* Bombay: Oxford University Press.

Singh, K. 1997. 'Property Rights and Tenures in Natural Resources.' In *Natural Resource Economics. Theory and Application in India,* edited by J. M. Kerr, D. K. Marothia, K. Singh, C. Ramaswamy and W. R. Bentley, 131–160. New Delhi and Calcutta: Oxford and IBH Publishing Company Ltd.

Stoker, G. 1998. 'Governance as Theory: Five Propositions.' *International Social Science Journal* 155: 17–28.

Sutton, R. 1999. *The Policy Process: An Overview.* Working Paper 118. London: Overseas Development Institute.

Tang, S. Y. 1991. 'Institutional Arrangements and the Management of Common Pool Resources.' *Public Administration Review* 51(1): 42–51.

Tang, S. Y. 1992. *Institutions and Collective Action: Self-governance in Irrigation.* San Francisco, California: Institute of Contemporary Studies.

Thompson, J. H. 1998. *Forging the Prairie West.* Oxford University Press (OUP Catalog number 9780195410495), accessed at https://ideas.repec.org/b/oxp/obooks/9780195410495.html on February 25, 2018.

Tiffen, M., Mortimore, M. and Gichuki, F. 1994. *More People, Less Erosion: Environmental Recovery in Kenya.* Chichester, UK: John Wiley and Sons.

Uphoff, N. 1993. 'Grass-roots Organizations and NGOs in Rural Development: Opportunities with Diminishing States and Expanding Markets.' *World Development* 21(4): 607–622.

Vani, M. S. 2009. 'Groundwater Law in India: A New Approach.' In *Water and the Laws in India,* edited by R. R. Iyer, 435–476. New Delhi: Sage Publications.

Vasavada, S., Mishra, A., and Bates, C. 2001. 'How Many Committees Do I Belong To?' In *A New Moral Economy for India's Forests,* edited by R. Jeffrey and N. Sunder, 151–180. New Delhi: Sage Publications.

Venkateswaran, S. 1995. *Environment, Development and the Gender Gap.* New Delhi: Sage Publications.

World Bank. 1994. *Governance: The World Bank's Experience.* Washington, D.C.: The World Bank.

World Resources Institute. 2003. *World Resources 2002-2004: Decisions for the Earth: Balance, Voice and Power.* Washington, D.C.: World Resources Institute.

World Watch Institute. 2002. *State of the World 2002.* Washington, D.C: World Watch Institute.

Young, O. 2000. 'Institutional Interplay: The Environmental Consequences of Cross-scale Interactions.' Paper presented at the 8th Annual Conference of the International Association for Study of Common Property, Bloomington, Indiana.

2

How are policy choices made and implemented?

Wildavsky, the eminent political scientist, noted, '...policy analysis is one activity for which there can be no fixed program, for policy analysis is synonymous with creativity, which may be stimulated by theory and sharpened by practice, which can be learned but not taught. In large part, it must be admitted, knowledge is negative – it tells us what we cannot do, where we cannot go, wherein we have been wrong, but not necessarily how to correct these errors. After all, if current efforts were judged wholly satisfactory, there would be little need for analysis and less for analysts (Wildavsky 1979: 3, 9).'

In Chapter 1, we examined the rationale for the study of public policy and in particular, the need for the study of policy processes. We introduced the policy sciences as a field of study comprising both the process and the prescriptive dimensions of public policy. In this chapter, we further explore the characteristics of policy analysis and describe its evolution as a field of enquiry. We then review different models of policy choice and theories of the policy process. These models are conceptual lenses for studying policy and explaining how policy processes take shape. They provide an analytic framework for the analysis of public policy. These models help us structure our thinking on policy; however, none of them is necessarily superior to the others. It is for us, as students of public policy, to critically evaluate each of them and examine their relevance for the study of public policy processes. Policy processes can be explained using one or a combination of these.

The organisation of this chapter is thus: we start with a review of some characteristics of policy analysis: it is applied, client-oriented and politically sensitive. We then look at how policy analysis has emerged as an inter-disciplinary field, drawing from but at the same time deviating from conventional disciplines. The evolution of policy analysis as an applied inter-disciplinary field is traced to the disenchantment with conventional disciplines on the supply side and the quest for the explanation of unsatisfactory development performance on the demand side.

We then move on to examine what is meant by a model, and why we should be interested in modelling social phenomena. The objectives of developing models of policy processes are described. We review some of the earlier models of the policy process: the systems approach and the streams metaphor followed by the punctuated equilibrium model.

The linear, or stages, model of the policy process – perhaps the most widely used and understood representation of the policy process – is then introduced and contrasted with the interactive model. Some of the weaknesses of the linear model are examined. We see how it creates a false dichotomy between the stages of policy formulation and implementation; in doing so, it limits our understanding of the politics of policy, or of the relationship that different stages in the policy process have with each other. It fails to provide us with a set of tools to look at the management of change. We then review the interactive model of the policy process and examine how it overcomes these limitations and helps us get a better understanding of the politics of policy.

This is followed by a discussion of the premise of rationalism in policy-making. The rational model of policy choice is described and its weaknesses elaborated; we look at why complete rationality in policy-making may be difficult to accomplish in practice and in fact, why it rarely is accomplished.[1] We examine how other models of policy choice seek to overcome these limitations. In this context, we review briefly the incremental model, the mixed scanning model, the view of policy as a social experiment and policy as social learning. In the last part of this chapter, we focus on different theories that seek to explain the role of groups in policy-making. Three different theories are described: group theory, elite theory, and public choice theory.

In the public policy literature, the expressions 'models of policy analysis' and 'models of the policy process' seem to be used interchangeably. Suffice it to say here that as models, these are representations both of policy choice, that is, how policy-makers choose among a number of policy options, as well as of the processes underlying these. Rationalism, incrementalism, mixed scanning, policy as social experiment and policy as interactive learning could be seen as models of policy choice; they explain how policy-makers choose

---

1 This observation was corroborated through discussions with several participants in the Post-Graduate Programme in Public Policy and Management offered by the School of Public Policy and Governance at MDI Gurgaon.

among a number of policy options. Linear and interactive models of the policy process, on the other hand, are models or theoretical representations of policy processes; they explain how policies evolve and move forward. They seek to answer the question: what does a policy process entail?

2.1 Characteristics and evolution of public policy analysis

Hogwood and Gunn (1984) note that policy analysis is not a single discipline nor should it represent a loose assembly of disciplines; if it is to deal with real, many-sided problems, it must develop an inter-disciplinary or multi-disciplinary approach, which should combine in a synergistic manner elements from many disciplines. In policy analysis, the effort is to be inter-disciplinary and applied, and to break through the frontiers of a single discipline.

As noted in Chapter 1, public policy analysis helps us in describing policies as well as in assessing their causes and consequences. Dye (2002) lists some important characteristics of public policy analysis. According to Dye, public policy analysis involves

1. a primary concern with explanation rather than prescription; policy recommendations, if made at all, are subordinate to description;
2. a rigorous search for the causes and consequences of public policies; and,
3. an effort to develop and test general propositions about the causes and consequences of public policy and to accumulate reliable research findings of general relevance.

Policy analysis is applied, rather than pure, implying that it is problem-oriented and practical. We could see policy analysis as comprising the application of certain tools, concepts and frameworks to understand public policy issues. An extension of this observation, namely, that it is applied, is that it is client-oriented; in that it is carried out for a specific organisation, or individual who needs some specific type of analysis or information.[2] Typically, it entails planning that is politically sensitive.

The origins of public policy analysis lie both on the demand side and the supply side (Hogwood and Gunn 1984). On the demand side, the push came from inadequacies in the government and existing policy responses to address various developmental issues. On the supply side, the thrust came from dissatisfaction

---

2 This perhaps explains an important function that policy think-tanks perform. See the discussion on the prescriptive dimensions of public policy and the role of think-tanks in it, in Chapter 1.

in academic disciplines and a discontent within the social sciences. That is, conventional disciplines were found inadequate in terms of understanding why certain development interventions failed, or were limited in their impact.

Demand side factors

On the demand side, the rediscovery of poverty in the United Kingdom in the 1960s, a questioning of the effectiveness of governments' activity and expenditure and non-planning of important sectors such as higher education and road transport led to an interest in policy analysis. At the same time, there was growing attention to social problems in the United States. Conditions in these environments tended to be dynamic and complex, shaped by changing technology and politics. There was a growing feeling that techniques and personnel from business management and insights from academic analysis could contribute to greater effectiveness in the government. These factors created a demand for the analysis of public policy in order to be better able to interpret the causes of poor or inadequate performance of public policy and to improve its effectiveness.

Supply side factors

At the same time, there was disenchantment with the ability of conventional disciplines to provide answers to the kind of questions mentioned above. This disenchantment came from many quarters. Within political science, studies tended to centre around high levels of generalisation at the cost of remoteness from real problems, an over concern with scientific status (studying only subjects that were quantifiable) and exercises in comparative government.

In public administration, the interests of scholars remained confined to a concern with structures rather than processes, procedures rather than behaviour and decisions rather than policy-making. Studies in economics also tended to be characterised by a deep concern with techniques (obsession with 'scientific status'), hypothesis and generalisations, with rather limited attention to processes and the relatively 'softer' issues. Within management studies, the focus remained by and large confined to the corporate sector (business) while the realm of public policy-making had to confront different political complexities (dealing with the challenges of the public sector that had somewhat different political realities). Here, too, as in economics and public administration, the emphasis remained on techniques rather than processes and conventional management techniques failed to pay attention to the political management of the system.

Thus, on the demand side, there was need for satisfactory explanations of inadequate development performance and on the supply side, there was a failure within conventional disciplines to provide this. These factors together created ground for the emergence of policy analysis as an independent field of enquiry, seeking to address concerns regarding the effectiveness of public policy.[3]

2.2 The evolution of policy sciences

The classic literature that founded policy sciences is only about sixty years old, and goes back to Harold Lasswell's call for a distinctive policy sciences (Birkland 2005). In fact, the interest in policy sciences can be traced back to the publication of Lerner and Laswell's *Policy Sciences* in 1951. This was followed by a sustained interest in the field in the USA in the 1960s and in Britain in the 1970s.

Policy sciences is really an applied sub-field of traditional academic disciplines. This is borne out by the fact that over the years, policy sciences has emerged as an inter-disciplinary field, drawing upon, while deviating from several disciplines: economics, public administration, anthropology, political science, sociology and management. The policy sciences literature is inspired by a large variety of approaches and theories; these are based on different ontological, epistemological and theoretical stands (Huitema and Meijerink 2009).[4] On the one hand, policy sciences draws upon several disciplines; on the other, its emergence as a separate field had to do with the disenchantment in conventional disciplines and their inability to handle complex policy problems within the respective disciplinary confines.[5]

Birkland (2005) notes that this inter-disciplinary character can be seen to be a strength as well as a weakness. It is a strength because the discipline draws upon many different sub-disciplines and concepts and tools that are thus developed by scholars across disciplines can be applied to enrich our understanding of policy. On the other hand, this could be seen as a weakness because not having a distinctive discipline or shared language (across these

---

3 For a more detailed exposition of this, see Hogwood and Gunn (1984).

4 See also John (1998). John (1998) notes that policy science covers 'the totality of public decision-making' and investigates the complex links between inchoate public demands and the detailed implementation of policy choices' (John 1998: 3).

5 In general, this could be seen as argument in favour of inter-disciplinary studies; namely, that insights from one discipline are inadequate to further our understanding of the complexities of a development problem or issue, because of which a multi-faceted approach is needed.

disciplines) means that students of policy often study and discuss the subject in terms of their own training and their respective (sub)-discipline's language, rather than a shared language that all can understand.[6] The argument is that a shared language of policy sciences is yet to emerge.

There is a challenge in developing a shared understanding of public policy; this is primarily because different programmes in public policy are rooted in different academic disciplines, with different kinds of thrusts and emphases. For instance, public policy programmes rooted in economics tend to focus much more around concepts and ideas such as marginal costs and benefits, utility, efficiency, welfare, property rights, incentives and transaction costs. Public policy programmes rooted in political science do incorporate economic methods and ideas but they are also much more consciously 'political' in their approach and interpretation of the policy process. Political scientists and sociologists tend to think much more in terms of policy communities, networks and the exercise of power in political processes and the behaviour of certain groups that influence the policy process.[7] Likewise, when public policy is taught as part of a law school curriculum, the emphasis is on legal practice, and on the underlying theories of law, litigation, and the search for legal meaning and legitimacy. Since the discipline (policy sciences) is so new and because of its inter-disciplinary variation, Birkland argues, the field has yet to coalesce around a shared set of principles, theories and practices.

However, the debate on whether there is a common language of policy or not is perhaps immaterial, given that our interest is in understanding the many dimensions of public policy. To the extent that concepts and ideas developed across disciplines help us achieve this, we should perhaps view this as a strength of the policy sciences literature. In other words, we are talking here of a wide diversity of concepts, theories, tools and analytic frameworks that help us understand different dimensions of public policy, such as what drives policy change, of what ideas, stories or concepts certain public policies are an expression and why we see more policy developments in some areas than in others.

Table 2.1 summarises the different concepts and tools employed in different disciplines for the study of public policy.

---

6 This is a weakness, however, that can be overcome through conscious efforts by scholars of one discipline to appreciate the nuances of another. As an illustration of the differences in how economists and anthropologists, for instance, measure poverty, see Bardhan (1989).

7 We elaborate these concepts and their relevance in the analysis of public policy in chapter 3.

Table 2.1 Tools and concepts used across disciplines to study public policy

Discipline	Tools, concepts and frameworks employed for the analysis of public policy
Economics	Public choice school; rationalism in policy-making; new institutional economics perspectives; rent-seeking and transaction costs; game theory
Political Science	Incrementalism; mixed scanning model; policy as social experiment; policy as interactive learning; policy networks; epistemic communities; international regime; management of change
Anthropology	Development discourses; development narratives; discourse analysis; legal pluralism perspectives
Management	Force field analysis; management of change; exercise of power and influence
Sociology	Human agency; street level bureaucracy; use of language and labelling in policy-making

In this chapter, we make an effort to develop and understand some of the ways in which policy is commonly understood, articulated or spoken about. We do this by focusing on perspectives on policy, which are basically different ways of seeing policy and then on models of policy processes or policy choice, that help us characterise or talk about the how policy choices are made and implemented.

2.3 Perspectives on policy

A perspective is basically our way of looking at things. Allison (1971) notes that we tend to view policies and policy analysis through our own conceptual lens. There are different perspectives on policy, of which three deserve attention here.

The first of these, perhaps the most dominant and widely prevalent, sees policy as a single decision implemented in a linear fashion. This is commonly referred to as the linear or rational model, and is attributed to Simon (1957). It views a policy as a decision followed by subsequent stages of implementation. As we shall see later in this chapter while discussing the distinction between linear and interactive models of the policy process, the policy process is not always (rather, rarely so) neat and well-defined. That is, in practice, it is not always possible to separate the various stages of the policy process across distinct steps. However, the strength of this perspective is that it easy to understand and simple to follow. But its weakness is that it is simplistic and presents a somewhat sanitised view of public policy, looking at it in isolation from its social and political context.

The second perspective sees policy as consisting of a broad course of action (or inaction) that evolves over time during the process of implementation. This perspective sees policies more as part of ongoing processes of negotiation and bargaining between multiple actors over time (Dobuzinskis 1992). According to this perspective, policy change is led by trigger events and catalysed by policy entrepreneurs.[8] A major weakness of both these perspectives on policy, however, is that they remain silent on issues of power (Keely and Scoones 2003).

A third perspective sees a policy, therefore, as an inherently political process rather than the instrumental execution of rational decisions. This perspective sees policies as operating technologies, enmeshed in relations of power between citizens, experts and political authorities (Foucault 1991). A policy is seen as a political technology, comprising a series of patterns of related decisions to which many circumstances and personal, group and organisational influences may have contributed.

The notion of policy as a political technology also relates to the way policy is often depoliticised. If such depoliticisation is in the interest of the dominant group, the political problem is removed from the realm of political discourse and recast in the neutral language of science. Policy is then represented as objective, value free, and termed in legal or scientific language to emphasise this. The term 'technology of politics' refers to the way in which various means are used to work with a political agenda.

2.4 Models of the policy process: talking about policy choice and change

Models are defined as basic frames of reference (Allison 1971). A model could be defined as a conceptual lens or a bundle of related assumptions. It is a representation of something else, designed for a specific purpose (Bullock and Stallybrass 1977). It could be seen to be a simplified representation of some aspect of the real world (Dye 2002). Thus a good model is one that very closely represents the aspect of the real world that it is seeking to. This could be a

---

8 A more detailed discussion of the role of policy entrepreneurs and trigger events is reserved for Chapter 3. More recently, students of policy processes have started examining the role of policy entrepreneurs in catalysing change. For a review of the role of policy entrepreneurs in catalysing water reforms, see for instance, Huitema and Meijerink (2009).

physical object (for instance, model of an airplane) or a social phenomena (for instance, models of the policy process of the kind described in this chapter).

Objectives of model building

We build models to represent certain objects or phenomena. Models may serve purposes of physical representation, simulation, explanation, prediction, experimentation or hypothesis testing. There can be different purposes of model building. Hogwood and Gunn (1984) list a few of them as follows:

- Physical representation
  For instance, a physical model of the campus of an academic institute or a model of an airplane that serves as a miniature replica
- Simulation
  For instance, in laboratory settings
- Explanation
  A model explaining certain behaviour, for instance, the relationship between household income and spending on recreation
- Prediction
  Models used for predicting certain phenomena based on an understanding of some cause—effect relationships. For example, climate change models that predict the impacts of anthropogenic activity on climate and natural resources
- Experimentation
- Hypothesis-testing

Types of models

There can be different types of models; we could distinguish between descriptive models, prescriptive models and conceptual models. *Descriptive* models explain relationships, e..g, a model describing relationships across different economic trends, or a model linking gross domestic product (GDP) with energy consumption could be seen to be a descriptive model. These models perform an important function of assisting description, explanation and understanding.

Prescriptive models concern themselves with what *ought to be*. For instance, we often speak of a model husband, model student or a model teacher. The reference here is to how a teacher or a husband ought to be. The reference is somewhat prescriptive in nature; the focus is on how certain things should be like. Another definition of models refers to *ideal types*, some of which never exist in reality, or do so only rarely. They are theoretical conceptualisations of situations that may not exist in reality but that are often used as assumptions in certain types of analysis. For instance, in economics, we talk about perfect competition and pure rationality. Likewise, we often speak of charismatic authority in management and social sciences literature. Later in this chapter, we will look at rationalism as a kind of 'ideal type' of public policy model, an approach to policy-making that does not exist in reality, but something that serves as an ideal to live up to. While policy-making is rarely rational in real life, it is considered an ideal worth approximating. As we shall see later in this chapter, this is one reason why efforts persist to strengthen information databases and make processes of policy-making more 'scientific', objective and less 'political'.

The models that are used in policy analysis are *conceptual models* (Dye 2002). A conceptual model helps us locate a pattern of events and relationships and we interpret events in terms of that pattern. A conceptual model serves as some representation of social phenomena. It simplifies reality for us and we interpret social phenomena on those lines. When we talk of models of the policy process, we refer to representations of how the processes of policy formulation and implementation take place. These are intended to be representations of the processes of policy-making and implementation. Thus, how good or bad a model is, is judged by the extent to which it captures the policy process in the real world.

These models perform certain functions, namely, to

1. simplify and clarify our thinking about politics and public policy
2. identify important aspects of policy problems
3. help us to communicate with each other by focusing on essential features of political life
4. direct our efforts to understand public policy better by suggesting what is important and what is unimportant
5. suggest explanations for public policy and predict its consequences

These models assist our description of public policy processes and facilitate our articulation of how these processes unfold.

It is important, however, to note that there is no uniform model of choice in policy analysis, that is, a single model or method that is preferable to all others and that consistently renders the best solutions to public problems (Dye 2002). Each of these models offers a separate way of thinking about public policy and political life and each can help us understand different aspects of public policy. In essence, these models could be seen as explaining 'policy continuity and change (Huitema and Meijerink 2009: 23).' Processes of the formulation and implementation of policies can be understood using one or a combination of these models. As models, they structure our thinking on public policy.

The systems model of the policy process

The systems model of the policy process was pioneered by David Easton in 1960 in his book, *A systems analysis of political life*. The basic premise of the systems model is that the public policy process can be understood as the product of a system, influenced by and influencing the environment in which it operates. The system receives inputs and responds with outputs. The inputs are the various forms of issues, pressures, information and the like to which actors in the system react. Inputs to the policy-making system are the demands placed on the system to do something about a problem or to address a problem. Perhaps the most obvious input is voting: voting is the most common form of political participation and elected officials and the news media often proclaim the results as providing policy guidance or mandates to pursue particular policies. Other inputs include public opinion, communications to elected officials and public managers, the news media and interest group activity. The outputs are, in simplest forms, public policy decisions to do or not to do something.

The policy environment could be thought of as containing the features of the structural, social, political and economic system in which public policy-making takes place. Though the boundary between the political system and the environment is blurred, as the system and the environment overlap to some extent, within this general notion of the policy environment, one can isolate four 'environments' that influence policy-making: the structural environment, the social environment, the economic environment and the political environment.

The *structural environment* refers to the structure of the three branches of the government (executive, legislature and judiciary); the federal system's division of labour between federal and state governments, with the State's delegation of duties and powers to local governments; traditional and legal structures, that establish the rules of policy-making; laws structuring the way the government does its business and provides opportunities for public participation; legal decisions made by the Supreme Court that establish the boundaries of permissible government action and the role of courts in establishing the rules under which the policy-making process is conducted.

The *social environment* includes the nature and composition of a population and its ageing structure. As an example, demographic trends such as the changing age composition, sex ratio, and dependency ratio have implications for public policy-making in that they may create room for policies for social security, old age medical care and women's education. *The economic environment* includes the distribution of wealth in a society, the nature and distribution of capital, the size and composition of industry sectors, the rate of growth of the economy, inflation and the costs of labour and raw materials. The economic conditions prevailing in a country can influence its choice of policies. For instance, wealthier economies can, typically, spend much more on space research than poorer economies. Finally, the *political environment* refers to general perceptions about the government, public problems and the effectiveness in dealing with them.

Thus, the systems model provides a simple way of thinking about policy change in terms of inputs and outputs. There seems to be some social metabolism through which these different inputs translate into outputs, or policy decisions.

The streams metaphor

The streams metaphor was propounded by John Kingdon (1985), who argued that issues gain agenda status and alternative solutions are selected when elements of three streams come together: the politics stream (the state of politics and public opinion), the policy stream (potential solutions to a problem) and the problem stream (attributes of a problem). Further, policy change is shaped by whether the situation is getting better or worse, whether it has suddenly sprung into public and elite consciousness through a focusing event and whether it is solvable with the alternatives available in the policy stream.

Within any particular problem area or domain, these streams run parallel and somewhat independently of each other until something happens to cause two or more of the streams to merge in a window of opportunity. This window denotes the possibility of policy change. However, the opening of the window does not in itself guarantee that a change will occur. That trigger can be a change in our understanding of the problem, a change in the political stream that is favourable to policy change or a focusing event that draws attention to a problem and helps open a window of opportunity. Essential to understanding policy change, therefore, from a perspective of the streams metaphor, is the concept of window of opportunity that provides a context for policy change to happen and that is eventually caused through a trigger event.

Punctuated equilibrium

Punctuated equilibrium is an idea borrowed from evolutionary biology that suggests that policy-making is characterised by long periods of stability followed by relatively sudden shifts in attention to problems, thereby leading to opportunities for policy change. This concept was propounded by Baumgartner and Jones (1991). Baumgartner and Jones argue that the balance of political power between groups of interest remains relatively stable over long periods of time punctuated by relatively sudden shifts in public understanding of problems and in the balance of power between the groups seeking to fight entrenched interests. Policy change happens when policy monopolies or subsystems break down, leading to greater and more critical attention to issues. This, according to the punctuated equilibrium model will lead to rapid policy change. In other words, it is the disruption of an equilibrium or status quo that causes policy change to happen.

2.5 Linear and interactive models of the policy process

An important distinction that informs our approach to the study of policy processes in this book is the distinction between a linear and an interactive model of the policy process (Thomas and Grindle 1990). This distinction is a recurring theme in public policy literature (Mooij 2003; Sutton 1999; Thomas and Grindle 1990) and we devote this section of this chapter to a discussion of the same.

A linear model of the policy process is a conceptual framework that sees policy (formulation and implementation) in terms of a linear process or a set of steps that are followed from issue identification to agenda setting, policy formulation, implementation, evaluation and monitoring to termination or continuation. In this model, policy-making is seen as a problem-solving process which is rational, balanced and objective; decisions are made in a series of sequential phases. An interactive model of the policy process, on the other hand, sees it as an outcome of interactions among different actors.

Linear model of the policy process

In a linear model of the policy process, policy implementation is viewed as part of a linear process and a distinct sequential step that proceeds directly from the predictions and prescriptions given by the economist to the policy-maker, to policy selection by the appropriate decision makers, to implementation and then to assessment of outcomes (Meier 1991 cited in Crosby 1996). This model assumes that policy-makers approach the issues rationally, going through each logical stage of the process and considering the relevant information.

A linear model thus supposes that a reform proposal gets on the policy agenda for government action, a decision is made on the proposal and the new policy or institutional arrangement is implemented, either successfully or unsuccessfully. Warwick (1982) calls this approach to policy implementation the 'machine model'. With its roots in classic administrative theory, this model assumes that implementation is a quasi-mechanical exercise where implementers and organisational units form a delivery system for delivering services to programme clients, the 'beneficiaries'.

Sutton (1999) lists the various steps that could be seen as comprising the stages of the policy process, as encapsulated in the linear model, as follows:

- Recognising and defining the nature of the issue to be dealt with
- Identifying possible courses of action to deal with the issue
- Weighing the advantages and disadvantages of each of these
- Choosing the option which offers the best solution
- Implementing the policy
- Possibly evaluating the outcome

In a similar vein, Dye (2002) lists the following stages in a policy process, describing the policy process as a series of political activities.

1. Problem identification: The identification of policy problems through demands for government action.
2. Agenda setting: Focusing the attention of the mass media and public officials on specific public problems to decide what will be decided.
3. Policy formulation: The development of policy proposals by interest groups, and think tanks.
4. Policy legitimisation: The selection and enactment of policies through political actions by the institutions of the State.
5. Policy implementation: The implementation of policies through organised bureaucracies, public expenditures and activities of executive agencies.
6. Policy evaluation: The evaluation of policies by government agencies themselves, outside consultants and the public.

According to this model, a well-formulated plan backed by legitimate authority contains the essential ingredients for its own implementation. This model gives us the impression that once a policy goes through the various stages of policy formulation, it automatically passes through the subsequent stages of implementation, monitoring and evaluation. A policy backed by systematic stages of problem identification, agenda setting, evaluation of policy options itself has the ingredients for success. This model suggests a simple logical structure of the policy process in which a problem is identified, alternatives are weighed, the best alternative is identified and a decision is taken. It is presumed that the system for implementation is inbuilt. And, if there is any problem in implementation then institutions have to be strengthened.

This model is very simple to articulate, conceptualise and understand. In fact, its advantage is that it is a simple representation of the policy process and it provides a simple understanding of the various stages that a policy would pass through. From this perspective, it is very easy to employ and work with while researching public policy processes. However, its simplicity is also its main drawback when it comes to assessing how realistically it describes the public policy process. The model is known to suffer from several weaknesses; we review each of them below:

Dichotomy between policy formulation and implementation; the search for escape hatches

A weakness of this model is that it separates the stages of policy formulation and implementation and creates a false dichotomy between the two (Sutton 1999). A policy, according to this model, passes through distinct steps of policy formulation and implementation, in a sequential order. That is, it sees policy formulation and implementation as distinct steps and fails to recognize the influence that one has over the other.

A fallout of this representation of the policy process is that blame for policy failure is laid not on the policy itself but on political will or managerial failure in implementing it. The failure of policies to achieve the desired outcomes can be blamed on a number of factors such as a lack of political will, poor management or shortage of resources.[9] In a sense, it allows policy-makers to evade responsibility for poor policy outcomes by blaming them on poor implementation when the problem could be with the stage of policy formation itself.

The tendency to split policy-making and implementation as two distinct stages in a sequential process and the divided, dichotomous and linear sequence from policy-making to implementation stems from the view that politics surrounds decision-making while implementation is an administrative activity. This model seems to ignore the possibility that policies can change as they move from the bureaucracy to the local levels where they are implemented, as they normally do.

---

9 These factors are referred to as 'escape hatches' in policy sciences literature. See Sutton (1999). These factors serve as scapegoats or as excuses for non-implementation.

That is, policy formulation and implementation are more closely related than the linear model of policy process would make us believe. The model blinds us to the relationship among the various stages of the policy process.

Silent on the management of change

This model also remains silent on the management of change. The linear model of the policy process fails to unpack the process dynamics involved in policy formulation and implementation. The policy implementation process remains a black box. The model does not equip policy analysts to unpack the dimensions and processes of policy change, and to that effect, it remains ineffective in improving the implementation of public policies. By viewing the policy process as a mechanical exercise, it does not provide a framework to understand the dynamics involved in policy-making and implementation; in other words, it is of limited use in understanding how to make policy processes more effective or how better to bridge the implementation gap.

Separation of stages not relevant

Critics of the linear model also argue that the separation of the policy process into distinct stages is superficial. A policy idea may not reach every stage: a policy concept may reach the agenda stage but any ideas generated may not get beyond mere discussion. Likewise, it could also be argued that one cannot separate the implementation of a policy from the evaluation, since evaluation may be happening all the time that a policy is being implemented. The basic point here is that all policies may not necessarily pass through all stages, or necessarily in this order.

Interactive model of the policy process

In contrast to the linear model, an interactive model of the policy process focuses much more on the dynamics involved in policy processes. The interactive model views policy reform as a process, one in which interested parties can exert pressure for change at many points (Thomas and Grindle 1990). Understanding the location, strength and stakes involved in these attempts to promote, alter or reverse policy reform initiatives is central to understanding the outcomes. A policy reform initiative may be altered or reversed at any stage in its life cycle by the pressures and reactions of those who oppose it. In particular, bureaucratic opposition often comes from resistance to change or loss of power and may range from overt opposition to quite sabotage or inaction. In fact, most policy-making could be seen as a process of incremental distribution of wealth and power (Hempel 1996). This process creates forces of support and resistance that influence the actual outcomes. Rather than a linear process in which policies pass sequentially from one stage to another, this model sees the process as a circular and interactive one, in which policy outcomes are shaped by the balance of power among different actors.

In an interactive model of the policy process, policy implementation is understood as a process in which different actors participate in the implementation of policy. Mackintosh (1992) views this process-oriented framework as one in which policy implementation is an ongoing, interactive and complex process whose outcomes can be extremely variable. This variability results from the motivations of different actors involved (governments, managers, and 'beneficiaries') and how they articulate their interests and mobilise resources for their furtherance. These actors interact with each other to further their own goals and interests, some supporting the policy implementation and others resisting it. The progress of reform is shaped by the net outcome of these interactions. The interactive model of the policy process thus provides a framework for studying the political economy of reforms.

This model is perhaps more useful than the linear model, since it facilitates a better understanding of the processes through which policies are formulated and implemented. It is perhaps a much more realistic representation of public policy processes than the linear model and gives us a better insight into the politics of policy and the management of public policy. It emphasises the importance of garnering support for reform processes and highlights the interaction between the stages of policy formulation and implementation.

Role of street level bureaucracies

It is important to note that the interactive model of the policy process allows for a deeper understanding of the role of what are called street-level bureaucracies or individuals and agencies engaged in policy implementation at the lowest (or the field) level.[10] These include schools, police, welfare departments, lower courts, legal service offices, accountants and others. On account of the

---

10 The concept of street-level bureaucracies was propounded by Lipsky (1980) to describe the lowest rung of civil servants, that is those members of the bureaucracy who are engaged with the implementation of a public service and have a direct interface with the recipients of the public service or the beneficiaries. A detailed discussion of the role of street-level bureaucracies is reserved for Chapter 4, where we examine how the motivations, intentions and attitudes of lower segments of the bureaucracy shape policy implementation.

constraints on their time and bureaucratic procedures at the local level, street-level bureaucracies observe considerable flexibility in implementing policies. The role and motivation of street-level bureaucracies is an important factor shaping the gap between the actual and intended policy outcomes.

Garnering support for reform

When our understanding of public policy is based on the interactive model of the policy process, it serves as a sounding board that the planning of the implementation process should be part of the policy formulation itself. That is, an essential factor contributing to the success of public policy is the extent to which policy-makers can foresee the likely constraints to public policy implementation and take necessary measures to garner support for policy reform or overcome resistance. When we are aware that policy outcomes are shaped by the exercise of power among a large number of actors, we are more likely to take steps to overcome resistance and garner support.

Most policy reform proceeds on the assumption of linear models of policy-making: an issue is identified, a subject is put on the agenda for policy reform and a new policy is framed and put on the implementation table. Very little effort is made to garner support and resources for implementation or to foresee bottlenecks. Crosby (1996) argues that one reason why policies fail is that policy implementers are generally excluded from the process of formulation and policy selection. They have little ownership of either the policy or the process. Further, they have minimal control over the diverse resources needed to carry out the policy mandate, lack the appropriate organisational resources and often must operate in an environment hostile to the changes mandated. For effective policy implementation, it is necessary that potential problems are considered well in advance of implementation itself and that appropriate procedures are designed into the programme (Hogwood and Gunn 1984). It can help the policy process to foresee who are likely to resist the reform efforts and how best to mobilise support for the same. At the risk of sounding clichéd or rhetorical, a good policy is one, that, among other things, can be implemented.

Interaction between policy-making and implementation

This model helps us to better understand the relationship between processes of policy-making and implementation and the influence that one has over the other. Unlike the linear model, policy-making and implementation are no longer seen as distinct steps in the policy process but are seen as inextricably related. Policies are reformulated in their implementation as different actors bring to the policy process their own interests, perceptions, motivations and agenda. The policy that is implemented on the ground is different from the policy that leaves the corridors of policy-making.

The interaction between policy-making and policy implementation is quite complex (Hogwood and Gunn 1984): it is shaped by the interaction of the policy with its setting (Chan and Wong et al. 1995). The study of implementation of policy, therefore, needs to be taken far more seriously. Hogwood and Gunn (1984) argue that implementation should be seen as part of the policy process itself. Many policies are reformulated in the process of implementation (Hempel 1996). At the same time, the content of public policy almost invariably reflects the process by which it is made and implemented (Hempel 1996).

The interactive model is a more realistic description of the policy process than the linear model. Besides, policy forumulation based on the assumptions of the interactive model of the policy process is more likely to be effective as it provides a tool to policy-makers to anticipate resistance and mobilise support. Very often well-formulated policies may remain limited in their impact because they fail to mobilise support or anticipate resistance. In other words, since the policy-making and implementation processes are closely related, managing and planning the implementation process needs to be part of the policy formulation process itself, rather than being seen as two distinct steps, as the linear model makes us believe.

Abandon the linear model?

Should the above described critiques of the linear model lead us necessarily to abandon it? The criticisms of the linear model of the policy process notwithstanding, it can be asserted that the linear model does provide an analytic tool to unpack the elements of a policy process, that is, it gives us an answer to a rather broad question 'what (stages) does a policy process comprise?'

It is important to note that the two models need not necessarily be seen as mutually exclusive but the two can be combined to retain the advantages of both. That is, we can unpack each of the stages in the linear model of the policy process to see what forces and interactions shape them. We work within the overall framework of the linear model but unpack each stage or step of the policy process to uncover the role of different actors in the policy process.

Mooij (2003) notes that the conclusion that there is something wrong with the linear model of policy-making does not necessarily mean that there are no stages in the policy process. According to Mooij, it is possible to reformulate stages in such a way that they do justice to the fact that the policy process is interactive rather than linear.

In the Indian context, a good example of this is provided by Mooij (2003) who cites the work of Sudan (2000) to explain the introduction of e-governance in Andhra Pradesh. These stages are listed as follows:

a. establishing a sense of urgency
b. creating a guiding coalition
c. developing a vision and a strategy
d. communicating the change vision
e. empowering broad-based action
f. generating short-term wins
g. consolidating gains and producing more change
h. anchoring new approaches in the culture

These stages suggest policy-making to be an interactive process, rather than a linear one, or one that is technical or automatic. The second option, according to Mooij, is to stick to the traditional formulation of stages, but to reconceptualise the stages, their boundaries and the relationships with subsequent stages. Stages are then conceptualised as arenas, each with their different sets of institutions, actors and stakes. Some actors may be important in some arenas while they are poorly represented in other arenas.

This conceptualisation of the policy process still helps us see it as comprising distinct stages while allowing us to recognise that at each stage, negotiations, dialogue and exercise of power take place among the various actors involved. Thus, insights from both these models can be combined to deepen our understanding of the public policy process and the two models need not be seen as mutually exclusive or water-tight. In other words, we can retain the various steps within the public policy process as conceptualised in the linear model but unpack each step to understand the role of the various actors, processes and institutions that shape it.

2.6 Rationalism: policy as rational output

While the models described above, in particular the linear and interactive models of the policy process, help us theorise about and characterise the policy process, the models that we turn to now are models of policy choice. That is, they describe how policy-makers choose among a number of policy options. If a policy-maker has a menu of options to choose from, what makes her decide in favour of one option over the others? What is it that leads to an elimination of different policy options and what is it that defines what the winning option will be?

The first approach to explaining policy choice is enshrined in the concept of rationalism. The notion of rationalism is centred around a conceptualisation or connotation of what constitutes a rational policy. A *rational policy* is understood to be one that achieves maximum social gain. According to a rationalist perspective on policy-making, governments should only choose policies resulting in gains to society that exceed costs by the greatest amount and refrain from pursuing policies if costs are not exceeded by the gains (Dye 2002). In other words, governments should only pursue policies that have the greatest benefit to society over the cost. Essentially, this has two premises. First, that no policy should be adopted if its costs exceed its benefits. Second, among policy alternatives, decision-makers should choose the policy that produces the greatest benefit over cost. Thus, rationalism is really a prescriptive model of the policy process, emphasising how policy choices should ideally be made rather than how they are made in practice. It presents an 'ideal type' approach to policy choice; it is prescriptive rather than descriptive in its tone.

For rationalism to hold good in practice, several conditions must be met. First, to select a rational policy, policy-makers must know all the society's value preferences, and their relative weights. Second, they must know all the policy alternatives available. Third, they must know the consequences of each of the policy alternatives professed. Fourth, they must be able to calculate the ratio of benefits to costs for each policy alternative. Fifth, and finally, they must be able to then select the most efficient policy alternative among the many options.

Is being rational realistic?

For years the rational actor model was widely assumed to be a primary method of decision-making in public and private organisations and the quest for this sort of rationality persists till today (Birkland 2005). However, several features of the rational model render it an unrealistic model of decision-making. Needless to say, the five conditions mentioned above are very difficult to meet in practice and so a rational policy could be considered, at best, to be some kind of an 'ideal type'.

There may be several barriers to rational decision-making, since the above mentioned five conditions are barely met in real life. First, this rationality assumes that the value preferences of society as a whole can be known and weighted objectively. That is, there must be a complete understanding of societal values. On the contrary, in real life, policy-makers may not have the time and resources or the commitment to objectively value each of the options available and sometimes even the requisite skills to carry out such activities might be absent. Further, a rational policy may turn out to be highly inefficient if the costs involved in arriving at it are exorbitant. In the rational model of the policy process, the problem is seen as technical, the climate as consensual and the process as controlled. On the other hand, when policy-making is seen as an inescapably political activity, as it usually is, policy is seen as a bargained outcome, the environment as conflictual and the process itself characterised by diversity and constraints (Gordon, Lewis and Young 1997).

To cut a long story short, rationalism is a difficult way of making policy choice in real life, on account of the implications for time, energy and resources to arrive at a rational policy choice. In a socially, ethnically and economically diverse country as India, making rational policy choices would necessitate generating huge amounts of data, which would require enormous resources and manpower. Besides, the process of coming to such a 'rational' decision could itself be a long and time-consuming one; by the time such decisions are reached, there could even be a loss of opportunity and a huge time lapse. In a satirical vein, one could ask whether it is 'rational' to make 'rational' policy choices. Besides, attaching some weights to the value preferences of different potential recipients of policies requires policy-makers to make some value judgements. Thus, contrary to what the term suggests, being rational in this sense of the term is never a neutral, value-free activity but one in which the biases of policy-makers will always have some room to play. Even if governments may lack the resources and manpower to arrive at rational policy choices, this task could always be outsourced to consultants or specialists. However, even then policy choice may eventually turn out to be a matter of political expediency and decisions based on rationality could take a back-seat. The policy choice may be influenced more by the positions of the government on certain issues or a question of posturing.

Even though rationality is difficult to attain in practice, does this mean that as a goal in policy-making, rationality should be abandoned? Birkland (2005) provides a convincing and emphatic negative answer to this question. This explains why endeavours continue in order to develop information systems and analytic techniques in order that we can move towards improved, more rational decision-making. Besides, the rational model of policy analysis provides a simple analytic tool that policy scientists might be comfortable with.

As Gordon, Lewis and Young (1997) note, 'The power and survival ability of the rational system model is surprising, given that its assumptions have been undermined by empirical studies of the policy process, and that its predictive record is uneven. The main explanation for its continuing existence must lie in its status as a normative model and as a 'dignified myth' which is often shared by the policy-makers themselves. Acceptance of the rational model helps the researcher towards a comfortable life: it enables him or her to engage in direct debate with the policy-makers on the basis that information provided by the researchers will be an aid to better policy-making. If, however, as we believe, policy-making systems approximate more closely to the political model, these prospects can only be superficially attractive (Gordon, Lewis and Young 1997: 7).' Rationalism could be seen to provide a justification for much of the policy advice that underlies policy studies of a prescriptive nature.

2.7 Alternatives to the rational model

Given that the rational model of policy analysis seems unrealistic and that policy-makers may not have the time, energy and resources to make rational policy choices, how are policy choices made in real life? If rationalism is an ideal type, then what is real? Given that the necessary conditions for rationalism to hold are barely met in practice, how do policy-makers choose among the various options available to them? In the absence of systematic information on the value preferences of citizens, the weights assigned to them and the potential benefits of various policy options, what policy choices do policy-makers make?

Incrementalism

One alternative is provided by the *incrementalist model*. This model postulates that major changes (in policy) occur through a series of small steps, or increments. Thus, the policy process is seen as being one of 'muddling through' (Lindblom 1979, 1959). As against the rational model of the policy process, which postulates that policy-makers weigh and choose among a large number of alternatives the one alternative that is the best or most rational, this model postulates that policy-makers tend to choose options that differ only marginally from existing policies. That is, policy-makers make policy choices that are only marginally different from the prevailing policies; they seek to maintain the status quo by and large and tamper with policies only marginally.

Incrementalism views public policy as a continuation of past government activities with only incremental modifications. Contrary to what is postulated by the rational model, in practice, constraints of time, information, and cost may prevent policy-makers from identifying the full range of policy alternatives and evaluating their consequences. Constraints of politics may prevent the establishment of clear-cut societal goals and the accurate calculation of costs and benefits. Under these conditions, policy-makers choose policies that are only marginally different from the existing ones and seek to maintain the status quo.

Incrementalism is conservative in that existing programmes, policies, and expenditures are considered as a base and attention is focused on new programmes and policies and on increases, decreases or modifications of current programmes. Not all policy changes are considered; only those that cause little physical, economic, organisational and administrative dislocation. A 'good policy' is one that all participants agree on rather than what is best to solve a problem. It is one that causes the least disruption of the status quo rather than one that is arrived at by systematically weighing the costs and benefits of the various alternatives, and choosing the one with the greatest social gain over social costs, as rationalism postulates. From a perspective of this model, therefore, long-term policy change comes from a series of small, incremental steps. Thus the major characteristic of this model is that it focuses on small changes to existing policies, rather than radical changes.

Having understood what is implied by incrementalism, we should understand why policy change tends to be incremental. Incrementalism persists because it allows policy-makers to stay in their comfort zone. It allows them to play safe, and to maintain the status quo. More often than not, incrementalism may be politically expedient.

Policy-makers generally accept the legitimacy of established programmes and tacitly agree to continue previous policies. There can be several reasons for this (Dye 2002). First, as noted above, policy-makers may not have the time, information or money to investigate all the alternatives to policy. Second, policy-makers may also accept the legitimacy of previous policies because of uncertainty about the consequences of completely new or different policies. Third, there may be heavy investments in existing programmes that preclude any really radical change. Fourth, incrementalism may be politically expedient. Finally, small changes are easier to be accepted by the recipient population or the intended beneficiaries of the public policy.

Two major problems with the theory (and to some extent the practice) of incrementalism are, first, that some problems actually may demand bold decisions and second, that some goals simply cannot be met with incremental steps (Birkland 2005). In certain areas of public policy, drastic changes may be needed from the current or established approaches and incrementalism may not be the best approach to move forward.

Mixed scanning model

A midway between the rational and incrementalist model of the policy process is the *mixed scanning model* (Etzioni 1967). This model postulates that the policies chosen are not those that are marginally different as in the incrementalist model or that policy-makers choose the best among several alternatives as in the rational model; instead, only a few policies that are different from the existing ones are chosen for in-depth examination. That is, this model provides some kind of a midway between rationalism and incrementalism. According to this model, in practice, neither do policy-makers evaluate all options for their costs and benefits nor do they make small changes in existing policies; instead, they pick up a few options and evaluate them for their relevance.

Policy as social experiment

A somewhat similar perspective is provided by the *policy as social experiment model*, that views social and policy change as a process of trial and error (for a review, see Weiss and Birckmayer 2006). Based on the experimental approach of natural sciences, this model is based on successive hypotheses being tested against reality. According to this model, policy change happens through constant experimentation, through trial, retrial and innovation, rather than through a selection of the most rational course of action. That is, a policy change is introduced, and then modified through a process of trial and error. In essence, this model postulates that policies evolve through a process of improvisation. To classify a policy change as incremental or a social experiment requires an understanding of the motivation behind the change and the process through which that change was effected.

Policy as interactive learning

The *policy as interactive learning model* views policy as a process that promotes interaction and sharing of ideas among those who make policy and those who are influenced most directly by the outcomes. An example is provided by Fiorino (2001), who reviews the evolution of environmental policy in the USA as a perspective to develop three different kinds of learning: technical, conceptual and social learning. Technical learning entails the search for new policy instruments, more regulation, enforcement, legalistic, bureaucratic codes and hierarchical relations, often leading to adversarial relations among the actors. Conceptual learning is a process of redefining policy goals and adjusting problem definitions and strategies: new concepts such as pollution prevention, ecological modernisation and sustainability enter the lexicon of public policy. Social learning focuses on interactions and communications among the actors. It builds on cognitive capacities of technical learning and rethinking of objectives and strategies that occurs in conceptual learning but it emphasises relations among actors and the quality of dialogue. When we see governments involve stakeholders in consultation for the initiation of new or modification of existing policies, we see the model of policy as interactive learning reflected. Here, we see a conscious effort at involving stakeholders and seeking inputs from them.

It is particularly important to understand the distinction between the interactive model of the policy process and the view of policy as interactive learning.[11] When we talk of policy as interactive learning, we refer to deliberate efforts by policy-makers to involve relevant stakeholders in the policy process. That is, there is an effort to deliberately learn or seek inputs into the policy process. The interactive model of the policy process, on the other hand, refers to the politics of policy; the exercise of power and influence by various actors to influence the policy choices. This is not to say that the two are mutually exclusive; even in an interactive learning mode, the balance of power among different actors will give more space to some than to others to influence the policy process.

2.8 Role of groups in policy-making

Much of the discussion in public policy literature deals with the influence that certain groups have over policy-making. Actors interact and bargain with each other, and thereby produce a particular policy outcome (Mooij 2003). Actors can be individuals, pursuing their own material interest or they can be collective (interest) groups. Three theories focus on the role of certain groups in the policy processes, namely, group theory, public choice theory and elite theory.

Group theory

Group theory begins with the proposition that interaction among groups is the central fact of politics. Individuals with common interest band together, formally or informally, to press their demands on governments. Politics is essentially the struggle between groups to influence public policy.

According to group theory, public policy at any point of time is the equilibrium reached in the group struggle. This equilibrium is determined by the relative influence of groups, which in turn, is determined by their number,

---

11 From my own experience with teaching participants in the public policy programme at MDI Gurgaon, these two often turned out to be a subject of confusion.

wealth, organisational status, strength, leadership, access to decision makers and internal cohesion. Policy-makers are seen as constantly responding to group pressure. Policy change results with the change in the relative influence of any interest group; policy will move in the direction of change desired by those with the most relative weight.

In many ways, this theory provides a similar explanation of policy change as does the interactive model of the policy process, seeing policy change as culminating from the relative strength of different actors engaged in policy processes, and bringing to bear on it their own interests and agenda. In Chapter 1, while discussing the salient features of the public policy-making process in India, we have examined how coalitions of certain groups have caused policies to be developed in their favour, even when the numbers of such people are small relative to the larger number of people fractured along the lines of caste, class and social groupings.[12] Group theory is particularly relevant in explaining policy change in countries like India where social and economic divisions can be strong.

Elite theory

Elite theory suggests that policy is shaped by the values and preferences of a small group of people, the social elite. Elites refer to politicians and bureaucratic officials who have decision-making responsibilities and whose decisions become authoritative for society (Thomas and Grindle 1990). This theory is based on the premise that people are apathetic and ill-informed about public policy. Public policy really turns out to be the preferences of the elites; public officials and administrators merely carry out the policies decided on by them. Implicit in elite theory is the stature, authority and influence that a nation's elite enjoy and that enables them to exercise control over policy-making processes.

According to elite theory, elites actually shape mass opinion on policy questions more than masses shaping elite opinion. Policy change occurs through changes in the value systems and beliefs of the elite. Elites are drawn disproportionately from the upper socio-economic strata of society. This does not necessarily mean that public policy will be hostile toward

---

12 This is to be distinguished from the role of epistemic communities, who may be invited into positions of prestige and power on account of the specialised knowledge and skill sets that they possess. Likewise, they need to be distinguished from policy networks, that refer to groups of people bound by common values, ideals and belief systems which they bring to the policy process. See the discussion in Chapter 3.

the masses' welfare but only that the responsibility for mass welfare is seen as resting on the shoulders of the elite. The welfare of the masses, in fact, could be an essential part of the elite value system. Elitism also implies that broadly there will be consensus among the elite, though competition might centre on a very narrow range of issues. Elite theory would somewhat tend to provide a similar explanation of policy change as would the incremental model of the policy process. Since elites are conservative and have a general interest in preserving the status quo, change is likely to be of a very incremental nature.

Public choice theory

Another theory that is applied to study group behaviour in public policy is public choice theory. Public choice could be understood to be the economic study of non-market decision-making, especially the application of economic analyses to public policy-making. Public choice theory, simply understood, is an application of neo-classical economics to understand public policy-making. This is similar to our discussion in Chapter 1 of the application of neo-classical economics to the design of institutions for governance and similar criticisms apply here.

The basic premise of the public choice school is that just as rational, utility-maximising individuals act in the market to pursue their self-interest, so do they in the corridors of policy-making. This goes on to explain phenomena as rent-seeking and opportunistic behaviour.[13]

According to public choice theory, therefore, interest groups, like other political actors, pursue their self-interest in the political market place. Public choice theory challenges the notion that individuals act differently in politics than do they in the market place. All political actors seek to maximise their personal benefits in politics, just as they do in the market place. Individuals might come together in politics for their own mutual benefit just as they come together in the market place and by agreement (contract) among themselves they can enhance their own well-being in the same way as trading in the market place.

This is akin to what Moore (1999) describes as interest group economism. Public choice theory assumes that

a. actors pursue mainly short-term self-interests;
b. individuals aggregate in interest groups that are exclusive in membership;
c. policy is made by the interaction of competing interest groups;

---

13 See also the discussion on New Institutional Economics in Chapter 1.

d. high levels of information are available; and,

e. each policy decision is a separate event, unrelated to other policy decisions.

Further, public choice theory deems that the government must provide and perform certain basic functions that the marketplace is unable to handle. These include the provision of public goods and addressing externalities.

Critics of this model tend to see this as a reductionistic and simplistic way of approaching policy processes. It is seen as a gross simplification of phenomena that are socially embedded, and inherently political. Mooij (2003) describes this model to be a 'grossly simplified version of a public choice paradigm' (Mooij 2003: 7), especially among economists who wish to state something about politics as well, using the tools and techniques developed in economics and applying an economic model to the realm of politics.

The basic critique is that this is a simplistic and reductionistic way of studying policy processes that are deeply political and shaped by power relationships among several actors. It is akin to posing the question: can the tools of marginalism and cost-benefit analysis that we apply to study the behaviour of rational, utility-maximizing consumers in the market be applied to study more complex phenomena such as collective action, decision-making and the framing of public policy?

2.9 The Indian context of policy-making and implementation: is there a 'one size fits all' model?

It is important to note that none of these models is superior to the others, or 'the best' and none of these models will be able to explain all kinds of policy change. At their best, these models help us understand policy choices that are made by policy-makers, that is, how policy-makers choose among a number of policy options. What factors influence the actual choice of policy from among a number of policy options? How do policy-makers narrow down the policy space? What considerations help eliminate some policy choices, while focusing on others? To that extent, they help us understand the nature of the polity and policy-making environment.

Characterising the nature of the policy process in the Indian context is further limited by the paucity of explicit studies of public policy processes (see also the discussion in Chapter 1). However, we find certain policies or policy changes to be more appropriately explained by one of these models, some by another and some by a combination of one or more of the above. It may also be that as countries move through different stages of development, policy processes are explained better by different models.[14] Policies may pass through different stages and a different model may be able to better explain each of them.

The different theories dealing with the role of groups in policy-making help us understand aspects of agenda setting. Who are the various groups that influence public policy and how do they influence the agenda of policy-making? Who are the actors that bring certain subjects to the attention of policy-makers? Likewise elite theory, group theory and public choice theory also help us understand why certain subjects come up on the policy agenda. The processes of decision-making or the processes through which policy-makers choose among a number of alternatives, on the other hand, are explained through rationalism, incrementalism and the mixed scanning model.

Policy-making tends to be incremental, for instance, where policy-makers seek to maintain the status quo or where gradual changes are necessary to garner support and acceptability for policy changes. Changes in small steps sometimes make it easier for the recipients of policy to accept these changes. For instance, incremental withdrawal of subsidies or incremental increases in the price of fuels (petrol or diesel) are easier to implement rather than drastic changes that can evoke public outcry. Incrementalism tends to be the nature of the policy process where the stakes can be high, where large numbers of people are affected and where drastic departures from existing policies entail substantial risks, including loss of vote banks. The reason that we use the expression 'phasing out of subsidies' is that it points or refers to a gradual, incremental withdrawal rather than a drastic roll-back. Administrative reforms is another area where the approach to policy change has been incremental on account of political expediency. These are areas where governments try to play safe or 'not to rock the boat'.

Policy as social experiment is the nature of the policy process involving, for instance, the introduction of new technologies, where policy-makers seek to experiment with innovation and modify policies based on responses. The odd-even rule to regulate vehicular traffic introduced in Delhi a few months ago could be seen to be an example of policy as social experiment. A new policy is introduced, the experience with it is noted and based on the experience,

---

14 For instance, a point that was brought out by one of the participants in the course on public policy analysis was whether the linear model of policy analysis is a better representation of policy change in communist countries while the interactive model in more reflective of democratic and open societies. While it may be possible to answer such questions intuitively, they require perhaps more systematic scientific investigation.

modifications are sought. In India, the modification of the National Rural Employment Guarantee Act (NREGA) to the Mahatma Gandhi National Rural Employment Guarantee Act (MNREGA), the introduction of the Aadhaar Card, the Voter Identity card, the mid-day meals scheme and the closure of the Bus Rapid Transit System (BRTS) could all be seen as cases of policy as social experiment. A policy initiative is introduced: based on the experience, changes are made in it. Alternatively, unsure of the consequences, a policy approach is tried on a small and pilot scale and based on the experience, it is scaled up or modified. Cases of pilot experiments of new policy approaches could be considered examples of policy as social experiment.

Both incrementalism and policy as social experiment may result in marginal changes; however, the distinction between the two comes from the motivation in the changes sought. Incrementalism is motivated by an urge to maintain the status quo while policy as social experiment is motivated by an urge to improvise based on the experience with policy implementation. Further, incrementalism involves changes in existing policies while policy as social experiment may involve a new initiative introduced for the first time that subsequently evolves based on the experience with its implementation.

Some moves, however, represent a far cry from incrementalism. This is where the government made bold policy choices or 'major moves' that represented a drastic departure from the past. In the Indian context, the balance of payments crisis in 1991 prompted the devaluation of the Indian rupee; more recently, the introduction of the Goods and Services Tax (GST) and the drive to demonetise the Indian economy represent major breaks from the past, a distant call indeed from the premise of incrementalism. These are areas where fiscal or other constraints require immediate shock treatment; or, where small steps would defeat the purpose that is better served by a sudden break from the past. For instance, in the demonetisation case, the professed intention was to track black money. Done in increments, the purpose would not have been met. A sudden move to demonetise caught the public unawares.

While the above models focus on policy choice, taking the policy implementation process as a black box, the interactive model explicitly takes implementation as a part of the policy process. Aspects of policy support and resistance can be studied through the interactive model or through group theory. If we are interested in studying the politics of policy, then it is the interactive model that would assist our analysis.

Several recent examples of policy change can be explained using the interactive model of the policy process. One such example is provided by the case of the debate around land acquisition in India and how different actors have influenced policy development in this regard. Recent years have seen the subject of land acquisition grab the attention of the media as well as policy-makers and the public. The policy for the development of Special Economic Zones (SEZs) as well as large-scale urbanisation necessitate the acquisition of large tracts of agricultural land around major cities. Though land acquisition has been an essential ingredient of processes for urbanisation and industrialisation, it was the acquisition of land for the Tata Group of industries for the development of a car plant at Singur and the protests against it led by Mamata Banerjee, the leader of the Trinamool Congress, that gave the subject great visibility in the media and brought it to the attention of the public at large.

The basic concerns related to the forced acquisitions of agricultural land as well as the compensation that farmers received for it, which was often below the market rates. This process of land acquisition had its legal basis in the Land Acquisition Act of 1894, that allowed the State to acquire land for a 'public purpose'. The Land Acquisition Act (1894) allowed the acquisition of private lands for public purpose without a clear definition of 'public purpose'; besides, citizens could not really question the acquisition, only the compensation and the way the 'market value' for the land was fixed. Under the Act, the definition of 'public purpose' for which land could be acquired included land acquired for a non-state body like a company.

These concerns were sought to be taken care of through two of the proposed legal interventions, namely, the Land Acquisition (Amendment Bill), 2007 and the Rehabilitation and Resettlement Bill, 2007. The new bill sought to redefine 'public purpose' as land acquired only for defence purposes, infrastructure projects or for any project useful to the general public where 70 per cent of the land had already been purchased from willing sellers through the market (that is, where at least 70 per cent of the purchase of the land required had already been made on the basis of voluntary sales by land-owners, as against the forced acquisitions by the state). In other words, the proposed bill did not permit government to acquire land for private companies except when the company had already acquired 70 per cent of the required land through voluntary sales by landowners.

The second modification concerned the compensation. Under the earlier law, the District Collector's award of compensation was final unless altered by a civil court. However, the new bill sought to bar the jurisdiction of civil courts on all matters related to land acquisition and envisaged the setting up of a Land Acquisition Compensation Disputes Settlement Authority at the state and central levels to adjudicate disputes resulting from land acquisition proceedings. It also stated that payment for acquired land must be made within one year from the date of the declaration of acquisition, after which a penalty would have to be paid.

The essence of the proposed changes was that they sought to amend the Land Acquisition Act of 1894 and make it more sensitive to the concerns of the landowners without creating hurdles for industry. There was broad consensus in favour of the amendment in Parliament. However, the introduction of the bill was stalled by the Trinamool Congress. The leader of the party, Mamata Banerjee, stalled the introduction of the bill on grounds that the government should not have any role whatsoever in the land acquisition process but that industry should deal directly with the landowners and acquire 100 per cent of the land that it needs by itself. The main reason understood for this was that Mamata had gained huge political mileage by leading land-related agitations of farmers against the land acquisition for corporate giants in Singur and Nandigram districts in the state of West Bengal. She opposed the introduction of the bill in the belief that support for these bills would undermine the political capital she had gained by leading farmer agitations against land acquisition in this state.

A few months after this, the Confederation of Indian Industries (CII) recommended three-pronged provisions for effective land acquisition legislation and for this it proposed changes in the Land Acquisition (Amendment) Bill.[15] It suggested a provision for setting up land bank corporations to facilitate acquisition and disbursement of land for industrial use. The CII proposed that the Bill's provision that the State could only acquire land for a private sector project if the company had already acquired a minimum percentage of the land would make it difficult for industry to set up projects.

The CII took the position that agglomerating land from numerous owners is not a task which the corporate sector could do effectively, especially in the absence of proper land records and with small and scattered land holdings. Any attempt on the part of the government to transfer this task squarely on industry, without improving the system, would badly affect industrial development and overall economic growth in the country. The CII advocated state land bank corporations to serve as institutions dedicated for

15 http://www.business-standard.com/india/news/cii-for-changes-inland-acquisition-bill/378780/, accessed on December 7, 2009.

acquiring unproductive and other lands for industrial purposes and provide a transparent and viable solution to the problem. The job of the state land bank corporations would be to scientifically acquire large tracts of non-cultivable and other lands, develop these as land banks for the future and have a transparent mechanism to pass these on to the private sector. Further, the CII recommended national digitisation of land records and planned zoning of land, as archaic land records are a big hurdle for land acquisition and compensation disbursement. Simultaneously, the CII recommended ex-ante zoning of land so as to have a clear mapping, identification and segregation of the land for various purposes, over a 100- to 150-year period. In order to avoid controversies, such zoning and acquisitions by land bank corporations must be made ex-ante, that is, before it is allocated to any particular private sector entity.

The processes described above played a vital role in the repeal of the Land Acquisition Act of 1894 and could be seen as important milestones in the journey to the Land Rehabilitation and Resettlement Act of 2017; they describe the politics of policy, namely, the role that different actors play in the policy process. They show on the lines of Thomas and Grindle's (1990) interactive model of the policy process, that policy-making is not a linear, step-wise process but an interactive one in which different actors bring their own interests and agenda to the policy process. The policy outcomes are shaped by the interactions among different actors.

The Right to Education Bill provides another illustration of this process.[16] The draft of the bill was first put on the website of the Ministry of Education and Human Resources as well as on the websites of various NGOs. Comments were sought from the general public. Originally the law commission had suggested 50 per cent reservation in private schools. The private schools lobby protested and the union government put the bill on back burner on the grounds of paucity of funds. Even state governments rejected the model policy of Right to Education for paucity of funds, the underlying reason being protests by private schools. But due to constant campaigning by NGOs and public pressure, the government had to make it as one of its promises to be fulfilled within hundred days. Thus, the policy sailed through Parliament but with a change in reservation from 50 per cent to 25 per cent. Further, instead of giving detailed outlines for

16 This example was contributed by Seema Sahai, doctoral candidate at the School of Public Policy and Governance at MDI, Gurgaon, and I thank her for this.

grassroots enactment, it has given much leverage to local self-government to implement the policy. This again shows how the balance of power among the various actors influences the process of policy formulation and how different interest groups seek to further or protect their own interests in the policy process.

Policy reforms in several sectors, such as water, irrigation, power, infrastructure, that affect the public at large, can be explained using the interactive model of the policy process. In sectors where the stakes are high and large numbers of people are affected by changes but also where there is room to affect the course of policy, the policy process is a highly interactive one. On the other hand, where the nature of the sector is specialised, the extent to which the public at large is impacted in their day-to-day life is small and where the scope to influence policy is restricted, policy-making is likely to be linear. Very often, the policy-making process could be linear but the implementation process could be an interactive one; that is, when the policy comes to the ground, different actors may oppose it, leading to altering of the policy outcomes. The nature of the policy process may also change from predominantly linear to interactive; for instance, in early stages of planned economic development, policy-making in India was much more linear; as the scope for civil society engagement increased and the range of actors influencing policy choices expanded (see the discussion on shift from government to governance in Chapter 1), policy processes became more interactive.

2.10 Conclusion

A model, as stated earlier in this chapter, is a simplified representation of a real-life situation. These models of policy analysis essentially seek to provide an analytic framework through which the analysis of public policy processes could be carried out. It is for students of public policy to examine which of these best describes their experiences with policy formulation and implementation and what the major strengths and weaknesses of each of these models are. Essentially, these models structure our thinking on the analysis of public policy and provide a set of tools that inform our approach to the analysis of public policy. They inform our analysis of public policy and help articulate the nuances of public policy processes. They may also help us understand the evolution of public policies under different governments and facilitate the comparison of policy processes across time and nations. Characterising the nature of the policy process requires a deep understanding of the processes behind the policy, thus making a call for stronger research on this front.

References

Allison, G. T. 1971. *Essence of Decision*. Boston: Little, Brown.

Bardhan, P. 1989. *Conversations Between Economists and Anthropologists: Methodological Issues in Measuring Economic Change in Rural India*. New Delhi: Oxford University Press.

Baumgartner, F. R. and Jones, B. D. 1991. 'Agenda Dynamics and Policy Subsystems.' *Journal of Politics* 53(4): 1044–74.

Birkland, T. A. 2005. *An Introduction to the Policy Process: Theories, Concepts and Models of Public Policy-making*. Second edition. New York: M. E. Sharpe.

Bullock, A. and Stallybrass, O. 1977. *The Fontana Dictionary of Modern Thought*. London: Fontana/Collins.

Chan, H. S., Wong, K., Cheung, K. C. and Lo, J. M. 1995. 'The Implementation Gap in Environmental Management in China: The Case of Guangzhou, Zhengzhou and Nanjing.' *Public Administration Review* 55(4): 333–340.

Crosby, B. L. 1996. 'Policy Implementation: the Organizational Challenge.' *World Development* 24(9): 1403–1415.

Dobuzinskis, L. 1992. 'Modernist and Postmodernist Metaphors of the Policy Process: Control and Stability vs. Chaos and Reflexive Understanding.' *Policy Sciences* 25(4): 355–380.

Dye, T. R. 2002. *Understanding Public Policy*. Tenth edition. Delhi: Pearson Education.

Etzioni, A. 1967. 'Mixed Scanning: A Third Approach to Decision-making.' *Public Administration Review* 27(5): 385–392.

Fiorino, D. J. 2001. 'Environmental Policy as Learning: A New View of An Old Landscape.' *Public Administration Review* 61(3): 322–334.

Foucault, M. 1991. *The Foucault Effect: Studies in Governmentality*. Chicago: University of Chicago Press.

Gordon, I., Lewis, J. and Young, K. 1997. 'Perspectives on Policy Analysis.' In *The Policy Process: A Reader*, edited by M. Hill, 5–9. London: Harvester WheatSheaf, Prentice Hall.

Hempel, L. C. 1996. *Environmental Governance: The Global Challenge*. Washington, D.C.: Island Press.

Hogwood, B. A. and Gunn, L. A. 1984. *Policy Analysis for the Real World*. Oxford: Oxford University Press.

Huitema, D. and Meijerink, S. 2009. *Water Policy Entrepreneurs: A Research Companion to Water Transitions Around the Globe*. Cheltenham: Edward Elgar.

John, P. 1998. *Analysing Public Policy*. London: Cassell.

Keeley, J. and Scoones, I. 2003. *Understanding Environmental Policy Processes: Cases from Africa*. London: Earthscan.

Kingdon, J. W. 1985. *Agendas, Alternatives and Public Policies*. Second edition. New York: Harper Collins.

Lerner, D. and Laswell, H. 1951. *Policy Sciences*. Stanford: Stanford University Press.

Lindblom, C. E. 1959. 'The Science of Muddling Through.' *Public Administration Review* 19: 78–88.

Lindblom, C. E. 1979. 'Still Muddling, Not Yet Through.' *Public Administration Review* 39: 517–525.

Lipsky, M. 1980. *Street Level Bureaucracy: Dilemmas of the Individual in Public Services*. New York: Russell Sage Foundation.

Mackintosh, M. 1992. 'Introduction.' In *Development Policy and Public Action*, edited by M. Wuyts, M. Mackintosh and T. Hewitt, 1–9. Oxford: Oxford University Press in association with Open University.

Meier, G. M. 1991. *Politics and Policy-Making in Developing Countries*. San Francisco: Institute for Contemporary Studies Press.

Mooij, J. 2003. 'Smart Governance? Politics in the Policy Process in Andhra Pradesh, India.' Working Paper 228, Overseas Development Institute, U.K.

Moore, M. 1999. 'Politics Against Poverty?' *IDS Bulletin* 30(2): 33–46.

Simon, H. A. 1957. *Administrative Behaviour*. Second edition. London: Macmillan.

Sudan, R. 2000. 'Towards SMART Government. The Andhra Pradesh Example.' *Indian Journal of Public Administration* 46(3): 401–16.

Sutton, R. 1999. 'The Policy Process: An Overview.' Working Paper 118, Overseas Development Institute, U.K.

Thomas, J. W and Grindle, M. S. 1990. 'After the Decision: Implementing Policy Reforms in Developing Countries.' *World Development* 18(8): 1163–1181.

Warwick, D. P. 1982. *Bitter Pills*. New York: Cambridge University Press.

Weiss, C. H. and Birckmayer, J. 2006. 'Social Experimentation for Public Policy.' In *The Oxford Handbook of Public Policy*, edited by Robert E. Goodin, Michael Moran, and Martin Rein, 806–831. Oxford: Oxford University Press.

Wildavsky, A. 1979. *Speaking Truth to Power*. New York: John Wiley.

3

Where does policy change come from?
Context, ideas and people

In this chapter, we look at various factors that explain the policy choices made by policy-makers. We recall from our discussion in Chapter 2 that policy-makers may not evaluate all the policy options available to them. In this chapter, we review concepts in the public policy literature that explain policy choice. These concepts help us understand why certain policy choices are favoured by policy-makers. If policy-makers have a number of options to choose from, what factors decide why some options will be eliminated and some will prevail? In other words, what is the process of the narrowing of policy space?

Policy choices can be seen to have their genesis in certain ideas or streams of thought called development discourses or in stories called narratives. These narratives or discourses provide legitimacy to policy choices and lead policy-makers to choose certain options over others. In Chapter 2, we reviewed different theories that explain the role of groups in the policy process. In this chapter, we look at how specific groups called epistemic communities, advocacy coalitions or policy networks affect policy development, along with individuals and organisations called change agents. These individuals and groups provide a mechanism through which narratives and discourses enter the policy process and lead governments to make certain choices.

First, however, we examine the global context of policy-making, and review two important trends that are shaping this context: the emergence of the 'good governance paradigm' and the globalisation of governance. Both these trends have had an important impact on recent policy developments in India and abroad and can be seen as influencing policy choice in several areas of public policy. These provide the broader context in which policy processes take shape.

The organisation of this chapter is thus: we start with a review of the global context of policy-making. In this regard, we review two important concepts, namely, the good governance paradigm and the globalisation of governance. We examine the trends shaping the globalisation of governance. Having discussed the global context of policy-making, we review the factors that shape policy choice. Policy changes can be seen to be located in certain ideas or streams of thought called discourses or certain stories that establish causality and acquire the status of established wisdom called narratives. Within a context of the good governance agenda and the globalisation of governance, policy change is brought about by individuals called change agents, policy networks or epistemic communities. These individuals and groups translate these narratives and discourses into policy choices.

3.1 Policy-making in developing and developed countries: is there a difference?

In Chapter 2, we reviewed different models of the policy process, most of which have been developed in the west. Mooij (2003) raises a pertinent question on whether there is such a thing as 'a third world policy process', given that most theories and concepts that seek to explain policy change have been developed by western policy scientists.

Drawing upon Horowitz (1989) and partially on Thomas and Grindle (1990), Mooij (2003) concludes that while there are several similarities, several important differences can be noted between policy-making in developed and developing countries. The first of these involves regime legitimacy. Since many Third World regimes, such as those in Africa and Latin America, are fragile, State legitimacy itself may be open to question. As a result, on top of other objectives, the goal of many policies in developing countries may simply be to protect or enhance regime legitimacy. This creates an additional stake in the policy process. Second, the main policy concerns are often different, since developing countries face such challenges as enhancing access to basic education, health and ameliorating disease and hunger that are distinct from those faced by the developed world. That is, the priorities for public policy to address tend to be different.

Third, developing countries tend to have a large State structure, implying that the State is inordinately important as compared to society. This, however, should not, in itself, necessarily be taken to mean that the State is strong or effective. Fourth, Mooij notes that the capacity to effectuate policy tends to be rather weak in developing countries. The State may be hampered in its ability to effectuate policy by the scarcity of resources (financial, managerial or technical). Fifth, in many developing countries, there are often large groups of people excluded from participation in the policy process. Thus, policy processes tend not to be as inclusive as in the developed world. Sixth, and related to the previous point, the mode and channels of participation are often less well established or clearly circumscribed. The seventh point is that generally, in developed countries, much more importance tends to be given to expert knowledge than in developing countries. Finally, many developing countries have a higher importance of foreign development models to pursue and this may be accompanied by a high dependence on foreign experts. We shall come back to this point later in this chapter when we talk about the concept of policy transfer.

To the above, we may add another and final eighth point, as noted by Thomas and Grindle (1990), namely, that while in many developed countries, the main area of policy contestation is the process of policy formulation itself, in developing countries it is the process of policy implementation that witnesses most struggles and contestations. Greater contestation and exercise of power takes place in the realm of policy implementation, where different actors bring their own interests and agenda to the policy implementation process. This, as we noted in Chapter 1, is one of the important reasons for the need for a greater importance being attached to the study of policy implementation processes in the developing world. We shall revisit this point in Chapter 4, where we note the role of different actors in shaping policy outcomes through their perceptions, motivations and actions.

3.2 The good governance paradigm

The concept of 'good governance' has now come to be widely used. It is used by bilateral and multilateral organisations, NGOs, academicians and researchers. It is a recurring theme in national and international conferences and provides a basis for directing financial resources in specific directions. An understanding of the concept of good governance is also essential for understanding processes of policy formulation since many recent public policy interventions can be seen to be located, or at least, draw their justification from the good governance agenda. Many policy changes in India and abroad can be seen to be located in the notion of good governance. The good governance paradigm has been instrumental in providing the broad context in which policy choices are made; it has also been fundamental in altering the balance of power between the State, markets and civil society as actors in governance.

The 'good governance' paradigm was floated and espoused by the World Bank in the 1990s in response to the below satisfactory results in some of the reform programmes supported by the World Bank.[1] In this context, improving systems of governance came to be identified as a means for bringing about sustainable economic development. It was argued that for better economic management, fundamental changes were needed within the political system and the mere injection of financial resources was far from enough. The infusion of financial resources needed to be matched by changes in the political system and by appropriate institutional reform. The concept of good governance was propagated as a means to secure more effective utilisation of financial resources that were being injected by the World Bank into the economies of the developing world.

The World Bank's vision of good governance envisages a bureaucracy imbued with professional ethos, an accountable executive arm of the government, a strong civil society participating in public affairs and citizens behaving under the rule of law (Shylendra 2004). More lately, there has been a broadening of this concept by official aid agencies incorporating political dimensions so as to include and emphasise participatory development, democratic systems that promote transparent and accountable societies, and civil society participation. In essence, the concept has been widened in order to include notions of civil society participation in public affairs.

As per a recent definition by the Organisation for Economic Cooperation and Development (OECD), good, effective public governance helps to strengthen democracy and human rights, promote economic prosperity and social cohesion, reduce poverty, enhance environmental protection and the sustainable use of natural resources, and deepen confidence in government and public administration.

Prescriptive and descriptive dimensions of good governance
The term good governance is used both in a prescriptive and in a descriptive sense (Shylendra 2004). In a descriptive sense, this phenomenon is seen as emerging due to a changing role of State in developed as well as in developing countries. This is happening in a context of neo-liberal ideologies, globalisation and liberalisation. The State is cutting back expenditure, and other actors are acquiring a pre-eminent role, leading to what is called a pluralisation of the State.

In a prescriptive sense, the good governance paradigm refers to enabling the right manner of exercise of power for attaining better economic development in a country as prescribed (World Bank 1994). It entails a right manner

---

1   For a detailed discussion of the genesis of the concept, see also Mathur (2008).

of exercise of power for economic development as well as simultaneously enhancing the scope for participation and democratic processes.

In this sense, it could be seen as comprising a wish list of elements that are essential for improving governance systems. Four important ideas are thus emphasised in the thrust on good governance. These are as follows:

1. Improving public sector management
2. Ensuring accountability of public and private sectors
3. Creating an appropriate legal framework for development
4. Promoting transparency and information

Though the concept is used widely, it is perhaps for the same reason that it also has its critics: the term is used loosely, often without a clear understanding of its connotation; further, the term is seen as being excessively prescriptive. A number of criticisms can be levelled against the 'good governance' paradigm, that we review below.

The first is the 'holier than thou' attitude that it seems to postulate. It is seen by some as being excessively prescriptive, as imposing certain preconceived notions of how governance should be carried out. It presents a wish-list, a sort of utopia to which governments may aspire. Further, many argue that adhering to its prescriptions reduces the policy space that developing country governments have. It is seen to be part of an agenda espoused by multilateral institutions dominated by countries of the west. Besides, 'good governance' has come to be seen as a broad, umbrella concept. The term tends to be used rather loosely and at times it constitutes little more than rhetoric; it is used widely by those who wish to garner support or visibility for their programmes, but often with little understanding of what the term entails and how that would be operationalised. It has become a sort of cliché, a buzzword, that provides hope of an alternative future but with little of a roadmap on how to get there. Another critique of this notion is the emphasis it places on securing the rule of law, as if State law itself were sacrosanct. We shall revisit this idea at greater length in Chapter 4, while discussing the constructs of legal pluralism, wherein we look at State law more critically and in relation to non-State laws and institutions that may often take precedence over it and in fact, may be more appropriate or relevant to people's needs, priorities and culture.

Nevertheless, we could see the concept of good governance as useful in that it provides some kind of an ideal to live up to. It gives governments and institutions of the State some kind of a blueprint for improving service delivery and reforming the institutions of the State. It provides an ideal to aspire for, just like the concept of rationalism in policy-making discussed in

Chapter 2. It is an ideal model of governance or represents a prescriptive form of it. For reasons that we argued rationalism in policy-making to be relevant despite being unrealistic, the good governance paradigm also retains its sheen for academicians and practitioners.

3.3 International governance: the global context of policy-making

Governance can be studied at different levels: national, local or international. We have referred in Chapter 1 to national and local governance while talking about governance through the State and local institutions. We now turn our attention to institutions and mechanisms that shape international governance.

How do nations collectively pursue their interests at the global level in the absence of an international government or State? One answer to this question is provided by the regime theory or the international relations perspective in the political science literature (Sutton 1999). Regimes can be defined as sets of implicit and explicit principles, norms, rules and decision-making procedures around which actors' expectations converge in a given area of international relations.[2]

An international regime could be considered to be a set of principles, norms, rules and procedures accepted by States which helps them to realise common interests. International regime theory shows how States, acting in their own self-interest, can come together to work towards some basic common interests in the absence of a regulating authority, such as an international government. Sutton (1999) notes different approaches to how regimes function. One perspective focuses on power-based approaches that are shaped by a dominant country; knowledge-based (cognitive) approaches emphasise the importance of normative and causal beliefs that decision-makers hold; and, finally, interest-based (neo-liberal) approaches emphasise how international regimes help states achieve their individual interest.

Another perspective on global governance is provided by legal anthropological approaches from a standpoint of legal pluralism, that points to the interface of state, customary and international law.[3] When we study the globalisation of governance from a perspective of legal pluralism, we look at how international and transnational law exercise influence on national law. Increasingly,

---

2 Principles are beliefs of fact, causation and rectitude. Norms are standards of behaviour defined in terms of rights and obligations. Rules are specific prescriptions for action while decision-making procedures are prevailing practices for making and implementing collective choice. See also the discussion in Chapter 1.

3 See the discussion on the concept of legal pluralism in Chapter 1.

international and transnational law have come to exercise an influence on national law and policy, causing the locus of control over decision-making to shift outside the political boundaries of States, pointing to the globalisation of governance. Further, as international law gets implemented at the local level, it gets diluted and is mediated through the influence of local law and other institutions, pointing to the 'glocalisation of law' (Randeria 2003).[4]

The globalisation of governance

Apart from the 'good governance' paradigm, another trend that has been significant in shaping the context of public policy formulation is what is referred to as the 'globalisation of governance'. It has caused control and autonomy over policy-making to move beyond the frontiers of nation-states and has also caused some convergence in policy choices made by nations across the globe. Many argue that it has been an important factor leading to a constricting of policy space while others suggest these claims to be exaggerated.

The globalisation of governance is an interesting and controversial concept, given that both the terms 'governance' and 'globalisation' have many meanings and connotations. They are terms on which it is hard to come to a consensus regarding their meaning. On globalisation, Cerney, Menz and Soederberg (2005: 9) note '...There are almost as many definitions as there are scholars and actors writing and thinking about globalisation'.

Globalisation has been defined as '...the closer integration of the countries and peoples of the world which has been brought about by the enormous reduction of costs of transportation and communication, and the breaking down of artificial barriers to the flows of goods, services, capital, knowledge and (to a lesser extent) people across borders (Stiglitz 2002: 9).' Bertucci and Alberti (2003: 17) define globalisation as 'the increasing flows between countries of goods, services, capital, ideas, information and people that produce cross-border integration of economic, social and cultural activities.' They note that it creates both opportunities and costs for the actors involved and for this reason it should not be demonised or sanctified; nor should it be made a scapegoat for the major problems affecting the world today.

Gelinas (2003), noting the many ways in which the term can be interpreted, sees globalisation as a system, a process, an ideology and an alibi. As a system,

---

4 One example of this might be to see how the same programmes funded by multilateral institutions are implemented in different countries, such that they get colored by local institutions, policies and norms.

it represents the total control of the world by supranational economic interests. As a process, it represents a series of actions carried out in order to achieve a particular result.

As an ideology, it represents a coherent set of beliefs, views and ideas determining the nature of truth in a given society. Its role is to justify the established political and economic system and make people accept it as the only one that is legitimate, respectable and possible. As an alibi, globalisation is presented as a natural, inevitable and irresistible phenomenon, which lets major economic and political decision-makers off the hook.

While it is common to see globalisation as a predominantly economic phenomenon represented by the integration of world markets, it should actually be seen as a multi-faceted phenomenon with political, economic, technological and cultural dimensions (Giddens 2002). Giddens refers to a process of 'reverse colonisation', implying that the non-western countries have come to exercise an influence over developments in the west; examples of this can be seen in the Latinizing of the non-west, the emergence of a globally-oriented high tech sector in India or the selling of Brazilian television programmes in Portugal. Cerney, Menz and Soederberg (2005: 2) see globalisation as 'essentially a political process of convergence'. When we talk about globalisation, we refer to a process of convergence globally, be it in the realms of culture, religion, political systems or the economy. Cultural globalisation, for instance, means that the world tends to wear similar clothes, enjoy the same music and eat the same food.

In general, over the last two decades, there has been increasing recognition that a new global economy has emerged as a result of two long-run broad trends converging: globalisation, and advances in information and communication technology (Clarke 2006). This 'new economy' is different from the old economy in that knowledge has become the primary ingredient for economic growth rather than traditional productivity inputs such as labour and natural resources. The characteristics of this new economy include a rising knowledge intensity in all industries, including in the service sector, a corresponding decline in the material resource intensity of economic activity, and a global focus resulting from the increased international flows of capital, technology and skilled labour.

There have been wide-ranging debates on the implications of globalisation for the sovereignty of nation-states, economic development and well-being, global power relationships and cultural hegemony. In fact, globalisation is still seen by many in the developing world as merely the latest stage in the exploitation of the Third World by the west, a project from which the rich countries gain at the expense of the poor (Giddens 2002). To many living outside the west in America or in Europe, globalisation looks pretty much like westernisation, or perhaps Americanisation, since America is now the biggest superpower with a dominant economic, cultural and military position in the global order. From this perspective, many of the visible cultural expressions of globalisation are entities such as McDonald's, Coca-Cola and CNN that have made deep inroads all over the world and are seen as symbolic representations of American culture invading global culture.

Globalisation, it is held by its critics, mainly advances the interests of the United States and other western countries. Questions are also raised about the benefits that globalisation has brought to the world, especially to poorer economies. African countries have experienced problems, it is argued, not because of the growth of globalisation but perhaps because they have been left out. According to Sachs (2005), however, the authenticity of the anti-globalisation movement can be questioned by the observation that globalisation, more than anything else, has reduced the numbers of extreme poor in India by two hundred million and in China by three hundred million since 1990. Far from being exploited by the multinational companies against which the movement is targeted, these countries have achieved unprecedented rates of growth on the basis of foreign direct investment and the export-led growth that followed. Further, countries with higher levels of FDI per capita are also the countries with higher GNP per capita and this holds true for countries across the world, in Latin America, Africa and Asia. Likewise, countries with open trade have grown much faster than countries with closed trade and rising per capita incomes in most countries have generally been associated with a rise in the ratio of trade to GDP.

Globalisation processes are propelling many changes not only at the national level as described above but also internationally. Political problems tend to become more transnational, governance activities tend to become more supranational and political legitimisation is increasingly affected by transnational processes and norms; however, even then, as argued by Koenig-Archibugi (2005), States retain the key resources needed for effective governance. There is no consensus among analysts about the extent to which political authority and governance capacity have migrated to transnational or supranational level. There is evidence that major parts of the world are indeed moving in a post-national direction; however, it needs to be understood perhaps that this process is neither linear, nor consistent across sectors and regions, nor irreversible.

There is, nevertheless, a growing realisation that governments are not the only and not necessarily the most important actors in governance. Various developments contribute to this awareness: namely, the rising role of supranational bureaucracies in policy formulation and implementation, as well as trends towards international legalisation and adjudication; the circumstance that an increasing number of public agencies other than national executives, such as central bankers and securities regulators, establish trans-governmental networks with their counterparts in other countries; the self-regulatory activities of business actors, which create a number of transnational governance mechanisms; the growing role of NGOs and transnational advocacy networks in identifying transnational problems, formulating policy options and assisting other actors in policy implementation; finally, the fact that civil society, companies, national public agencies and inter-governmental organisations are forming multi-stakeholder policy networks that seek consensual solutions to social problems, such as the World Commission on Dams, the Global Alliance for vaccines and immunization, and the UN Global Compact. These trends provide a backdrop and context in which policy choices are made and processes of public policy-making need to be studied.

We could use the term 'globalisation of governance' in two different ways. The first is to refer to trends in convergence in governance across the world, through similar trends in paradigmatic shifts towards markets, privatisation, local institutions and partnerships as appropriate modes of governance, as described in Chapter 1, and the global spread of democracy, as described in the following sections of this chapter. The second is to refer to the emergence and rising importance of multilateral institutions such as the World Trade Organisation (WTO), the International Monetary Fund (IMF)) and the World Bank, the growing influence of transnational corporations and the rising influence of NGOs on governance processes internationally. These organisations and institutions, that operate at the global level, have a bearing on governance processes at the national level. Where previously the nation state exercised considerable control over the making of public policy, the rise of transnational corporations, the increasing role of international NGOs and that of global governance agencies such as the WTO, IMF and World Bank has resulted in a reconfiguration of political power in which the State is no longer the predominant actor. Globalisation has thus become, as put by Peine and McMichael (2005: 19) 'discursively a form of governing itself.'

In this part of the chapter, we will review the trends that point to the globalisation of governance, namely,

1. the growing role of multilateral institutions
2. the rise of transnational companies
3. the increasing influence of international NGOs
4. the importance of international summits and conventions
5. the spread of information and communication technology
6. the spread of democracy
7. the role of type 2 partnerships

The growing role of multilateral institutions

An important trend shaping public policy in recent years has been the increasing role of multilateral organisations that urge governments to follow similar courses of action across the globe. This has implications for not only national level governance but also local livelihoods and vulnerability; the impacts of these institutions as well as the policies and laws that they urge governments to formulate and implement trickle down from global to local levels.

A case in point is the neo-liberal agenda in the form of a heightened role of markets as espoused by the World Bank in the 1980s. This took the form of conditionalities attached to financial support programmes, which many argue shifted the locus of control over decision-making from the national to the international arena. The new economic policies that India embraced in the 1990s could be seen to be located in the neo-liberal discourse espoused by the World Bank and other international institutions.

The three main institutions that are known to govern globalisation are the IMF, WTO and the World Bank (Stiglitz 2002). The IMF and the World Bank have indeed been at the centre of the major economic issues of the last two decades, including the financial crises and the transition of former communist countries to market economies. These organisations originated as a result of the United Nations Monetary and Financial Conference at Bretton Woods, New Hampshire in July 1944, as part of a concerted effort to finance the rebuilding of Europe after the devastation of World War II. The IMF was founded on the belief that there was a need for collective action at the global level for economic stability. It was based on the premise that markets can work badly, and therefore, concerted efforts are needed to stimulate aggregate demand. However, as paradox would have it, as Stiglitz notes, it now favours market supremacy with ideological fervour. Founded on the belief that there is a need for international pressure on countries to have more expansionary policies, such as increasing expenditures, reducing taxes or lowering interest rates to stimulate the economy, today the IMF typically provides financial support to countries only if and when they engage in policies like cutting deficits, raising taxes or raising interest rates that lead to a contraction of the economy.

Those who congregated at Bretton Woods did so in the backdrop of the economic depression of the 1930s; the economist John Mayard Keynes provided a simple explanation that this could be avoided by governments by stimulating aggregate demand. The IMF and World Bank then became the key missionary institutions to preach the lessons of free market and these ideas were reluctantly pushed on developing countries that badly needed their loans and financial support. In the 1980s, the Bank went beyond just lending for projects to providing broad-based support, in the form of structural adjustment loans but did this only when the IMF gave its approval, and with that, gave IMF imposed conditions on the country. The IMF was supposed to help only in times of crises; however, developing countries had a recurring need for help so the IMF more or less became a permanent part of life in most of the developing world.

The World Bank and the IMF, further, were driven by the collective will of the G-7. The agenda of the IMF was to prevent another global depression, by putting pressure on countries that were not doing their fair share to maintain global aggregate demand, by allowing their economies to grow into a slump; it would also provide liquidity in the form of loans to those countries unable to stimulate aggregate demand with their own resources.

Though the ideas and intentions behind the creation of the international economic institutions were sound, they gradually evolved over the years into something very different from what was originally intended. The Keynesian orientation of the IMF, which emphasised market failures and the role for government in job creation was replaced by the free market mantra of the 1980s. This was part of the New Washington Consensus, a consensus between the IMF, World Bank and the US treasury about the right policies for developing countries, that signalled a radically different approach to economic development and stabilisation.

Critics argue that these institutions are dominated by commercial and financial interests in the industrially wealthy countries of the world, that is, they are not representative of the nations that they serve. Though they serve the developing countries, they are headed by representatives of the developed world. At the IMF, it is the finance ministers and central bank governors while at WTO, it is trade ministers that represent the trade interests of these countries; each of which is considered to be closely aligned with certain interests in them. Disillusionment under the international system of globalisation under the aegis of the IMF further grows as the poor face cut-backs in welfare expenditure in different parts of the world (Stiglitz 2002).

In this background, Sachs (2005) makes a case for an 'enlightened globalisation': a globalisation of democracies, multilateralism, science and technology and a global economic system designed to meet human needs. Pointing to the globalisation movement, he notes that it has indeed made its mark for the good in so far as it has exposed the hypocrisies and glaring shortcomings of global governance and for ending years of 'self-congratulation by the rich and the powerful (Sachs 2005: 355).' He makes a call for a greater role for international institutions in ending global poverty, noting that they have the experience to do so as much as the technical sophistication and internal motivation of a highly professional staff. '... Yet they have been badly used, indeed misused, as creditor-run agencies rather than international institutions representing all of their 182 member governments. It is time to restore the international role of these agencies so that they are no longer the handmaidens of creditor governments, but the champions of economic justice and enlightened globalisation (Sachs 2005: 366).'

What does the rising influence of such international institutions mean for public policy? It has been argued by the likes of Chang (2006) that the rising influence of multilateral institutions like the IMF and the World Bank as well as the growing number of international conventions and regimes has led to the shrinkage of policy space to dangerous levels for most developing countries, to the point that their ability to achieve economic development is itself being threatened. The current phase of shrinkage in policy space started in the 1980s, when the World Bank and the IMF massively expanded their programme loans in the aftermath of the debt crisis in 1982 in the form of structural adjustment programmes and broadened the scope and enhanced the strength of the conditionalities attached to their loans.

Chang takes an extreme view, asserting that these days there is virtually no area of public policy in which the Bank and the Fund do not have very strong influence (democracy, judicial reform, health, education and so on). At the same time, aid policies of the developed countries have also contributed to the shrinking of the policy space. This policy space is further reduced through the actions of developed countries in the WTO. Chang concludes on a pessimistic note that '...urgent action is needed. if nothing is done, the policy space available for developing countries will shrink to virtually nothing over the next several years, which could spell the end of development.'

This view has, however, been challenged by sceptics such as Shalini Randeria who argue that the State selectively implements what it wants to, and in doing so, exercises discretion to suit its convenience. In other words, Randeria notes that the claims regarding the loss of state sovereignty in the context of the increasing influence of multilateral institutions are exaggerated. Randeria observes that the State does not completely succumb to the prescriptions of multilateral institutions; instead, it exercises discretion in implementing what international institutions urge it to. Thus, the whole point about nation-states losing their sovereignty to international institutions needs to be taken with a pinch of salt. The State has varying room to manoeuvre or to manipulate policy reforms, giving rise to the notion of the 'cunning state' (Randeria 2003).

An important point that surfaced when this issue was posed to participants in the public policy programme being taught at MDI's School of Public Policy and Governance who were asked to engage with the above positions in light of their own experience with policy-making was that the institutions of the State do have room to manoeuvre at the stage that they enter into agreements with international institutions. That is, there is scope for negotiation and protecting State interest. Much depends on the diplomacy and tact with which this process is carried out. The process of securing financial support from international donors could be seen as an inherently political process, with considerable scope for bargaining, negotiation and room to manoeuvre. In the current age of globalisation of governance, much depends on the negotiation skills of those in positions of power and at the negotiating table with donors and funders. Much on the lines of what we argued while discussing the linear model of the policy process in Chapter 2, the process of securing financial support and accepting reform conditions is not one stage in a linear process of policy-making but itself a potentially interactive one, in which different actors have space to negotiate and protect their interests.

Many participants felt that the truth may lie somewhere between the positions advocated by Chang and Randeria, namely, that of the loss of state sovereignty and the notion of the cunning state. Generalisations may not be possible and the experience in this context may depend largely on the negotiation skills of those negotiating with donors and funders as well as the economic status and health of the recipient country that defines its bargaining strength and room to manoeuvre.

Very often, donor funding can be used as an excuse to initiate the kinds of policy changes desired by governments. In other words, governments frame certain policies that trickle down to the lower levels of government in the guise of conditions mandated by donors and funders. Many participants also felt that the perceived conditionalities may not be implemented in toto at the first go, but may be implemented incrementally. That is, the influence of donor and funder thinking trickles down into the corridors of policy-making slowly. Very often, interest in the donor-supported programme disappears once the donor funding ceases; that is, once the programme comes to a close, governments as well as the beneficiaries lose interest in it. This, of course, poses challenges for the viability and sustainability of the interventions. This is a common problem, for instance, in the context of donor-funded programmes for the formation of natural resource management user groups, wherein very often these groups collapse after the period of the donor-funded programme is over.

In my own research on the reform of irrigation systems in India, I have seen the influence of donors, funders and multilateral institutions in influencing the direction and pace of reform. For instance, the World Bank played an important role in irrigation reform programmes, particularly, those aimed at the establishment of water users' associations in a large number of States such as Haryana, Karnataka and Odisha. While interviewing members of the Irrigation Department in Haryana, segments of the irrigation bureaucracy pointed out that the chief reason for the formation of water users' associations (WUAs) was that it was mandated under the World Bank's WRCP and barring that, there was little motivation for the formation of WUAs (Narain 2003). A crucial issue for governments that are recipients of financial support programmes is whether they are able to articulate for themselves the rationale for certain interventions, or whether they are carried out primarily under external pressure.[5] Governments need to reflect on their own motivations in implementing reform programmes; another issue, as noted above, is the room to manoeuvre for governments in their negotiations with international institutions.

The rise and role of transnational corporations

International corporations have grown in size, number and significance over recent years and their growth has also redefined the relationship between the State and the market. It has created a shift in the balance of power between the State and private enterprise and has emerged as an important factor diluting State authority in recent years. The point of debate relates to whether private corporations can amass sufficient strength to overtake the State in terms of authority.

At the beginning of the 1980s, the best funded and positioned multinational

---

5 For more on the role of donors and funders in influencing reforms in the irrigation sector in India, see Narain (2009).

corporations (MNCs) acquired the status of transnational corporations (TNCs) (Gelinas 2003). Many of these mega enterprises are known to stand beyond or above the nation-state. With increasingly numerous mergers, takeovers and alliances, the concentration of wealth at the top reached such a degree that economic power succeeded in liberating itself from the national legal framework and from governmental control. The information revolution of the 1980s, marked by an extraordinary influx of new telecommunications, computerisation and automation, played an important role in transforming MNCs into TNCs. These tools allowed them to go beyond the former limits of time, space, borders, languages and cultures.

These TNCs share a number of features in common, as identified by Gelinas (2003): a huge direct foreign investment capacity of over $ 4 billion, embodied in a network of subsidiaries and subcontractors everywhere around the world; a financial strategic potential for carrying out mergers and forging alliances capable of concentrating supply and demand in order to neutralise and ideally eliminate competition; and, a capacity to relocate and delocate production units anywhere in the world where labour is cheaper and where environmental and social laws and regulations are least restrictive.

Globalisation has indeed encouraged participation by private organisations in governing processes. Many States accepted economic interconnectedness across political boundaries and States such as Britain, USA and Australia, New Zealand and Canada adopted market-driven neo-liberal policies of privatisation and deregulation (Higgins and Lawrence 2005). A part of this shift involved private-sector agencies assuming an increased influence in processes of governing.

Can or will transnational corporations rise above State authority? Transnational corporations have indeed risen in significance. They may not be involved directly in governing; however, they emerge as players in governance through their impact on lobbying for policy change, as also their ability to flout rules and regulations with impunity or to bend them in their favour. The growing might of transnational corporations relative to nation-states can be gauged by the fact that the largest companies in the world today have an annual turnover higher than the Gross Domestic Product (GDP) of all but a few nations. They are said to have usurped some powers that should belong to sovereign democratic States; they are able to roam the world in search of the cheapest source of labour and raw materials and are able to ride roughshod over the interests of the poor nations in doing so, just like colonial nation-states did in the past.

Sceptics of this view, however, argue that the power of big companies can be easily exaggerated by those who say that corporations run the world. Nations, especially, when they act collaboratively, have far more power than corporations and will continue to do so for the indefinite future. Nations have control over territory, corporations do not; nations establish frameworks of law, corporations do not; nations control military power, while corporations not so. As globalisation advances, therefore, it actually becomes more difficult for the big companies to act irresponsibly rather than the other way round. Further, people increasingly act both individually and collectively: in personal life and in social life, in interest groups, ethnic and value groups, classes and fractions of classes, in both public and private sectors; and, in doing so, they have an ability to counter the forces of globalisation. By attempting to manage, manipulate and own diverse processes of globalisation, people are able to defend their interests and to pursue their goals.

Another reason for this position, that questions the 'unfair' sweep of globalisation, as we shall see below, is the rise of NGOs, which have the capability to monitor what companies do, in any part of the world and to bring sanctions to bear upon them. Organisations such as Oxfam or Greenpeace have been global in scope in their activities. They have the potential of bringing corporate malpractices to public attention and mobilising opposition to them. Thus, according to this view, globalisation is to be seen not so much as an all-pervasive, powerful process, dominated by a few large and powerful actors but one in which people have ample room to manoeuvre or to find their own space.

The more important issue, then, in the context of our discussion on the globalisation of governance, as noted by Sachs (2005) is not so much whether one would be pro-globalisation or anti-globalisation. Instead, the issue is how governments in liberalising economies are able to evolve policy frameworks to penalise defaulting corporate giants and multinationals against which such movements are targeted. 'Where the anti-globalisation movement has a powerful point to stress is how multinational corporations often go well beyond their market demands to maximise shareholder wealth subject to the market rules of the game and instead, expend substantial efforts, often hidden under the table, to make the rules of the game themselves. Economic reasoning justifies market-based behaviour by companies if the rules of the game are sound. There is nothing in economic reasoning to justify letting the companies themselves set the rules of the game through lobbying, campaign financing and dominance of government policies (Sachs 2005: 358).'

Role of international NGOs

The emergence of international and national and regional organisations, NGOs and transnational networks based on shared interests has further shaped the globalisation of governance. Five decades ago, about 1,000 NGOs operated mostly at the local level; at the turn of the century, the United Nations reported that almost 30,000 NGOs operate internationally. Moreover, NGOs are invited to participate in global meetings such as the World Summit on Sustainable Development (WSSD) (2002), that can be taken as a good indication of the growing recognition of their role and position.

NGOs have begun to play an important role in challenging authoritarian rule and pushing donor governments towards a more proactive role against repressive regimes. Schmitz (2006) notes that during the past decades, NGOs and intergovernmental organisations (IGOs) along with bilateral donors have made human rights and democracy major goals of their external interventions in Africa and elsewhere. Transnational NGOs such as Amnesty International (AI) began in the 1960s to report on human rights conditions around the world, pressuring reluctant donor governments and multilateral agencies to monitor the domestic conduct of aid recipients. The end of the Cold War and the global diffusion of democratic governance in the early 1990s further pushed human rights and democracy to the centre of many aid programmes. In Kenya and Uganda, human rights NGOs have for long mobilised against repression and built alliances with domestic dissidents. More recently, donor governments have pushed for press freedom, multipartyism and a more independent judiciary while multilateral agencies increasingly view good governance as a prerequisite for economic development.

Since the mid-1990s, there has been an impressive increase in the research on the participation of non-state actors in global governance, especially on NGOs and business actors. There has been a proliferation of studies on the role of NGOs in areas such as human rights, rules of war, humanitarian emergencies, gender equality, economic development, demography, health policy, business regulation, environmental protection among others. NGOs are considered to be ubiquitous, having established their presence in almost all international policy domains; they are well entrenched in traditional areas such as development policy, humanitarian assistance and environmental protection but their presence is increasing also on previously less accessible issues like finance and arms control. Further, recent research has highlighted the fact that civil society organisations, companies, national public agencies and intergovernmental organisations often form what have been called multi-stakeholder policy networks that seek consensual solutions to social problems in specific sectors.

International summits

The globalisation of governance has been shaped as well by a series of international summits that urge governments to act on important environmental and social policy issues. In the environmental arena, for instance, this was triggered off by *Our Common Future,* the report of the Brundtland Commission in 1987. Starting with the Earth Summit at Rio (1992), this led to a series of international summits. Though there is debate over the relative importance and significance of these summits and a detailed discussion of this might be beyond the scope of this book, it cannot be denied that they have emerged as an important factor in shaping governance at a global level and influencing policy development at the national level. International summits often place pressure on nation-states to align their policies with what are perceived to be development priorities internationally; here, too, we notice the gradual shrinkage of policy space for developing countries. Though in recent decades Brazil, India, China (the so-called BRIC nations) have begun to acquire some prominence in the international political environment, the balance of international power continues to favour the developed nations of the west.

The role of international summits is essential for the analysis of the understanding of globalisation of governance for two reasons: first, these summits place pressure on nation-states to make specific policy choices, thereby constricting their policy space. Second, they lead to some kind of convergence in policy choices and governance processes globally.

The spread of information and communication technology

The process of globalisation in general, and of governance in particular, has been further shaped through the rapid spread of information and communication technology (ICT), as well as its wide acceptance and use. The spread of ICT has clearly been one of the most defining processes of the new millennium. It has been credited with accelerating the processes of globalisation on the one hand and facilitating better access to local information on the other. Though significant asymmetries exist with regard to access to this resource and the pattern of disposal of e-waste is a stark reminder of the North–South divide, the role of information and communication technology in accelerating processes of growth and development is hardly a subject of contestation.

The spread of ICT is indeed bringing several benefits to a wide cross-section of users (Orbicom and IDRC 2009). In poor as well as in rich nations, the use of mobile phone has facilitated the expansion of markets, social business and public services. It has facilitated the emergence of an entire range of economic services, such as micro-finance and insurance, marketing and distribution, employment and personal services as well as public services. By providing better access to information, ICTs have lowered transaction costs and strengthened livelihoods. At the same time, the use of ICT has facilitated a better delivery of public services, as seen in the case of telehealth and distance education. Telemedicine projects in Mozambique, Uganda and Bangladesh have improved medical care in remote and poorly equipped areas (World Watch Institute 2002). Using low-cost equipment, rural doctors can send x-rays or laboratory results to medical experts at hospitals in larger cities and obtain advice about treatment. The use of ICTs has also impacted other dimensions of human well-being, by widening the net of political participation and accountability. Though the internet is making slow progress in some of the poorest parts of the world, it can be extremely useful to accelerate its dissemination (World Watch Institute 2002). Through the spread of ICTs, political developments in one part of the world travel much faster to another; changes in governance systems and procedures can be quicker in influencing similar developments elsewhere.

There also exist, however, the perils of the use of ICT as well as impending dangers, such as the use of mobile phones to span violence, cyber crime and terrorism and the vulnerability that arises from a reliance on and the disruption of communication (Orbicom and IDRC 2009). Thus, the imperatives for building and employing an appropriate regulatory and policy environment as well as good communication infrastructure can hardly be overemphasised. At the same time, there are global asymmetries in access to this resource (World Watch Institute 2002). The United States, where the internet was developed, continues to dominate this electronic network. Most of Africa is still left out of the global network, plagued by a lack of infrastructure, particularly telephone lines, and high connection costs. Further, these asymmetries extend to disposal of this waste. The wired world generates a tremendous amount of hazardous waste: a computer monitor, for instance, contains four to eight pounds of lead (World Watch Institute 2002). Large volumes of used computers, circuit boards, and monitors discarded in the United States are sent to China, India and Pakistan for recycling and disposal, exposing workers to toxins and poisoning groundwater supplies.

The spread of democracy

Another important global trend in recent years has been the spread of democracy that has been influenced by the advance of global communication. Since the 1970s, the number of democratic governments has more than doubled. Democracy has spread to more than 30 new countries. These changes began in Mediterranean Europe with the overthrowing of military regimes in Greece, Spain and Portugal. The second group of countries where democracy spread in the early 1980s was in South and Central America; 12 countries in this region established or re-established democratic governments, including Brazil and Argentina. In Asia, democratisation has been going on since the early 1970s in countries such as South Korea, Taiwan, the Philippines, Bangladesh, Thailand and Mongolia.

What is more important now, however, is what some call 'democratising democracy', which would mean devolution, greater transparency and having effective anti-corruption measures at all levels. It implies constitutional reforms and the promotion of greater transparency in political affairs; there is a need for greater democratisation of democracy itself. Broadly, the notion of democratisation of democracy is consistent with the ideas enshrined in the concept of good governance, discussed earlier in this chapter. Much like the paradigmatic shifts in thinking on appropriate forms of governance worldwide, the spread of democracy in many countries of the world reveals some convergence in governance processes internationally.

The rise of type 2 partnerships

Type 2 partnerships received a major boost after the Johannesburg Summit of 2002. These partnerships were seen as an important means of fulfilling the commitments entailed in and agreed upon in the Johannesburg Plan of Implementation (Nischal and Narain 2004). Such partnerships include public-private initiatives as well as coalitions of international organisations, governments and NGOs (World Resources Institute 2003). They have certain characteristics; namely, that they are voluntary and self-organised. They are not formally negotiated and thus do not require universal consensus. They can range from simple agreements for exchange of information to initiatives that plan and fund infrastructure projects, education programmes or scientific studies. At the time of writing this book, the Commission for Sustainable Development (CSD) Secretariat listed the names of over 300 partnerships that relate to commitments contained in the implementation plan.

The emphasis on type 2 partnerships stems essentially from the realisation that State efforts on their own are inadequate to accomplish the Millennium Development Goals (MDGs) and need to be supplemented by efforts from actors other than the State.

The deliberations at the World Summit on Sustainable Development (WSSD), the preparatory process that led to the summit, the Millennium Summit and the Monterrey Conference, were all driven by the challenge of finding solutions for reducing poverty. The creation of global partnerships for development in terms of its impacts on human well-being and environment is seen as a potent tool that may be harnessed to attain the global development goals.

During the course of preparations for the WSSD, it was widely accepted that governments alone were unable to deliver implementation. It was felt that accomplishment of perceived targets required approaching issues from a multitude of perspectives, which could only be acquired through integration of efforts and building of consensus among the concerned actors at the global level. Based on this, early on in the preparatory process the UN Secretariat determined that there would be two types of outcomes of the Johannesburg summit: (1) Type 1, negotiated by the UN Member States and (2) Type 2 initiatives/partnerships, which are voluntary instruments for achieving specified targets agreed at the summit.

Perhaps the strongest rationale for type 2 partnerships is built on the premise of their role in bridging governance deficits. As noticed earlier in Chapter 1, the emphasis on type 2 partnerships globally at the turn of the millennium is a reflection of the realisation that neither of the State, markets nor local institutions are capable of addressing development challenges on their own; instead, there is need for partnerships across actors at a global level to accomplish these goals.

As forms of governance, these partnerships are intended to play a role in harnessing the strengths of the different involved actors (governments, industry, corporates and NGOs) in accomplishing the Millennium Development Goals. Different actors in reform processes have different strengths; they differ in their abilities to catalyse change, effect direct action, mobilise political support and garner material and human resources (Krishnan and Narain 2003). For instance, NGOs have a good understanding of local socio-political dynamics, bureaucracy–user linkages, markets and institutions. They are uniquely positioned to provide critical linkages between the State and civil society. This role is exercised at two levels: first, by influencing policy change through advocacy and second, by implementing new technologies, programmes and policies.

However, NGOs tend to be local in their approach and are usually limited in their ability to produce reform on a larger scale, typically being constrained by resources and geographical reach. That is where government support is needed in synergising scattered local initiatives so that a significant dent is made on reform processes. Besides, NGOs need a supportive environment from the State to carry out their activities. The corporate sector can support these initiatives not only through a direct involvement, for instance, in the social sector but also by providing financial resources to support both research and action. Besides, the corporate sector can supplement NGO interventions by capitalising, where relevant, on its geographical reach through its wide presence or distribution networks. The involvement of diverse stakeholders brings with it the strengths of each, which need to be mobilised well to ensure the success of partnerships. Table 3.1 provides a listing of the strengths of different actors in partnerships.

Table 3.1 Strengths of different actors in partnerships: what different actors can uniquely do and provide

Industry	Resources for research and action Corporate responsibility for environment Direct action in spread of civic amenities
NGOs	Advocacy for policy reform Mobilising local action Implementation of programmes and policies Introduction of new technologies Feedback to government
International Organisations	Promote networking and consensus building among governments and institutes Set guidelines for setting targets and monitoring Fund research and action
Research Institutes	Carry out Process Documentation Research Provide feedback to government and policy-makers Consolidate and disseminate research and databases
Government	Support civil society action Promote networks among research institutes, NGOs and civil society groups Provide enabling policy and regulatory frameworks Provide funds for relevant initiatives

Source: Krishnan and Narain (2003)

There are several areas in which type 2 partnerships can have an important role to play. One such area is the diffusion and dissemination of technologies for rural development. The role of technologies in sustainable development can hardly be debated; it is well understood that technological innovations can do much to raise productivity and tackle problems of disease, water supply, sanitation, hygiene and hunger. Recent decades have seen significant technological progress, with dramatic advances in medicine, agriculture, energy, genomics and information and communications technology (UNDP 2002). However, several other frontiers need to be crossed, such as, and importantly, low-cost energy for poor communities and cures for sleeping sickness and vaccines for HIV/AIDS. Technological innovations could accelerate progress towards Goals 1-7 in the MDGs.[6] Investments in global technology for reducing poverty and reaching the goals need to be expanded to match the needs.

It is interesting to note that while one of the key objectives behind the formation of type 2 partnerships has been the garnering of financial resources from actors than the state, Hale and Mauzerall (2004) conclude that little partnership financing has actually come from new sources. Most still comes from the government and less than 1 per cent from the private sector. They give a number of suggestions to make type 2 partnerships more effective, namely, establishing a learning network, increasing the transparency of partnerships, increasing private sector and small stakeholder participation and aligning partnership activities with multilateral priorities.

3.4 Policy transfer analysis
The globalisation of governance and the rising role of multilateral institutions as well as their implications for the erosion of policy space in developing countries has led to an increased interest in the subject of policy transfer analysis. Policy transfer analysis is a theory of policy development that seeks to make sense of a process or set of processes in which knowledge about institutions, policies or delivery systems at one sector or level of governance is used in the development of institutions, policies or delivery systems at another sector or level of governance (Evans 2004). There are three different types of processes of transfer: voluntary transfer or lesson-drawing, negotiated transfer and coercive transfer.

Negotiated policy transfer refers to a process in which governments are compelled by influential donor countries, global financial institutions,

---

6 For description of MDGs, see 'United Nations Millennium Development Goals,' United Nations, www.un.org/millenniumgoals/

supranational institutions, international organisations or transnational corporations to introduce policy change, in order to secure grants, loans or other forms of inward investment. Though an exchange process does occur, it remains a coercive activity because the recipient country is denied freedom of choice. Another form of indirect policy transfer can be seen when governments introduce institutional or policy changes due to a fear of falling behind neighbouring countries. For example, Japan's economic miracle in East Asia proved inspirational to neighbouring countries as Singapore, South Korea and Malaysia. Direct coercive policy transfer occurs when a government is forced to introduce constitutional, social and political changes against its will and the will of its people, under pressure from foreign agencies. Each of these forms of policy transfer entail different levels of autonomy for the State and different forms of its relationship with the international community, with implications for State sovereignty.

3.5 A new role for the State?

Since globalisation entered popular academic parlance in the 1980s, there has been substantial debate on whether this signals the end of the State as a form of sovereign authority or the reconfiguration of State powers. The emergence of the global economy, the rise of transnational bodies, international law and hegemonic power blocs contribute to a change in the role of the nation-state. As seen above, the rise of transworld regulatory bodies as well as the range of multilateral regional schemes have all contributed to trends in globalisation with new questions for state sovereignty. While regionalism is not simply a result of globalisation and may, in fact, be seen as part of a reaction against globalising tendencies, it incorporates mechanisms of governing that extend well beyond the State.

It could be argued that globalisation does not necessarily reduce the role of the nation-state but that it instead leads to its redefinition. In a context of globalisation, States need to take on a different role. Improving and reforming public administration and governance is critical to making globalisation and governance work for all, alleviating poverty and income inequality and advancing human rights and democracy.[7] Thus, States need to promote

---

7 For a review of the changing role of the State in India in the context of globalisation, see Nayar (2009). Nayar argues that the role of the State has been redefined in the period of globalisation and has far from 'shrunk'. For a discussion of the changing role of the State vis-a-vis the corporate sector and civil society organisations, see also Mathur (2008).

decentralisation and strengthen social policies: in particular, social safety nets, reinforce social capital, promote an efficient public administration, develop an effective strategy for resource mobilisation and improve tax administration systems. States must establish, maintain, refine and reform an enabling framework for private initiative as well.

3.6 Who brings about policy change? Where do these ideas come from?

The good governance agenda and the globalisation of governance as shaped by the rise of multilateral institutions, transnational corporations, transnational NGOs, international summits, the spread of ICT and the global spread of democracy provide a context for understanding the processes of public policy formulation. Within this context, policy change is brought about by specific individuals or groups called change agents, policy networks or policy communities. They propagate certain sets of beliefs or ideas, often called discourses, or spread certain stories called narratives that provide policy-makers with convincing ideas for policy choices. This is the subject of the following sections, to which we now turn our attention.

Change agents

A change agent is defined as one who sees change as an opportunity rather than a threat, who will be instrumental in managing change and taking it forward (Sutton 1999). A change agent gives direction and momentum to the implementation of new policies and methods. Change agents can be instrumental in bringing about policy change through intensive lobbying and advocacy with the government; they influence policy development through their efforts at persuasion and pressure on governments as well as through organisation and mobilisation of civil society. In Chapter 1, we referred to the concept of policy advocacy. Policy advocacy is carried out, in large part, by change agents, who pressurise governments for reform using their skills of persuasion and pressure.

In the Indian context, one is familiar with the names of many activists and leaders that were instrumental in bringing about social change. Anna Hazare, known for spearheading watershed conservation efforts in Maharashtra, Dr. Verghese Kurien, known for pioneering India's white revolution, and Sam Pitroda, known for pioneering change in the field of information technology, could all be considered change agents. Social activists like Aruna Roy have acted as change agents in the implementation of the National Rural Employment

Guarantee Act (NREGA). Arvind Kejriwal played a key role in the execution of the Right to Information Act.

Besides, there are several NGOs working for the formation and mobilisation of self-help groups and in the field of micro-credit and natural resource management. They have often lobbied with governments for policy change. Non-governmental organisations such as the Centre for Science and Environment have come to the fore with their agenda of lobbying with the government to bring about policy change. NGOs such as Viksat and Development Support Centre have lobbied for policy change in the irrigation sector in Gujarat, while the Center for Applied Systems Analysis in Development (CASAD) has lobbied for policy change in Maharashtra on the same front (Narain 2003). NGOs have played a role also in process advocacy, pushing for alternative approaches to the public policy formation processes, as seen in the case of Sahayog, that has lobbied for making processes of irrigation reform more participatory in States such as Karnataka (Mollinga 2001).

The concept of change agents is relevant for the analysis of policy change. Policy change entails an element of risks; policy entrepreneurs or change agents bear this risk. Policy change requires skills of perseverance and persuasion, which change agents bring to the policy process.

Epistemic communities

Haas (1992) defines an epistemic community as a network of knowledge-based experts or groups with an authoritative claim to policy relevant knowledge within the domain of their expertise. Members of an epistemic community hold a common set of causal beliefs and share notions of validity based on internally defined criteria for evaluation, common policy projects and shared normative commitments. Epistemic communities serve as channels through which new ideas circulate from societies to governments as well as from country to country.

An epistemic community could be considered to be a group of technical experts who have access to privileged or specialised information and share and discuss ideas among themselves. Inherent in the concept of epistemic communities is an element of exclusion; others are excluded, they do not have access to this information. Epistemic communities may include individuals, NGOs and research communities. They have powerful influences on policy-making, expressing political opinions and having links with governmental decision-makers.

Epistemic communities can influence state interest by

    a.   elucidating cause and effect relationships and providing advice about the likely results of various courses of action following a shock or crisis;

b. shedding light on the nature of complex inter-linkages between issues and on the chain of events that might proceed from failure to take action or from instituting a particular policy;

c. helping to define the self-interests of states or factions within it; and,

d. helping to formulate policies through framing of alternatives and defining implications of possible actions

Epistemic communities gain importance because of asymmetries in information; they have access to knowledge that others are deprived of. Policy-makers depend on them for a specialised knowledge to which they may not have access otherwise. They can put pressure on politicians and if politicians agree, they can invite them into positions of power.

In the Indian context, the notion of inter-linking of rivers as a form of public intervention to address the twin problems of water scarcity and abundance could be seen as influenced by the water technocracy. These proposals are claimed to be based on a scientific, technical expertise that belongs to only a few, who have used that as a basis for advocating proposals for the linking up of rivers to address the nation's twin problems of drought and flooding. Likewise, people with a specific technical or subject knowledge may be roped in as members of specific committees constituted by the government. These members are present on these committees on account of their specialised knowledge of a subject, that is their exclusive prerogative and a potential source of great influence on policy-making. A group of senior economists invited to advise governments on issues of economic policy or senior defence or space scientists invited by the government to advise it on matters of space and defence policy could be examples of epistemic communities. There is a certain aura of exclusion about such groups; they are closed and closely knit groups. This exclusion arises from the very specialised nature of the knowledge that is needed to inform policy in such sectors. Epistemic communities are likely to have a stronger role in those areas of policy-making where the potential of civil society to influence policy choices is limited; these are areas where the policy-making process tends to be more linear.

Policy networks

A policy network is a group of individuals and organisations, that share similar belief systems, codes of conduct and established patterns of behaviour.[8] It is built

---

8 See Kickert et al. (1997).

around an open and flexible system of relationships. Networks can be studied and dissected to determine who the dominant actors are, for example, networks in the USA that deal with energy are dominated by business groups and those relating to health policies are dominated by professional bodies (Sutton 1991). The extent of integration can, of course, vary across networks. Policy networks could also refer to the system of relationships that links the policy community together.

The concepts of policy networks and epistemic communities are important in that they help understand the role of interest groups in the policy process; they also provide a mechanism for bringing in narratives and political interests into the policy process. Pre-budget time is one occasion when many policy networks swing into action.

Distinguishing policy networks from epistemic communities
The difference between a network and epistemic community is that a policy or epistemic community is a more tightly knit group of elite experts who have access to certain information and knowledge that is not available to those excluded from the group. The way to distinguish between epistemic community and policy network is that an epistemic community is typically held together by its access to or understanding of specialised knowledge to which others do not have access; a network is bound together more so by a shared set of ideals, values and belief systems. A policy network tends to draw upon a larger group of people from a wider cross-section than does an epistemic community. We could understand the epistemic community to be a more closely-knit group of people bound together by their specialised knowledge than a policy network.

Advocacy coalitions
The advocacy coalition framework (ACF) is an approach to studying the policy process, that contends that two to four advocacy coalitions typically form in a particular policy domain when groups coalesce around a shared set of core values and beliefs. These groups engage in policy debate, competing and compromising on solutions based on their core values and beliefs. Policy is the result of competition and debate between the advocacy coalitions.

The advocacy coalition framework was developed by Paul Sabatier and has been further refined and developed, going through a number of amendments through joint work by Paul Sabatier and his colleague Jenkins-Smith.[9] The ACF assumes that policy elites have well-integrated belief systems linking

---

9 See, for instance, Sabatier (1993).

fundamental, distributional and substantive values. Actors will also conceptualise the severity of the causes of policy problems and devise different approaches for addressing those problems. These beliefs, in turn, are shaped by an individual's socialisation, education and organisational and institutional experiences.

The ACF is built around three hypotheses. First, that on major controversies within a major policy sub-system, the organisation of allies and opponents will be rather stable over periods of a decade or so. The political glue holding a coalition together is the group's agreement over certain policy core beliefs. The second hypothesis is that actors within an advocacy coalition will show substantial consensus on issues pertaining to the policy core, although less so on secondary aspects. The third hypothesis is that an actor or coalition will give up secondary aspects of his or her belief system before acknowledging weaknesses in the policy core.

The ACF addresses three different beliefs covering different levels of the topical scope. *Deep core* beliefs are composed of ontological and normative beliefs. *Policy core* beliefs consist of a coalition's normative commitments and causal perceptions across the sub-system under analysis. *Secondary aspects* refer to implementing polices that will address the problem.

According to the advocacy coalition framework, the sub-system is guarded by stable coalitions and policy core beliefs. In order for a major policy change to occur, an outside force must interrupt the system. This force is known as *exogenous perturbation* and can occur in the form of changes in socio-economic conditions, change in public opinion, a change in the system-wide governing coalitions or outputs from other sub-systems. External shocks, particularly ones that are large, often directly influence other political sub-systems resulting in changes in policy core beliefs and causing a realignment of actors in different coalitions.

The concepts of epistemic community, change agents and policy networks help us understand and articulate the role of different individuals and actors in policy formulation processes. They help us examine how policy change is contributed to by individuals or groups of individuals who bring to the process their beliefs, values and expertise that serves as an input into the policy process. In other words, these concepts help us understand the role that different individuals or groups of people play in the policy process.

Development discourses

We now turn our attention to a discussion of how ideas influence policy choices; in this context, we will discuss the relevance of two concepts: narratives and discourses.

A discourse can be considered to be an ensemble of ideas, concepts and categories through which meaning is given to phenomena; discourses shape certain problems, distinguishing some aspects of a situation and marginalizing others (Hajer 1995). It represents a collection of ideas that represent specific ways of thinking about a policy issue. A development discourse describes a way of thinking and outlook, a system of values and priorities that marginalises other possible ways of thinking (Sutton 1999). A discourse can also refer to dialogue, language and conversation or to the analysis of language used in policy-making.

Discourses, by presenting specific ways in which problems need to be approached, draw the attention of policy-makers to those ways of intervening, thereby shaping policy choices, and narrowing the policy space. Grillo (1997) lists some prominent development discourses. These are:

1. *Discourse of the state-engendered order in development,* involving the intervention of experts located in the UN agencies and embodied in multilateral and bilateral aid agencies: this discourse emphasises the supremacy of the State as an actor in governance, and dominated thinking on appropriate ways of governing till the 1980s.

2. *Market-engendered spontaneous order discourse,* institutionally located in the IMF and the World Bank. This discourse emphasises the supremacy of the free market as a mechanism for allocating resources and shaped policies for liberalisation in India and elsewhere in the 1990s.

3. *Discourse of the public sphere,* found in NGOs, research institutes and charities- constructed on the optimistic, reason-informed pursuit of formal and substantive democracy. This discourse emphasises the value of civic engagement and civil society participation in governance processes.

It is interesting to note that chronologically, these discourses acquired prominence at different points of time. The discourse of the State-engendered order in development dominated thinking on public policy through most of the period prior to the 1980s, when the market-engendered spontaneous order discourse took precedence. The discourse of the public sphere has acquired greater significance in recent years, especially in the period of and after the 1990s. The changing dominance of these discourses corresponds to the paradigmatic shifts in thinking on appropriate forms of governance.

Discourses influence policy choices in that many policies get their legitimisation from these discourses. By drawing the attention of policy-makers to specific issues that deserve attention and to specific ways of intervening, they provide a basis and legitimisation to policy choice. As noted above, the neo-liberal discourse emphasising the free market was behind policies for liberalising the Indian economy in the early 1990s. Likewise, policies for reservation for the backward classes can be seen to be located in the discourse on affirmative action. The discourse on gender empowerment has been crucial in shaping policies for reserving seats for women in civic bodies. The discourse on climate change has been influential in shaping policy choices favouring clean technologies as well as to promote financial and technological transfers from the North to the South. Thus, the analysis of discourse provides an entry point to study how policy evolves. Policy choices can be seen to be located in dominant discourses of their time; they are embedded in and derive their legitimacy from certain discourses.

Development narrative

A development narrative is a story that gains the status of conventional wisdom.[10] These narratives are essentially stories that individuals, organisations and the development community as a whole tell themselves and to others in order to see patterns in ambiguity or to make sense of the uncertain environment in which development takes place. They are stories that tend to theorise about the nature of social reality by establishing causality. These stories are repeated so often that they acquire the status of conventional wisdom. These stories then are used to provide a justification for policy choices. Policy choices made by policy-makers are seen to have their genesis in such narratives.

A narrative could be seen as a story that is used to develop or justify a policy intervention. A common example is the 'tragedy of the commons',[11] that influenced efforts at nationalisation and privatisation of natural resources like land and water. The essence of the narrative is that in the absence of institutions or rules to regulate the use of common pool resources, they will be overexploited (see also Chapter 1). If every shepherd grazing his herd of sheep on a pasture land were to increase the size of his flock, the grazing land would diminish and disappear in due course. This narrative, that gained the status of established wisdom, became the basis for public policy interventions for establishing state or private property regimes over what would be open access resources. Subsequently, the work of Ostrom (1990, 1992) and other scholars demonstrated the potential of community-based

---

10 For a detailed discussion on the role of development narratives in influencing public policy formation, see also Sutton (1999) and Roe (1991).

11 See Hardin (1968) and the discussion on the need for institutions for the management of common property resources. See also Ostrom (1990, 1992).

institutions for natural resource management. The fact that communities were capable of governing their own resources became a basis for policies for decentralised natural resource management. This narrative provided a legitimacy or justification for policies that sought to create user groups for managing natural resources. Narratives shape the framing of the issue; they influence what the problem is presented to be and compel policy-makers to make corresponding policy choices.

Narratives can provide new ways of understanding a problem and thus assert alternative ways of intervening. For instance, Amartya Sen's well known narrative about famine caused not by the physical absence of food, but by the lack of entitlement provides a fresh insight into what governments and policy-makers need to do to tackle famine: focus on institutions and entitlements; expand access; and, not necessarily 'produce more food'. It tells us 'where the problem lies'; narratives influence what the problem is presented to be.

These narratives persist primarily for three reasons. First, that they are consistent with certain scientific theories. For example, the tragedy of the commons occurs when there is a departure from the concept of carrying capacity. That is, the narratives may derive from certain scientific theories and explanations of relationships. Second, they simplify complex development processes and bring some order to them (Roe 1991). They serve as some kinds of stories that simplify the reality around us. In other words, they provide a simple way of characterising social processes or articulating them. Narratives are a way of dealing with the uncertainty and ambiguity that characterises development activity. They provide a pattern through which certain events can be interpreted and certain relationships can be explained. They help us to articulate specific kinds of development problems. They are, thus, able to transform a chaotic reality into an ordered and comprehensible sequence of events.

Third, narratives are often transmitted and perpetuated through policy networks and communities. This would typically be because they serve certain interests. They are known to serve the interest of certain groups or epistemic communities and transfer ownership of the development process to them. Certain groups and communities may propagate narratives in order to preserve their identity and position.

Just like development discourses, narratives serve an important function in policy development (Roe 1991). They reduce the policy space. Narratives develop to simplify the ambiguity; to bring order to chaos and uncertainty. They often are used to provide some sort of a blueprint for development. In the Indian context, it is possible to look at how certain development narratives have influenced policy choices. For instance, 'small family, happy family' constituted a narrative that could be seen to be located behind policies aiming at population stabilisation. It established a causality; namely, that with limited resources, it is easier to bring up a smaller family than a larger family.

Malthusian prophecies abut population growth outstripping food production were also often used as a basis for justifying policies for population stabilisation. 'Gram Vikas, Desh Vikas' (development of a village leads to development of the nation) could be seen to be another narrative that forms the basis of interventions for the development of rural areas.

Narratives behind water scarcity have been the basis for justifying large-scale water interventions such as the much hyped about and debated Sardar Sarvoar Dam (Mehta 2005). Drawing on her work in a village in Kutch district of Gujarat, Mehta (2005) notes that popular narratives concerning outmigration, over grazing and dwindling rainfall have gained wide currency at the local and State levels. While undermining the role of anthropogenic forces in aggravating water scarcity, these notions benefit politicians, business and industrial constituencies and certain voluntary agencies. They perpetuate the notion of dependency on water wonders like the Sardar Sarovar Dam.

In the field of natural resource management, the idea that programmes cannot be successful unless they build upon the participation of the resource users became a narrative, or what we may call a 'counter-narrative' to the 'tragedy of the commons'.[12] These narratives by establishing cause–effect relationships create a sense of urgency among policy-makers to act in specific ways, to the exclusion of other policy options.

One way to study the evolution of policy, therefore, is to look at how the dominant narratives surrounding the policy issue change with time. For instance, in the 1970s the dominant narrative around agriculture was shaped by the imperatives of increasing agricultural productivity. This resulted in an emphasis on high-yielding varieties of seeds and input intensive agriculture. This is no longer the dominant narrative in Indian agriculture as the results of high-input agriculture on diminishing long-term productivity have come to be seen. The dominant narratives now are about organic farming. It is interesting to see that at any point of time, there will be narratives and counter narratives. It is the dominant narrative that influences the final policy choice. Thus, one way to study policy change is to see how the dominant narrative surrounding a policy issue changes.

---

12 For the role of such narratives in influencing policy formation in the irrigation sector in India, see Narain (2009).

The concept of narratives and the tendency to use them excessively, however, has certain limitations. First, there could be a strong pressure to produce and reproduce simplifying narratives, especially in situations where difficult and ambiguous decisions have to be made. Further, development narratives can often lead individuals and organisations to make wrong assumptions about the cause of a problem and from this draw irrelevant lessons. This happens typically when there are efforts to transplant development model blueprints from one setting to another, where they may not be valid. In other words, development narratives may be misleading when they are hurriedly understood and sought to be applied. They can mislead when attempts are made to over-generalise a situation. Conventional wisdom can blind us to alternative options and opportunities. There are problems when narratives lead to simplistic overgeneralisations, excluding other potentially relevant policy options.

Roe (1991) gives a very good example of this in the form of the Grameen model of micro-credit. There has been an assumption that the blueprint of the Grameen model can be applied in any country or community regardless of social/cultural, economic or political contexts, as in Bangladesh. The false lesson learnt is that it will be successful in all circumstances. The purported success of the Grameen model of micro-credit persists because of its popularity among international donors. Micro-credit programmes competing for funding and support find that applying the favoured Grameen model gets their foot in the door with big donors, regardless of how accurately the model will apply to their specific situations.

Roe (1991) notes that development policies are often based on arguments, scenarios and narratives that may not stand up to closer scrutiny. Frequently the narratives are directly contradicted by experience in the field. In spite of this, the narratives persist and continue to inform policy-making. The most obvious reaction is to dismiss the narratives as myths or ideologies and to call for more rational policy-making or a more learning-based process. However, Roe suggests that this will not have any great effect, because the ideals of rationality and learning would not automatically fulfil the needs that the narratives do, and thus are likely to be discarded in practice. Instead, Roe notes that it is necessary to first try and understand why policy so often leans on narratives, and why policy-making apparently 'learns less and less' over time, before attempting to reform it. Roe suggests that the best way of reforming outdated narratives is to engage with them, either by trying to improve the narrative itself or by introducing counter-narratives. It is interesting to note, however, that new scientific evidence will lead to challenging established narratives.

Difference between a discourse and a narrative

A discourse is different from a narrative in that it is wider in concept; it is more of a philosophy. A narrative is narrower; more of a story. Discourses relate to modes of thought, values and fundamental approaches to issues whereas narratives help define an approach to a specific development problem. Nevertheless, narratives could be part of wider discourses. Narratives can lend the necessary support to a discourse by complementing it. A narrative could sometimes be seen to be a story that provides legitimacy to a discourse. For instance, the idea that the infusion of financial resources was not enough to steer economies out of low levels of development was used as a narrative by the World Bank, on which came to be founded the discourse on 'good governance'. Similarly, 'historical injustice' can be seen as the narrative underlying the discourse on affirmative action. The narrative of the bad, inefficient and corrupt State was embedded in the neo-liberal discourse that advocated the free market as an alternative to the poor performance of the State.

3.7 The case of water privatisation: where it comes from and why it persists, though it benefits only a few

We conclude this chapter by drawing upon the work of Urs and Whittell (2009) on the experience of water privatisation in Bengaluru that provides a very good example of the influence of narratives and discourses on the reform process as well as the role of the individuals and organisations who articulate them. The growing scarcity of water has compelled policy-makers and neo-classical economists alike to emphasise the need to price it correctly to reflect its scarcity value, paving the way for privatisation of water services in Bengaluru. However, this gives rise to problems of an ethical nature: if water were priced and sold in the market, would it flow through the taps of the poor, who are at present the most deprived and typically outside the ambit of the provision of water supply? '… Can the universal need for water to live and some people's desire to profit from its sale be reconciled (Urs and Whittell 2009: 2?).' This has been the central thread in their work analysing the experience of water privatisation in the city.

Urs and Whitell note that the 'reform agenda' of privatising Bengaluru's water supply has been advocated by a network of transnational NGOs, multilateral institutions, donors and funders who have found allies amid sections of the government and politicians. Neo-liberal discourses of privatisation, advocated by multilateral institutions and some transnational NGOs have found acceptance among and allies amid sections of the government. This has triggered off Bengaluru's privatisation process, often to the detriment of the poor and the marginalised.

Bengaluru has indeed grown well in recent decades as India's 'Silicon Valley', a picture vividly painted by the authors.[13] In a drive to build Bengaluru into a 'world-class city' the concerns of the poor have been sidelined, as obviously they do not apparently exist in 'world-class cities', or even if they do, they are not part of their landscape as depicted in brochures and glossy hand-outs.

Narratives such as those of a world-class city provide a justification for the appropriation of resources from the peripheral areas to support their expansion. These narratives are propagated by groups of people who use these narratives to justify policies for urban expansion. These efforts at turning Bengaluru into a 'world-class city', Urs and Whitell note, have been led by coalitions of politicians, industrialists, donors and funders and have led to marginalisation of the poor, as seen in their large-scale eviction and dislocation. Hiding behind glossy pictures of the city is the large number of poor, no matter what criterion you adopt to identify them, who live in slums in the centre as well as the periphery of the city. They inhabit what have been described as the city's 'shadow areas'. Those who live here, even though they have been involved in building the city itself, are treated with suspicion and disrespect and struggle for access to ration and basic amenities.

The growth of Bengaluru's urban sprawl in which peripheral lands have been gradually engulfed has dealt a fatal blow to the water access of those who live on the periphery. People have lost access to water when the land on which the water sources were located were auctioned off. Water has unfortunately received relatively little attention from the State's parliamentarians. Indeed water only catches the attention of politicians in the context of inter-State water disputes; political parties have not engaged with the movement against privatisation per se. At the same time, the public space to voice dissent against privatisation of water has been severely constricted. The only protests that are heard seriously are those of the middle and upper middle classes; the voices of the poor are taken for granted. Urs and Whitell (2009) note that the resources needed to provide water supply to all are available; only the political will to mobilise them is needed. In the long run, though, this can only be achieved when the pressure to do so comes from the citizens for whom the supply is intended.

---

13 This growth has been led by a process of land acquisition from the peripheral areas, engulfing the agricultural lands and changing the landscape in favour of glitzy malls and high-rise buildings, housing the offices of multinational giants, that are the hallmark of modern Indian cities. However, Urs and Whitell (2009) note that the infrastructure has not kept pace with the phenomenal expansion of the city and its outgrowths.

The analysis of the privatisation policy process by the authors suggests that a few dominant actors can steer the policy formulation process in a certain direction, often to the detriment of the marginalised. Further, even when the results with certain policy interventions might be limited, certain actors (and the discourses that they propagate) can provide a justification for the continuation and persistence of those interventions. Worldwide, the privatisation of water has led to widespread protests; the quality of water service provision has in some places actually deteriorated and private companies have failed to honour their commitments. Supplies have been disconnected when people could not pay, even when conditions of ill-health and insecurity demanded that they receive continued access to it. Privatisation has nevertheless persisted neither because it is theoretically sound (based on the narrative of the bad State) nor because it has had positive effects but because it reflects the interests of some powerful groups who advocate a neo-liberal 'reform' agenda.[14]

Similar claims are often made by scholars of the urbanisation process in India, namely, that the neo-liberal agenda and processes of globalisation have led to the growth of modern Indian cities and have compelled governments to follow policies to protect the interests of a dominant few at the expense of the poor and marginalised; further, that this has often fuelled discontent and resentment. Banerji Guha (2009) and Baviskar (2002), for instance, argue that current processes of urbanisation have led to the displacement and marginalisation of the poor. 'Theories and praxis of neo-liberal urbanism and the enforcement of regulatory regime in cities and their regions are getting intrinsically associated with such resistances and struggles signifying a radical politics of contestation that would finally decide for who the cities and their spaces are meant for...the city space is converted into a globally designed space of economic regeneration and contradiction, marginalisation and flux... In the process of restructuring space as part of the reconceptualisation of contemporary 'urban', displacement and dispossession of the poor and weaker

---

14 In fact, water privatisation is known also to have led to further marginalisation of women, as noted by Mishra-Panda (2004). The MDGs mention both gender equality and provision of water. Over the years, women have disproportionately borne the burden of water privatisation policies in the form of price hikes, water cut-offs, deteriorating water quality and health and sanitation hazards; women have resisted efforts against privatisation. The government has often granted licences to the private sector, especially to MNCs, in the urban fringe areas for sale and industrial use. In this regard, Mishra-Panda notes that the State should restrict issuing such licences, especially in those areas having fertile agricultural lands and where groundwater is the only source available to the local population.

sections have surfaced as a fundamental aspect, aided by other methods of marginalisation… (Banerji Guha 2009:106).'

3.8 Conclusion

In this chapter, we looked at different terms and concepts that help explain the processes of policy choice. In other words they help us answer the question: where does policy change come from?

We started the chapter by reviewing the global context of policy-making. We reviewed the paradigm of 'good governance', that has been instrumental in shaping policy choice especially in developing countries. Many public policy changes can be seen to be located in the good governance paradigm. The good governance paradigm has led many countries to reform their systems of civil service and public delivery, streamline the State, improve incentive systems, accountability and weed out corruption. Policy choices favouring decentralisation and civil society engagement can be seen to have their genesis in the good governance agenda. The good governance agenda gives legitimacy to policy choices made by the State.

At the same time, policy-making takes place in a context of globalisation of governance, shaped by processes at a global level in terms of the rising role of multilateral and bilateral institutions, transnational companies and international NGOs. The globalisation of governance has thrown new challenges for the sovereignty of the State and led many to argue that the rising stature of multilateral institutions and their increasing presence has led to the erosion of the autonomy of the State, to the point that the policy space facing most countries has been considerably reduced. This view has been challenged by other scholars who argue that the State has considerable space or room to manoeuvre in that the State only selectively implements what it is urged to.

The globalisation of governance shaped by the rising role of international institutions, international NGOs, large transnational corporations and the spread of ICTs, has altered the relationship among the major actors in governance, that is, the State, markets and civil society. Often it has led to the dilution of State authority and raised new questions about the relative authority of the State vis-a-vis other actors in governance and policy-making processes. It has led to the erosion of the policy space, often by constricting the policy choices available to policy-makers.

Within this overall context, policy change is led by certain individuals or groups and is influenced by sets of ideas and beliefs that may be propagated by them. Policy reform may be led by change agents or groups of technical experts called epistemic communities or larger groups of closely tied people such as advocacy coalitions or policy networks. These groups influence policy development by propagating discourses or narratives. Discourses and narratives reduce the policy space by focusing the attention of policy-makers on a few selected policy options that are consistent with the ideas and courses of action embodied in them. Discourses and narratives provide a legitimacy to the choices made by policy-makers. They present certain policy choices as superior to the others while marginalising the latter. This is how policy-makers eliminate policy options while focusing on some.

This is how policy comes to be. What happens when these policies come to the ground? What factors shape processes of policy implementation? This is the subject of Chapter 4 to which we now turn our attention.

References

Andonova, L. B. and Levy, M. A. 2003. 'Franchising Governance: Making Sense of the Johannesburg Type II Partnerships.' In *Yearbook of International Co-operation on Environment and Development 2003/2004*, edited by O. S. Stokke and O. B. Thommessen,19–31. London: Earthscan Publications.

Banerjee-Guha, S. 2009. 'Shifting Cities: Urban Restructuring in Mumbai.' *Economic and Political Weekly* 31(2): 121–122.

Baviskar, A. 2002. 'The Politics of the City.' *Seminar* (New Delhi) August 2002.

Bernstein, J. 2001. 'Analysis of UNEP Executive Director's Report on International Environmental Governance (UNEP/IGM/1/2).' Paper prepared for the UNEP Civil Society Consultations on International Environmental Governance, Nairobi, 22-25 May.

Bertucci, G. and Alberti, A. 2003. 'Globalisation and the Role of the State: Challenges and Perspectives.' In *Reinventing Government for the 21st Century: State Capacity in a Globalising Society*, edited by D. R. Rondinelli and G. S. Cheema, 17–31. Bloomfield: Kumarian Press, Inc.

Cerny, P. G., Menz, G. and Soederberg, S. 2005. 'Different Roads to Globalisation: Neoliberalism, the Competition State, and Politics in a More Open World.' In *Internalising Globalisation. The Rise of Neoliberalism and the Decline of National Varieties of Capitalism*, edited by S. Soderberg, G. Menz and P. G. Cerny, 1–30. New York: Palgrave Macmillan.

Chang, H. 2006. 'Policy Space in Historical Perspective with Special Reference to Trade and Industrial Policies.' *Economic and Political Weekly* 41(7): 627–634.

Clarke, M. 2006. 'Are the Development Policy Implications of the New Economy, New? All That Is Old Is New Again.' *Journal of International Development* 18(5): 639–648.

Evans, M. 2004. 'Understanding Policy Transfer.' In *Policy Transfer in Global Perspective*, edited by M. Evans, 10–42. England: Ashgate.

Gelinas, J. B. 2003. *Juggernaut Politics: Understanding Predatory Globalisation*. London and New York: Zed Books.

Giddens, A. 2002. *Runaway World. How Globalisation is Reshaping Our Lives*. London: Profile Books.

Grillo, R. 1997. 'Discourses of Development: The View from Anthropology.' In *Discourses of Development: Anthropological Perspectives*, edited by R. Grillo and R. L. Stirrat, Introduction. Oxford: Oxford International Publications.

Haas, P. M. 1992. 'Introduction: Epistemic Communities and International Policy Coordination.' *International Organization* 46(1): 1–35.

Hajer, M. A. 1995. *The Politics of Environmental Discourse: Ecological Modernization and the Policy Process*. Oxford: Oxford University Press.

Hale, T. N. and Mauzerall, D. L. 2004. 'Thinking Globally and Acting Locally: Can the Johannesburg Partnerships Coordinate Action on Sustainable Development?' *The Journal of Environment and Development* 13(3): 220–329.

Hardin, G. 1968. 'Tragedy of the Commons,' *Science* 162: 1243–1248.

Higgins, V. and Lawrence, G. 2005. 'Introduction: Globalization and Agricultural Governance.' In *Agricultural Governance: Globalization and the New Politics of Regulation*, edited by V. Higgins and G. Lawrence 1–16. London and New York: Routledge.

Horowitz, D. 1989. 'Is There a Third World Policy Process?' *Policy Sciences* 22: 197–212.

Koening-Archibugi, M. 2005. 'Introduction: Institutional Diversity in Global Governance.' In *New Modes of Governance in the Global System. Exploring Publicness, Delegation and Inclusiveness*, edited by M. Koening-Archibugi and M. Zurn, 1–30. London: Palgrave Macmillan.

Krishnan, R. and Narain, V. 2003. 'Partnerships and Scientific Perspectives in Water and Energy.' In *Looking Beyond Johannesburg: Scientific Perspectives in Water and Energy*, edited by R. K. Pachauri and G. Vasudeva, 3–38. New Delhi: The Energy and Resources Institute.

Mathur, K. 2008. *From Government to Governance: A Brief Survey of the Indian Experience*. New Delhi: National Book Trust.

Mehta, L. 2005. *The Politics and Poetics of Water. Naturalising Water Scarcity in Western India*. Hyderabad: Orient Longman.

Mishra-Panda, Smita. 2004. 'Privatisation of Water: Towards an Understanding of Gender Dimensions.' Working Paper 185, Institute of Rural Management, India.

Mollinga, P. P. 2001. 'Power in Motion: A Critical Assessment of Canal Irrigation Reform, With a Focus on India. IPIM Working Paper/ Monograph Series No. 1. New Delhi: Indian Network on Participatory Irrigation Management.

Mooij, J. 2003. 'Smart Governance? Politics in the Policy Process in Andhra Pradesh, India.' Working Paper 228, Overseas Development Institute, U.K.

Nakayama, M. and Jansky, L. 2001. 'New Perspectives for the Management of International Water Systems.' *Global Environmental Change* 11(3): 246–250.

Narain, V. 2003. *Institutions, Technology and Water Control: Water Users' Associations in Irrigation Management Reform in Two Large-scale Systems in India*. Hyderabad: Orient Longman.

Narain, V. 2009. 'Where Does Policy Change Come From? And Where Does It End Up? Establishing Water Users' Associations in Large-Scale Irrigation Systems in India.' In *Water Policy Entrepreneurs: A Research Companion to Water Transitions Around the Globe*, edited by D. Huitema and S. Meijerink, 120–136. Cheltenham: Edward Elgar.

Nayar, B. R. 2009. *The Myth of the Shrinking State. Globalization and the State in India*. New Delhi: Oxford University Press.

Nischal, S. and Narain, V. 2004. 'Partnerships: The Way Ahead?' In *Partnerships for Sustainable Development: Addressing the WEHAB Agenda*, edited by R. K. Pachauri, 1–26. New Delhi: The Energy and Resources Institute.

Orbicom and International Development Research Center. 2009. *Digital Review of Asia-Pacific 2009-10*. New Delhi: Sage Publications.

Ostrom, E. 1990. *Governing the Commons. The Evolution of Institutions for Collective Action*. Cambridge: Cambridge University Press.

Ostrom, E. 1992. *Crafting Institutions for Self-governing Irrigation Systems*. San Francisco: Institute for Contemporary Studies.

Pachauri, R. K. 2004. 'Climate and Humanity.' *Global Environmental Change* 14(2): 101–103.

Peine, E. and McMichael, P. 2005. 'Globalisation and Global Governance.' In *Agricultural Governance. Globalization and the New Politics of Regulation*, edited by V. Higgins and G. Lawrence, 19–34. London and New York: Routledge.

Randeria, S. 2003. 'Glocalization of Law: Environmental Justice, World Bank, NGOs and the Cunning State.' *Current Sociology* 51: 305–328.

Roe, E. M. 1991. 'Development Narratives, Or Making the Best of Blueprint Development.' *World Development* 19(4): 287–300.

Roy, D. 2004. 'From Home to Estate.' *Seminar* 533: 68–75.

Sachs, J. 2005. *The End of Poverty: How We Can Make It Happen in Our Life Time*. London: Penguin Books.

Schmitz, H. P. 2006. *Transnational Mobilisation and Domestic Regime Change. Africa in Comparative Perspective*. International Political Economy Series. England: Palgrave Macmillan.

Sabatier, P. A. 1993. 'Policy Change Over A Decade Or More.' In *Policy Change and Learning: An Advocacy Coalition Approach*, edited by P. A. Sabatier and H. C. Jenkins Smith, 13–39. Bouler, CO: Westview Press.

Shatkin, G. 2007. 'Global Cities of the South: Emerging Perspectives in Growth and Inequality.' *Cities* 24(1): 1–15.

Shylendra, H. S. 2004. '*The Emerging Governance Paradigm and its Implications for Poverty Alleviation and Equity*.' Working Paper 182, Institute of Rural Management, India.

Stiglitz, J. 2002. *Globalisation and its Discontents*. New Delhi: Penguin Books.

Sutton, R. 1999. 'The Policy Process: An Overview.' Working Paper 118, Overseas Development Institute, U.K.

Thomas, J. W. and Grindle, M. S. 1990. 'After the Decision: Implementing Policy Reforms in Developing Countries.' *World Development* 18(8): 1163–1181.

UNDP. 2002. *Human Development Report 2002: Deepening Democracy in a Fragmented World*. New York: United Nations Development Programme.

UNEP. 2005. 'Pacific Environment Outlook.' Special edition for the Mauritus International Meeting for the 10-year review of the Barbados Programme of Action for the Sustainable Development of Small Island Developing States. Nairobi: United Nations Environment Programme.

United Nations Commission on Environment and Development. 1987. *Our Common Future*. Oxford: Oxford University Press.

Urs, K. and Whittel, R. 2009. *Resisting Reform? Water Profits and Democracy*. New Delhi: Sage Publications.

Weinstein, L. 2008. 'Mumbai's Development Mafias: Globalization, Organized Crime and Land Development.' *International Journal of Urban and Regional Research* 32(1): 22–39.

World Bank. 1994. *Governance: The World Bank's Experience*. Washington, D.C.: World Bank.

World Resources Institute. 2003. *World Resources 2002-2004: Decisions for the Earth. Balance, Voice and Power.* Washington, D.C.: World Resources Institute.

World Watch Institute. 2002. *Vital Signs 2002: The Trends that are Shaping Our Future.* Washington, D.C.: World Watch Institute (WW Norton and Co.).

4

What happens when policies come to the ground?

We noted in Chapter 2 that the linear model of the policy process creates a false dichotomy between the stages of policy formulation and implementation. Policy-making and implementation are seen as distinct activities, separate from each other. An interactive model of the policy process suggests, on the contrary, that policies can be reformulated in the implementation process and, therefore, the distinction between the processes of policy formulation and implementation is not water tight. In this chapter, we look more closely at the factors that influence the policy implementation process, as well as theoretical frameworks that help analyse the same.

The key question that we answer in this chapter is: How can we explain the difference between the intended and actual outcomes of public policy? What factors shape the implementation process? What analytic frameworks or conceptual approaches can be employed for the analysis of the implementation of public policy? In Chapter 2, we examined the importance of understanding the management of change; in this chapter, we look at different conceptual approaches and analytical frameworks that help analyse the management of change. In attempting to answer these questions, we draw upon concepts and frameworks developed in legal anthropology, development sociology and management literature.

4.1 Importance of the study of the implementation process

The interest in the study of implementation of public policy can be traced back to the publication of the book 'Implementation' by Pressman and Wildavsky in 1973. Prior to this, interest in public policy was confined more to the prescriptive dimensions of policy; earlier studies tended to be of decisions rather than of policies (Hogwood and Gunn 1984). The focus was on the moment at which the decision was taken or the policy was made. What happened after that was seen to be the concern of other disciplines such as public administration or management in the public sector. Since the 1970s, however, there has been a greater interest in studying what has been described by Dunsire as the 'implementation gap'.

Mathur (1998) notes that most public administration could be seen as the implementation strategy of public policy. This means that the effort at dichotomising policy and administration needs to be given up. The changed outlook also means that while administration owns a problem only after it has come out of the policy-formulation pipeline, implementation is treated as a continuous decision-making activity in which conscious linkages between choice of policies and strategies of implementation are made. Policy goals are linked in producing policy outputs. Implementation embodies the social and political processes that influence the course of administrative action.

'After the decision': the challenge of policy implementation

As noted in the preceding chapters, in most developing countries, the real challenges with regard to policy seem to appear after the policy decision is made and sought to be implemented (Thomas and Grindle 1990). That is, the main challenge is not in the prescriptive but in the process dimensions of public policy.[1] The linear model of policy-making has led donors to support substantial efforts to strengthen policy analysis in developing countries in the expectation that good analysis will translate into good decision-making and this, into good policy. Operationalising these expectations has taken the form of technical assistance contracts to build capacity in planning and policy analysis in many sectors. Inherent in these efforts is the assumption that sound policy-making itself will translate into good implementation; that is, a well-formulated policy itself has the ingredients for good implementation.

In practice, however, Thomas and Grindle note, the real issues arise 'after the decision', at the implementation stage. The outcomes of a policy intervention can be extremely variable, and this range of outcomes results from the fact that implementation is an interactive and ongoing process of decision-making by policy elites and managers in response to actual or anticipated reactions to reform initiatives. These officials could be potential strategic managers working within complex policy and institutional environments. Characteristics of

---

1 Refer also to our discussion in Chapter 1 that there is no dearth of policy prescription in countries like India. Many policy prescriptions seem to emanate from a large number of policy think-tanks. The crucial question is: why are they not implemented? This calls for a better and improved understanding of the reasons for the persistence of the implementation gap.

particular reforms determine the type of conflict and opposition that surround their implementation.

In Thomas and Grindle's interactive model, that builds upon a political economy approach to reform, pressures to put reform issues on the policy agenda are seen to come from many sources, including frequent reform-mongering by policy elites. The agenda represents a stock pile of proposed changes. Some items on the agenda are acted upon, but many are not, often because of the preferences, perceptions and actions of policy elites and their appreciation of the economic and political environment that they face.

Implementation is part of a process in which a new policy is particularly vulnerable. The fate of implementation is shaped in large part by whether the reaction to reforms takes place in the public arena or in the bureaucracy. The distribution of costs and benefits of a policy or an institutional change, its technical complexity, its administrative intensity, its short and long-term impact, and the degree to which it encourages participation determine whether the reaction or response to the initiative will occur primarily in a bureaucratic or a public arena.[2]

Brinkerhoff and Crosby (2002) note that the policy implementation process is at least as political as it is technical, and is complex and highly interactive. Besides technical and institutional analysis, it calls for consensus building, participation of key stakeholders, mechanisms for conflict resolution, compromise, contingency planning, and adaptation.[3] New policies often reconfigure roles, structures and incentives, thus changing the array of costs and benefits to implementers, direct beneficiaries and other stakeholders.

Political will and local leadership are understood to be essential for sustainable policy reform and implementation. No amount of external donor pressures or resources, by themselves, can produce sustained reform.[4] Without policy entrepreneurs or policy champions who are willing and able to be

---

2 This model explains policy choice differently from the rational or incremental models. According to this model, the choice of policy is shaped by the balance of power among the affected actors. That is, those policies are finally chosen that garner the necessary support for their introduction.

3 In terms of this explanation, the success of a policy depends in large part upon the extent to which an effort is made to address these issues at the policy formulation stage. That is, the management of the implementation process should itself be part of the planning and policy formulation stage. This, as we noted in Chapter 2, needs to be understood as a key relevance of the interactive model of the policy process vis-a-vis the linear model.

4 This may be an important reason behind the limited success of some donor funded programmes.

effective leaders for change, sustainable reform is not possible. When we see policy reform as a process, it means that policies are dynamic combinations of purposes, rules, actions, resources, incentives and behaviours leading to outcomes that can only be imperfectly predicted or controlled.

Unsuccessful policy implementation

It is useful and important, at this juncture, to distinguish between non-implementation and unsuccessful implementation of policies (Hogwood and Gunn 1984). In the former case, a policy is not put into effect as intended, perhaps because those involved in its execution have been uncooperative and/or bad or inefficient, or because their best efforts could not overcome obstacles to implementation, over which they had little or no control. In other words, the policy does not get executed. That is, it never does leave the corridors of policy-making. Unsuccessful implementation, on the other hand, occurs when a policy is carried out in full, and external circumstances are not unfavorable but none the less the policy fails to produce the desired outcomes or outputs. That is, the policy leaves the corridors of policy-making but on account of a number of reasons, it is not successfully implemented. In others words, there persists a gap between the actual and intended outcomes of the public policy.

4.2 Why should policies be difficult to implement?

According to Hogwood and Gunn (1984), the reasons for policy failure may be one or more of three: bad execution, misfortune or bad policy. Thus, the policy may be ineffectively implemented, which may be viewed by the implementers of the policy as bad execution. Or it may be due to unfavourable external circumstances that were beyond the control of the policy executors. The reason that is less commonly, or at least not as openly admitted, is that the policies themselves were bad in the sense of being based upon inadequate information, defective reasoning or unrealistic assumptions. In Chapter 3, we looked at the role of narratives in shaping policy choices. These narratives represent certain assumptions about cause–effect relationships. When these assumptions are flawed or constitute misrepresentations of reality, the policy choices on which they are based are likely to be faulty. For this reason it is necessary to challenge or question widely held narratives.

Hogwood and Gunn (1984) note that perfect implementation is unattainable in practice. This is for several reasons. First, the circumstances external to implementation may be outside the control of administrators because they are external to the policy and the implementing agency. Some of these obstacles may be physical. For instance, an agricultural programme may be set back by drought or disease. Likewise, there may be political opposition to a programme, which might be difficult for administrators to overcome. Second, policies that are physically and politically attainable may be hampered by inadequate availability of financial resources or by constraints of time. A common example is when unspent resources are available at the end of the financial year, and have to be spent in a hurry. Third, and following from the second, the required resources may not be available in the right combinations. Disrupted supply of one input may stall the success of a policy. Fourth, policies may be ineffective because they are misconceived in the first place. That is, they are bad policies to begin with. Such policies are policies that are based on an inadequate understanding of the problem, resulting from a poor appreciation of the relationship between cause and effect. Pressman and Wildavsky (1973) describe a policy as a hypothesis containing the initial conditions and predicted consequences. Thus, a policy is based on some premise, stating that '…if X happens, then Y should be a result.' A policy is bound to be ineffective if it is based on a poor understanding of the relationship between X and Y.

Fifth, and closely related to the above, policies may be ineffective when the cause–effect relationship is not as direct as is seemingly understood. Policies that have a long sequence of cause and effect relationships are likely to break down since the longer the chain of causality, the more numerous the reciprocal relationships among the links and the more complex the implementation becomes. In other words, more the links in the chain, the greater the risk that some of them will prove to be poorly conceived or badly initiated. Sixth, 'perfect implementation' requires dependency relationships to be minimal; this condition is also seldom achieved in practice. Implementation requires not only a complex series of events and linkages, but also agreement at each event among a large number of participants. Seventh, policy implementation may be hampered by a lack of understanding and agreement among objectives to be achieved.

Finally, perfect implementation requires three other conditions to be in place: that tasks are fully specified in the correct sequence, that there is perfect communication among and coordination of the various elements or agencies involved in the programme, and that those in authority demand and obtain complete compliance. When implementation involves innovation and the management of change, with major departures from previous policies and practices,there will be particularly high probability of suspicion, recalcitrance or outright resistance from affected individuals, groups and interests, especially if insufficient time has been allowed for explanation and consultation or if any previous experience of change has been unfortunate.

In the following sections of this chapter, we examine specific concepts and analytical frameworks that help us analyse and unpack the processes of policy implementation in greater detail and help us examine the discrepancy between the intended and actual outcomes of a policy. In other words, we look at the different ways in which we could study the 'implementation gap'. We start with analysing the role of the bureaucracy itself that shapes policy outcomes.

4.3 Street level bureaucracies and policy implementation

Policy implementation is shaped in large part by the actions of those engaged in its implementation, specifically, at the lowest level; that is, at the level characterised with the most direct interface of the policy with the citizens or with the clients or recipients of the public service. One reason that policies may not be implemented as intended may simply be that those engaged in policy implementation exercise discretion in the discharge of their duties and in the implementation of policies and programmes with which they are entrusted. In other words, the policies implemented are not the ones that are formulated; instead, policies are reframed in the course of their implementation by those in charge.

Max Weber, the German sociologist, conceptualised the bureaucracy as an institution bound by a well-defined set of rules, regulations and formal positions that routinises the process of administration. Bureaucracy is understood to be a form of organisation that emphasises precision, speed, clarity, regularity and efficiency. This is achieved through a fixed division of tasks, hierarchical supervision, and detailed rules and regulations that specify codes of conduct and lay down the modalities for dealing with matters of a routine nature.

According to Max Weber, the existence of the bureaucracy is necessitated by requirements of size, scale and complexity. Certain tasks require a well-defined organisation structure. A bureaucracy has several characteristics, some of which could be listed as follows:

1. A strong reliance on a system of rules and regulations
2. The presence of hierarchy in the organisation structure
3. Paper work
4. Professional qualifications and expert training

The bureaucratic form of organisation, thus understood, is known to have several advantages. These include a thrust on specialisation and a well-defined structure that imparts a measure of predictability and stability. Rationality and democracy are other understood advantages of this form of organisation.

However, it is understood also to have several demerits such as the existence of red tape, rigidity and inflexibility, a measure of impersonalisation, excessive standardisation and a somewhat mechanistic view of human activity.

This conceptualisation of the bureaucracy sees bureaucrats as individuals bound by an institutional framework of rules and regulations and adhering to them and conforming to them in the discharge of their duties. This view, however, was challenged by Lipsky (1980), who explained that bureaucrats, especially at the field level, exercise discretion in the discharge of their duties and the provision of services to their clients. They do not implement policies as they are designed to be implemented; instead, they exercise some discretion in the discharge of their duties, in keeping with the pressures and constraints on their time and resources.

The concept of street level bureaucracy was developed in Lipsky's book of the same title and further developed in work by two of his former research students, Weatherly and Prottas (Hill 2005). Lipsky used this concept to refer to bureaucrats at the field level, those engaged most directly in the implementation of policies and the provision of services to clients. In his book, Lipsky argues thus, '...the decisions of street-level bureaucrats, the routines they establish, and the devices they invent to cope with uncertainties and work pressures, effectively become the public policies they carry out (Lipsky 1980: xii).' He emphasised the role that street-level bureaucrats play in the implementation of policies, exercising considerable discretion such that policies get reformulated in the course of implementation. Thus, the policies implemented on the ground are different from those formulated in the corridors of policy-making. This provides a very useful conceptual entry point to explain the gap between intended and actual policy outputs as well as outcomes.

Lipsky argues that this process of street level policy implementation does not involve, as is typically believed, the advancement of the ideals many bring to personal service work but rather the development of practices that enable officials to cope with the pressures they face (Hill 2005). Street level bureaucrats develop methods of processing in a relatively routine and stereotyped way. They adjust their work habits to reflect lower expectations of themselves and their clients.

Such workers may seem like cogs in the wheel, as oppressed by the bureaucracy within which they work. Yet, to a researcher, they appear to have considerable autonomy and discretionary freedom. This is particularly true of many publicly employed semi-professionals: people like teachers and social workers who secure a degree of that autonomy allowed to professional workers. They also are able to exercise considerable discretion in the exercise of their duties and responsibilities and in the provision of public services. They make choices about the use of scarce resources under pressure; contemporary fiscal pressures upon human services make it much easier for officials to emphasise control than to put into practice service ideals. This freedom to make policy is used essentially to provide a more manageable task environment.

According to Lipsky, difficult work environments may lead to the abandonment of ideals and to the adoption of techniques that enable clients to be managed. Due to constraints on their time, and bureaucratic procedures at the local level, street-level bureaucracies exercise discretion in implementing instructions. One way of dealing with clients, according to Lipsky, is to categorise the clients on the basis of some stereotypes and then develop differentiated strategies of dealing with them. In terms of our distinction between policy outputs and outcomes presented in Chapter 1, street level bureaucrats influence directly the policy outputs, since they are engaged with the delivery of public services. That is, they influence policy outcomes through their influence on policy ouputs.

The concept of street level bureaucracies is useful in analysing policy implementation in that it draws attention to the role that bureaucrats themselves may play in policy implementation processes. An important factor that shapes policy implementation is the actions and attitudes of those involved in policy implementation. This can be an important reason why there is a gap between the intentions and outcomes of a policy, that is, policies are not implemented as they are initially conceived but rather as street level bureaucrats modify them in the course of their implementation. Therefore, analysing processes of policy implementation requires us to examine the attitudes, roles and perceptions of those engaged in policy implementation. The policies that are actually implemented in the field are not the policies that are framed by policy-makers; instead, they are 'devised' by those in charge of their implementation. That is, policies get reformulated as they move from the corridors of policy-making down to the field level where they interface with the clients or the recipients of public service delivery.[5]

Consider, for instance, a traffic policeman who is supposed to penalise all vehicles exceeding a certain speed limit. In practice, he may be unable to do so and may use some discretion because he may not have the energy or the willingness to penalise all of them. The police constable, the primary school teacher, the man operating a ration shop, a peon in a government department,

---

5   This observation reinforces our point about the false dichotomy between processes of policy formulation and implementation as considered in the linear model of the policy process. See the discussion in Chapter 2.

the polio *didi* (the nurse who administers polio drops), the forest guard and the *paatkari* (the employee of the Irrigation Department who has the direct interface with farmers by releasing water by opening the gates along the irrigation canal) all represent examples of the street level bureaucracy in the Indian context.

Though each of these officers has well-defined roles to perform along with the modalities, in practice, they may devise their own short cuts to the discharge of their duties. This is basically in order to deal with the constraints of their time, energy and resources. For instance, the police-man who visits our homes to verify our addresses has a well-defined role to perform and the modalities of doing this are also laid out. However, depending on the number of verifications that he has to do in a single day or location or the overall availability of time for him, he may devise his own short-cuts. In due course, these procedures may get institutionalised and even find acceptance within the bureaucratic and social contexts in which they function.

As noted above, a study of street level bureaucrats provides a very good conceptual entry point to understand policy implementation processes. Such a study would entail, for instance, ethnographies of the street level bureaucracy, looking at their day-to-day interactions with clients, their daily lives and schedules, the constraints on their time and their responses to them.[6] A study of street level bureaucracies can help paint a vivid picture of the policy implementation process and generate insights into where bottlenecks may lie and how the gap between the actual and intended policy outcomes and outputs can be filled. Besides, earlier in this chapter and elsewhere in the book, we have argued that planning the implementation process needs to be part of the policy-making process itself. Involving the street level bureaucracies can be one way of doing this. This could be both in terms of drawing on their experiences with policy implementation in the past but also by anticipating their interface with a policy when it comes to the ground. Involving those who will be in charge of policy implementation early on in the policy process could give some leads into the likely resources that need to be committed to the process as also to the constraints that policy implementation can run into.

4.4 Legal pluralism perspectives in policy implementation

Legal pluralism, a concept developed in legal anthropology, provides another analytic tool for the analysis of policy implementation. It draws attention to the

---

6 For examples of the study of the street level bureaucracy in the Indian context, see Wade (1992), Goel (2016) and Vasan (2002).

interface of policies emanating from the State with non-statutory institutions, customs and practices and how State-based policies may get diluted in the process of implementation as they encounter non-statutory forms of institutions, practices and organisational structures that are deeply embedded, have strong social sanction and often take precedence over statutory institutions.

Legal pluralism is an umbrella concept indicating the condition that more than one legal system or institution co-exists with respect to the same set of activities (von Benda-Beckmann 1999). Von Benda-Beckmann (1988) reserves the concept of legal pluralism to denote the duplicate nature of institutions, rules, and processes as also the relationship among them. It refers to a situation wherein many laws, institutions, rules, and practices may co-exist with regard to the same set of activities. For instance, statutory law may co-exist along with customary law and socially accepted conventions and practices.

Legal pluralism can be referred to as a concept, analytic framework or an empirical phenomenon. Three major ideas run in the writings on legal pluralism: first, there is a questioning of the legal centrist perspective of law; second, there is recognition of multiple regulatory orders; and, third, recognition of the omnipresence of legal pluralism.

First, there is a questioning of legal centrism, namely, that all legal ordering is rooted in State law (Griffiths 1986; Merry 1988; Spiertz and Wiber 1996). It is argued that statutory law is only one source of law. In contrast to a lawyer's perspective, law is not viewed as a unitary institution. It is recognised that there are many sources of law, laws are in a constant state of flux, many bodies of law are in conflict with each other and legal systems vary in terms of their internal cohesion. Further, what is called a legal system is hardly a system because it is not a coherent whole (Spiertz and Wiber1996).[7]

The second idea, and related to the first, is that of the co-existence of several normative orders. Griffiths (1986) draws our attention to the presence in one social field of more than one legal order. An individual finds himself at the converging point of multiple regulatory orders (Vanderlinden 1989). There is an interplay of plural normative frameworks in society; rules, law and institutional frameworks are independent social resources that actors mobilise to accomplish their ends (Spiertz and de Jong 1992).

Von Benda-Beckmann (1988) recognises the plurality of normative frameworks as a probable point of departure for empirical research and

---

7 Essentially, this means that not only are there different sources of law with different bases of legitimacy, but also that within State law, there can be many contradictions.

investigation. Merry (1998) notes the presence of competing and sometimes contradictory orders outside State law and their mutually constitutive relations to it; further, that these multiple regulatory orders are intertwined. Von Benda-Beckmann (1988), however, asserts that to say that they are intertwined would imply that they are distinguishable, which may often not be the case.

Third, there is recognition that legal pluralism is all pervasive (Griffiths 1986; Merry 1998). 'Legal Pluralism is the omnipresent, normal situation in human society (Griffiths 1986: 39).' Merry (1998) asserts that plural orders are found in all societies, the difference is only a matter of degree; that is, some societies may be more plural than others.[8]

A legal pluralistic analysis of public policy and institutions

A few observations are important in terms of a legal pluralistic analysis of law or policies. First, the premise of legal pluralism shifts focus from the legal system to the individual. Thus, the focus is not the legal system per se but on the individual who is confronted with different legal or normative systems.[9] Second, a legal pluralistic premise requires the recognition of different bases of legitimacy. Different legal systems have different bases of political authority or sanction. State law has its legitimacy in the State; customary law, conventions and practices have their legitimacy in a system of social sanction. Legal pluralism is, therefore, about the plurality of different bases of legitimacy: State, religion, social norms, customs or caste identities. These different bases of legitimacy assert their influence over an individual; this can give rise to situations of conflict.

As an analytic tool or conceptual lens, there can be many applications of legal pluralism to the analysis of public policy, institutions and governance. One aspect of governance in which the premise of legal pluralism is widely applied is in the context of discussion of rights and entitlements. First, it can help in a better understanding of property rights. Customary rights are often

---

8 For more on studies of legal pluralism, see the work and the website of the Commission on Legal Pluralism. The commission has an international conference that brings together a large number of scholars, lawyers, NGOs, activists and development practitioners engaged in the study of legal complexities. That is, they deal with or have an interest in the social significance of law, how people relate to law and how their lives are shaped by an interface of different legal systems.

9 This could be contrasted with new institutionalist perspectives on institutions that have as their focus an institutional framework and how that generates incentives for individual and group behaviour. See the discussion in Chapter 1.

found to co-exist along with rights sanctioned by the State. In fact, this can often be a cause of conflicts over natural resources. Further, legal pluralism helps us question the premise that no property rights exist. For instance, a situation where there are no State sanctioned rights could be interpreted to be a situation of 'no property rights existing', when in practice, there may be a system of rights and mutually constitutive obligations devised and followed by the community with a strong system of social sanction. That is, there may be no rights defined by the State; however, there may be well-defined norms and rights devised and understood by the community and strongly enforced and sanctioned by what we may choose to call the community's collective conscience.[10]

Second, it facilitates recognition of the notion of entitlements and extended entitlements. Statutory rights may be granted by the State. However, individuals may mobilise social relationships in order to make these rights more effective, marking a distinction between entitlements and extended entitlements. For instance, as noted in Chapter 1, in irrigation systems of northwest India, water rights are defined by statutory law but are realised through another normative system, namely, that of *bhaichara*-based organisation (Narain 2003).[11]

Third, legal pluralism can provide an analytic tool for the analysis of the interface of newly created statutory organisations with other pre-existing forms of social organisation. A public policy challenge in establishing new user groups is that it is important to take cognisance of pre-existing norms and practices pertaining to that field of activity. For instance, if we form a natural resource management committee in a setting where there already exist

---

10 This is, in fact quite true in the case of many community-based systems of natural resource management that exist outside of State control. There may be no State defined rights but communities may have their own systems of rights and access, which are accepted through social sanction and which structure the relationship of the community members with each other as well as with the resource in question.

11 Farmers are allocated a time for taking water during a certain day of the week by means of what is called a *warabandi* schedule. However, this time does not always match the crop-water requirements. So, farmers engage in time exchanges to make their water rights more effective. Though these time exchanges are prohibited under State law, they are widely practised and justified on the basis of their *bhaichara*, or social relations. We often talk about the distinction between the concretisation of rights and their materialisation. That is, rights may be defined in a certain way, often by the institutions of the State; however, they may be realised through other normative systems. See also Gerbrandy and Hoogendaam (2002).

some norms and practices for accessing and using that resource, then it is important to be aware of the implications of that for the formation of the new user group.[12] Fourth, legal pluralism can be applied to a gendered analysis of law, in how men's and women's access to law and interpretation of law can be different. Finally, in Chapter 3, we discussed the notion of good governance. The recognition of legal pluralism questions the premise of good governance and the rule of law, both of which tend to view State law as sacrosanct.

However, legal pluralism does not necessarily imply that institutions outside the State are sacrosanct, just or egalitarian. Many customary systems can in fact be more inequitable and unjust than statutory systems. Legal pluralism is only an analytic framework that sensitises us to institutions outside those engendered by the State, the role that they play in people's day-to-day lives as well as their relationship with statutory institutions.

In the context of the analysis of policy, and particularly of policy implementation, the premise of legal pluralism draws our attention to the fact that different sources of law and policy co-exist. There can be a discrepancy between the intentions of policy and its implementation. State designed policies may come into interface with other institutions, norms or practices and can get diluted in the process. Conversely, State devised policies may be supported by other institutional frameworks and the two can work in a mutually supportive manner. A formal policy framework may be easier to change but informal institutions not so easy to penetrate. For instance, policies for women's participation may come into interface with other norms/notions (such as the notion of *maryada*, that may inhibit women's participation).[13] The composition of resource management committees may be based on criteria different from those postulated by formal policy provisions.[14]

When we use a conceptual framework of legal pluralism for the analysis of policy implementation processes, we ask ourselves this question: When State law or public policy come to the ground, how do they interface with non-statutory institutions, norms and practices? What does this mean for the policy implementation process? Will local norms with a strong

---

12 As a good illustration of the consequences arising from the plurality of local organisations, see, as also noted in Chapter 1, a paper with an interesting title 'How Many Committees Do I Belong To?' (Vasavada and Mishra et al. 2001).

13 See Gupta (2005).

14 This is indeed often the case with regard to the formation of local resource management bodies.

social or religious sanction impede the implementation process? Or, will a 'new policy' take shape as the public policy articulates and interfaces with other norms and institutions on the ground? In other words, the policy 'implemented' on the ground is different from the policy that leaves the corridors of policy-making.

A good example of this was provided by one of the participants in the programme on public policy and management offered at MDI. This illustration came from a member of the IPS, the Indian Police Service. He referred to his experience in a district where it was not possible to ban the sale of a drug as it was offered to the Gods as part of a religious ceremony. Another good example is provided by the recent experience of Swachh Bharat. One of the important challenges in moving to open defecation free areas has been confronting the deeply embedded societal beliefs that encourage defecation in the open. State policies need to counter resistance among society to having toilets in their homes.[15]

A premise of legal pluralism does not necessarily endorse or glorify institutions and practices outside State law. Rather, it gives us an analytic construct to look at the relationship between State law and public policy with non-statutory institutions as well as to anticipate its implications for the policy implementation process.

Corruption: deviation from intended actions

A good example of discretion in the exercise and discharge of duties by the bureaucracy as well as of legal pluralism in the State apparatus is that of corruption. The dictionary meaning of corruption is, 'Influenced by, or using bribery; immoral, wicked'. Corruption is a normative concept and is situated against a perception of what is 'right', 'moral', 'correct', or 'legal'. Sometimes, it is difficult to observe, in that it is 'hidden'. The notion of corruption is intertwined with notions of accountability; it is seen as 'something to get rid of' in discourses on good governance; so much so, that it is interpreted often as the antithesis of good governance.

Corruption becomes institutionalised outside a bureaucratic set-up of rules and regulations. It is based on social capital: networks, trust, obligation and a reliance on informal networks.[16] It is important to note that it seeks its own legitimacy.

---

15 For other studies of legal pluralism in the Indian context, see Rajagopal (2005), Jentoft and Bavinck et al. (2009) and Moore (1993).

16 See the discussion on social capital in Chapter 1.

There are different perspectives and explanations of why corruption is found to exist. In the natural resource economics literature, for instance, the bureaucracy is seen as a nexus between users and the resource. Rent-seeking is seen as resulting from resources being under priced. Essentially, this means that as long as a public good or service is priced below the marginal value of it to the user, there will be an opportunity for those engaged in providing that good or service to appropriate the difference as an illicit payment. New institutional economics perspectives see corruption as the outcome of perverse incentives emanating from the prevailing institutional framework. In the irrigation management literature developed through socio-technical perspectives,[17] design structures in irrigation are seen as sources of control, and power. That is, those in charge of operating these structures wield considerable control over the release and availability of water and can use this position to extract illicit payments.[18]

Heinzpeter Znoj, in his study of corruption in Indonesia, identified several discourses surrounding corruption (Znoj 2007).[19] The *neo-liberal* discourse sees corruption as an informal market in State services, circumventing the State's own centralisation and over-regulation. According to this discourse, since the State is ineffective in providing services as intended, there appears an informal market for the services of the State. Corruption basically represents a market for such services. Therefore, according to this discourse, the less bureaucracy, the less opportunities for corruption. According to the *etatistic* discourse, on the other hand, the way to eliminate corruption is to strengthen the State's institutions and subject them to public scrutiny. Though this discourse recognises the causes of corruption to be similar to that identified by the neo-liberal discourse, it sees the solutions as somewhat different. As per this discourse, an independent judiciary with well-paid judges will help weed out corruption. Thus, it is not less State that is the solution but a more effective scrutiny of the institutions of the State. The civic religious discourse sees corruption as an outcome of a social pathology of lacking morality and civic virtues. According to this discourse, a religiously inspired civil society with high

---

17 See also the discussion in Chapter 1.

18 This may be seen as the explanation for the ability of lower staff or the Irrigation Department to extract extra payments for the release of water, for instance. This was often an important reason for the limited acceptability of irrigation management transfer programme in Maharashtra, wherein control over the irrigation system would move from the Irrigation Department to water user groups of farmers (Narain 2003).

19 See the discussion on discourses and their role in shaping public policy in Chapter 3.

ethical values can help eliminate corruption. The Islamist discourse, similarly, sees corruption as a sin that can be prevented if public life is organised around religious principles. According to the popular discourse, finally, politicians and bureaucrats 'eat' people's money; fate will eventually catch up with people, who will be punished in this or their next life.[20]

The solution to the problem of the existence of corruption, then, depends on how one sees its causes. For instance, in terms of Heinzpeter's analysis, according to the neo-liberal discourse, less state would automatically reduce corruption. As per the etatistic discourse, more scrutiny of the state may do the needful. The civic discourse would see corruption as being eliminated through ethical standards and moral values. As per the popular discourse, there would actually be no solution to this problem. That is, corruption will no longer be a public policy issue or one that can be addressed using specific policy interventions; instead, it would be a matter of individual choice and conscience wherein, it would be up to each individual to take responsibility for and bear the consequences of her actions.

Legitimising corruption

Heinzpeter's study further found that corruption was carried out under different names in Indonesia and those engaged in it sought a legitimisation of the same. The practice of corruption took different names such as 'gifts', 'mutual understanding', 'lobbying', 'taking one's share', 'co-operation', or 'help'. At the same time, corruption was found to be justified on the basis of insufficient payment. 'Subsistence corruption' for small officials was seen as a moral right. Bureaucrats were confronted with social expectations, to meet which, they used their social power to create extra income. Peer pressure was another reason why corruption was found to be rampant. The money in question was often called 'idle money', 'smoking money', 'smoothening money,' or 'fulus'.[21]

Corruption, as a form of exercise of discretion and power, remains very difficult to research, establish or assess.[22] The study of corruption is also methodologically quite challenging. At the same time, there are ethical issues in studying and reporting corruption or writing about it. That is, should a

---

20 This is similar to the law of *karma* in Hindu and Buddhist philosophy.

21 In the Indian context, expressions like *chai-paani*, indicating a pittance for tea and snacks are used to denote corruption.

22 For a recent review of issues surrounding the measurement and study of corruption, see also Sampford and Shacklock et al. (2006).

researcher who investigates corruption disclose the identity of those he discovers to be corrupt?[23] Corruption could be considered to be a case of legal pluralism in the sense that it takes place through a well established institutional system that exists parallel to the state system, that seeks its legitimacy.[24]

4.5 Actor-oriented approaches to the analysis of development policy and intervention

The actor-oriented approach to development policy and intervention is credited to Norman Long and his colleagues developed at Wageningen University, the Netherlands. Long advocates a departure from the linear, logical models of policy intervention to explore how policy and programme interventions are shaped by socially constructed and historically shaped meanings attached to development experiences. An actor-oriented perspective seeks to show that policy implementation processes are shaped by the socially constructed interpretation of programmes and interventions, both on the side of the implementers as well as the 'beneficiaries' or 'targets'.

Long (2002) argues that development intervention is often visualised as a discrete set of activities that takes place within a defined time-space setting involving the interaction between so-called 'intervening' parties and 'target' or 'recipient' groups. Such an image, according to Long, isolates intervention from the continuous flow of social life and ongoing relations that evolve between the various social actors, including the manifold ways in which local actors (both on- and off-stage) interact with implementing officials and organisations.

Development interventions, Long argues, should be seen not as isolated sequences of events from policy formulation to implementation, but instead as part of a chain or flow of events located within the broader framework of the activities of the state, international bodies and the actions of the different interest groups operative in civil society.[25] At the same time, they are linked to previous interventions, have consequences for future ones, and more often than not are a focus for intra- and inter-institutional struggles over perceived goals,

---

23 The author's position on this issue is that corruption can be studied using covert means, as long as confidentiality about the status of the members of the study is maintained and no harm is caused to them.

24 For a synthesis and review of cases studying the issue of corruption using a lens of legal pluralism, see Nuitjen and Anders (2007).

25 In this respect, it is somewhat similar in its basic premise to the interactive model of the policy process.

administrative competencies, resource allocation and institutional boundaries. Actor-oriented perspectives draw attention to the life worlds and interlocking ´projects´ of actors, and the development of theoretically grounded methods of social research that allow for the elucidation of social meanings, purposes and powers.

Long's actor-oriented approach requires delving more deeply into the social and cultural discontinuities and ambiguities inherent in the 'battlefields of knowledge' that shape the relations between local actors, development practitioners and researchers (Long 1989; Long and Long 1992).This image of the 'battlefields of knowledge' conveys the idea of contested arenas in which actors´ understandings, interests and values are pitched against each other. It is here that struggles over social meanings and practices take place. It is here too, where we see most clearly the emergence of various kinds of negotiated orders, accommodations, oppositions, separations and contradictions. Such battlefields embrace a wide range of social actors committed to different livelihood strategies, cultural interests and political trajectories.

By acknowledging the existence of 'multiple social realities' (that is, the co-existence of different understandings and interpretations of experience), it questions the ontological realism of positivist science (that is, of a 'real world' that is simply 'out there' to be discovered). Methodologically this calls for a detailed ethnographic understanding of everyday life and of the processes by which images, identities and social practices are shared, contested, negotiated and sometimes rejected by the various actors involved. The crux of this argument is that practitioners and researchers are both involved in activities in which their observations and interpretations are necessarily tacitly shaped by their own biographical and theoretical perspectives.

Cornerstones of an actor-oriented analysis

Long (2002) provides the following tenets of an actor-oriented approach to the analysis of planned intervention.

- Social life is heterogeneous or polymorphic. That is, it comprises a wide diversity of social forms and cultural repertoires, even under seemingly homogeneous circumstances.
- It is necessary to study how such differences are produced, reproduced, consolidated and transformed and to identify the social processes involved, not merely the structural outcomes.
- Such a perspective requires a theory of agency based upon the capacity of actors to process their own, and learn from others', experiences and

to act upon them. Agency implies a certain knowledgeability, whereby experiences and desires are reflexively accorded meanings and purposes and the capability to command relevant skills, access resources of various kinds and engage in particular organising practices.

- Social action is never an individual ego-centred pursuit. It takes place within networks of relations (involving human and non-human components), is shaped by both routine and explorative organising practices, and is bounded by certain social conventions, values and power relations.

- It would be misleading to assume that such social and institutional constraints can be reduced to general sociological categories and hierarchies based on class, gender, status, ethnicity and so on. Social action and interpretation is context specific and contextually generated. Boundary markers are specific to particular domains, arenas and fields of social action and should not be prejudged analytically.

- Meanings, values and interpretations are culturally constructed but they are differentially applied and reinterpreted in accordance with existing behavioural possibilities or changed circumstances, thereby generating 'new' cultural 'standards'.

- Related to these processes is the question of scale, by which is meant the ways in which 'micro-scale' interactional settings and localised arenas are connected to wider 'macro-scale' phenomena. Rather than seeing the 'local' as shaped by the 'global' or the 'global' as an aggregation of the 'local', an actor perspective aims to elucidate the precise sets of interlocking relationships, actor 'projects' and social practices that interpenetrate various social, symbolic and geographical spaces.

- In order to examine these interrelations, it is useful to work with the concept of 'social interface' which explores how discrepancies of social interest, cultural interpretation, knowledge and power are mediated and perpetuated or transformed at critical points of linkage or confrontation. These interfaces need to be identified ethnographically, not presumed on the basis of predetermined categories.

Long advocates an 'interface approach' to the analysis of development policy and intervention. According to Arce and Long (1992:214), an interface approach 'conveys the idea of some kind of face to face encounter between individuals with differing interests, resources, and power. Studies of interface encounters aim to bring out the types of discontinuities that exist and the dynamics and emerging character of the struggles and interactions that take place, showing how actors' goals, perceptions, values, interests and relationships are reinforced or reshaped by this process. For instance, in rural development interface situations, a central issue is the way in which policy is implemented and often at the same time transformed.'

Mooij (2003) describes Long's approach as a more anthropological approach of actors and bargaining processes that shows the role of groups in policy processes. An actor-oriented perspective shows how such macro-phenomena and pressing human problems result (intentionally and unintentionally) from the complex interplay of specific actors' strategies, 'projects', resource endowments (material/technical and social/institutional), discourses and meanings. In this way, it explains how the products of social action such as policy documents, technologies, commodity markets or socio-demographic patterns are constructed socially and culturally.

When applied to the analysis of policy processes, the actor-oriented perspective implies that intervention processes cannot be confined to the specific 'spaces' and functions delimited by official policies and plans. Nor should we assume that so-called beneficiaries reduce or limit their perceptions of reality and its problems simply to those defined for them by the intervening agency as constituting the 'project' or 'programme'. People process their own experiences of 'projects' and 'interventions' alongside their many other experiences and livelihood concerns. They construct their own memory of these experiences, as well as take into account the experiences of other groups within their socio-spatial networks. That is, they may learn from the differential responses, strategies and experiences of others outside the target population or specific action programme. The same holds true for those who work as implementers or facilitators.

Hence, according to Long, for many of the social actors involved, interventions have no clear beginning marked by the formal definition of goals and means nor any final cut-off point or 'end-date' as identified by the writing of final reports or evaluations. These considerations lead to the conclusion that we need to deconstruct the concept of intervention so that it is recognised for what it fundamentally is, namely, an ongoing, socially constructed and negotiated process, not simply the execution of an already-specified plan or framework for action with expected outcomes.

The value of the actor-oriented approach, when applied to the study of policy implementation processes, is that it shifts focus from the specific policy and the time period of its implementation, or its targeted beneficiaries to the wider social and political context in which the implementation takes place.[26] The implementation process is not confined to a specific time period or location but shaped by the past histories and experiences of those associated with it. In presenting this perspective, the framework departs drastically from the linear rational model of the policy process presented in Chapter 2 of this book. Instead it sees, much like the interactive model of the policy process, the process as being shaped by a complex interplay of social relations and power among the actors, as well as their past experiences and memories of the policy process.

4.6 The management of change

While the implementation of policy change is widely recognised as complex and difficult, policy reform failures could often be attributed to the lack of careful consideration of how the policy reform implementation is or should be organised. Crosby (1996) lists several characteristics of policy change that have considerable implications for implementation. First, the stimulus for change often comes from outside as a response to intractable economic crises that force governments to seek external assistance. Some of these proposed changes could mark a significant departure from established practices and policies in the target country. Second, policy decisions and implementation tend to be highly political. Change results in both gainers and losers, and the losers may be in a position to exercise resistance. Third, while the policy elite (bureaucrats and politicians) have the lead role in the initiation of policy change, those most actively involved in the formulation of policy change are technocrats. These technocrats operate under rather different decisional criteria than either the political or the administrative leadership. Fourth, policy decision-making is often a top-down, non-participative process, confined to a narrow set of decision-makers. Those with the responsibility for implementation are not involved with the process of policy formulation. The implementing official is simply the receptor of orders regarding policy change with little opportunities for input into the decision-making process and thus little sense of ownership of the policy decision. Fifth, reform minded policy-makers are frequently new to government and unfamiliar with the environment for policy formulation. Sixth, quite often adequate resources in order to carry out the policy change either do not exist or are located in the wrong places. Finally, government agencies may lack the necessary ability to easily adapt to the tasks required by policy change.

---

26 In the Indian context, the actor-oriented approach has been used to study energy use in the Indian household sector (see Reddy and Srinivas 2009).

The success of an implementation activity is shaped in large part by the extent to which these factors are considered and anticipated. Policies may fail in achieving their outcomes if any one or more of these activities are missing, or not carried out at the desired level. Here we revert to the interactive model of the policy process, wherein we observed that simply a policy decision is not enough in order to bring about change. Policies may suffer in their implementation if policy-makers do not pay sufficient attention to the carrying out of the activities necessary to support the implementation measures. Paying attention to the steps mentioned above, therefore, needs to be part of the policy-making process itself. Rather than see 'implementation' as a stage subsequent to or distinct from the policy-making process, it needs to be seen as part of the policy-making process itself.

Mobilising resources

Sutton (1999) argues that managing the implementation process is a complex activity that entails several crucial aspects. This includes securing participation of key stakeholders, devising ways for conflict resolution, securing compromise among diverse interests, carrying out contingency planning, resource mobilisation, and adaptation.

In the implementation process, political, financial, managerial and technical resources are likely to be needed to sustain the reform. It is important to recognise that mobilising these is part of the challenges to decision-makers and policy managers. Those opposing the policy change may attempt to block access to the necessary resources, thus stalling the reform and returning it to the policy agenda. Choices by policy elite and managers at this stage may have an important bearing on the eventual outcome of the reform initiative. To this effect, Thomas and Grindle (1990) suggest that policy-makers should themselves be included in the implementation process.

Reforms call for political, financial, and managerial resources as well as technical resources, and reformers must know which are needed and where they will be available. This requires the capacity to assess resource availability and consider how resources might be expanded or mobilised. Decision-makers, likewise, must weigh political resources for policy implementation; public managers must look at bureaucratic resources. It is important for policy-makers to not only enlist those who support and those who resist a reform, but also to assess the degree to which support and opposition can be mobilised, how powerful each group is and the sequence in which the information reaches people.

This review of resources (political, financial, managerial and technical) provides decision-makers or managers with a way to review systematically the resources available to support the implementation process in the face of various forms of opposition. Implicitly, by suggesting the relevant resources, it also provides a means of assessing the opposition. According to Thomas and Grindle, such a review is not adequate to ensure implementation; however, from this review can come a very specific strategy tailored to the particular environment in which the reform is being implemented. In other words, anticipating the reactions of different stakeholders and putting in place strategies to mobilise support and overcome resistance need to be part of the policy-making process. This could improve the effectiveness of the implementation and lead to a greater convergence between the intended and actual policy outcomes and outputs.

Identifying interest groups

An important step in the management of change is the identification of different interest groups. The identification of relevant interest groups is necessary for any policy change to happen and policies may fail in the absence of sufficient effort at consulting the various interest groups or developing platforms where proposals for change are debated and negotiated.

These interest groups could be clustered around
- State-centred forces, which in turn could comprise
  - Technocratic forces
  - Bureaucrats, or
  - State interests
- Society-centred forces, which could comprise
  - Classes
  - Parties, or
  - Voters

Skills for the management of change

Apart from the identification and involvement of stakeholders and the mobilisation of technical, human and financial resources, specific skills are required for the management of change at the organisational level. Insights on the management of change that we use in our analysis come mainly from the literature on organisational design and development.

At the organisational level, several skills are required for the management of change (Leigh 1988). These are mainly in terms of the exercise of power and influence and there can be differences in the manner in which power and influence are exercised.

There can be different sources of power, namely, position (power that is based on a formal position in an organisation, for instance, that of the Chief Executive Officer or President); expert (power based on technical skills, expertise or specialised knowledge, for instance, of engineers or scientists in a particular field); and finally, personal (this refers to power based on a person's individual attributes, personality traits or charisma). Correspondingly, there can be different forms of exercise of power, namely, personal power (this is power that is based on an individual's personality or charisma); expert power (based on technical knowledge or skill); and finally, position power (the legal or legitimate power drawn from a formal position).

A pertinent point for students of public policy to ask is what role power plays in the implementation of policies. Also, what is the kind of interface that different forms of power may have in shaping policy implementation and the kinds of tensions that may arise from the interface of different forms of power in an organisational setting.

Further, at an organisational level, the management of change requires the exercise of different methods of influence. These methods of influence could likewise be characterised as follows:

- Overt or open, verbal influence. This takes the following forms
  - Exchange (negotiation, bargaining or bribes)
  - Rules and procedures (as in a bureaucracy)
  - Persuasion
- Unseen or covert influence
  - Ecology (this refers to the relationship of individuals with their surroundings) and
  - Magnetism (invisible but felt pull of personal power)

Models of organisational change

Change can be triggered within organisations in different ways. From the management literature, there are seen to be different models of change in organisations.

- *The development model.* As per the development model, organisations pass through three phases in the normal course of their development, depending on the exercise of power and authority. These phases could be described as follows:
  - Autocratic
  - Bureaucratic
  - Democratic

- *Crisis model.* As per the crisis model, organisational change is not driven so much by passing through systematic stages, but more so by crisis. Transition is marked by a period of crisis, a different crisis being the cause in each stage. As per this stage, there are different phases in the evolution of an organisation. These could be listed as follows:
  - ○ Pioneer phase
  - ○ Phase of differentiation
  - ○ Phase of integration

These models provide an approach to analyse how change is received by and, in turn, how it influences organisations.

Finally, Sutton (1999) lists several activities that are essential for the seeing through of a policy intervention. These are as follows

- Data collection
- Analysis
- Reflection
- Developing a vision
- Concept building
- Identifying change agents, which could be
  - ○ Individuals to lead the change
  - ○ Task forces, groups or committees
- Recognising barriers to change
  - ○ Predict the reaction of individuals and groups to proposed changes
  - ○ Public resistance to change
- Building support for reform
  - ○ Energizing
  - ○ Involve people early and encourage their participation
- Reforming organisational structures
  - ○ Fitting new tasks into older organisational structures can be problematic
- Mobilising resources
  - ○ Can be retarded by those who resist change
  - ○ Once donor funds are exhausted, how do we continue?
  - ○ Dealing with resource crunch

Though this does not provide a blueprint for the management of change, it does provide us with a broad checklist of issues that need to be thought through in planning for policy change, apart from the policy formulation itself. The basic point is that the management of change should receive as much attention as the formulation of a new policy. In essence, we can improve the effectiveness of the implementation of public policy by foreseeing and planning the implementation process and ensuring the support of the various actors who are involved in the implementation process, or those who are likely to be affected by it.

4.7 Improving service delivery in India: some lessons for the management of change

Poor service delivery has often been identified as a critical lacuna in the implementation of public programmes in the country; a number of factors are understood to limit the effectiveness of public service delivery (World Bank 2006). A crushing salary burden in the civil services, weak capacity in key management positions, frequent transfers of civil servants and rampant corruption could be considered to be some of them. Further, the World Bank study notes the Civil Services to be under managed with weak mechanisms for accountability.

Nevertheless, the nation has seen several successes in improving service delivery and there have been several ways of doing so. Research on the implementation process shows that in most cases, an important reason for the success of these interventions was that they found support among those who would be affected by them. Promoting competition has been one way of accomplishing this, as seen with the reforms in the telecom sector. Another similar example has been the promotion of competition in marketing services to farmers through the e-*choupal* kiosks and the *choupal sagar* hubs initiative of corporate giant ITC. This initiative found wide support with farmers and that was a crucial determinant of its success. An important reason for this was that it freed farmers from exploitative practices at *mandis* and eliminated information asymmetries surrounding prices and marketing of agricultural produce. For ITC, it reduced transaction costs in dealing with farmers and helped establish long-term supply relationships.

E-governance, that helps simplify transactions, has been a second route to improving service delivery. *Bhoomi, eSeva* and *FRIENDS* provide some examples of this. The *e Seva* application succeeded in bringing under one roof the services of about 13 state and local government agencies, three central government agencies and nine private sector organisations. An important factor that facilitated the success of these efforts was that none of them was resisted by those who might have lost out as a result of these initiatives. In this case, too, the reform found steady acceptance among the actors and those who would be affected by it.

A much wider attempt at reforms, however, is known to have come about through restructuring agency processes. The Karnataka State Road Transport Corporation (KSRTC) and Metro Water (Hyderabad) had the interests of large numbers of voters at stake, and that ensured the sustainability of these reforms. In the case of the stamps and registration department in Maharashtra, the driver of reform came not from the public but from the highest levels of the State government that was eager to show that Maharashtra could showcase a major e-governance reform programme. These reforms took place in the form of a public-private partnership and were sustained by wide publicity.

Another innovative approach to reform has been through decentralisation: decentralising teacher management in Madhya Pradesh stands out as an example. Madhya Pradesh's reform in primary education succeeded because of several factors: the Chief Minister's vision of decentralised forms of governance, a stable tenure of the involved civil servants, the creation of an institutional vehicle to push reform and far-reaching changes in teacher service conditions. This had a major impact on the creation of accountability relationships among teachers, affecting an important, though, neglected facet of basic education, as often pointed out by scholars as Jean Dreze and Amartya Sen.

Lack of political will is often cited as a reason for programme failure, though often it only serves as an 'escape-hatch' for poor delivery. Tamil Nadu's reforms directed at improving human development were sustained by the perception among two political parties that social programmes would bring electoral returns as well as a common ideological emphasis on welfare policies. This enabled the State to surpass Karnataka in terms of overall human development outcomes between 1981 and 2001, beyond what could have been expected by economic growth alone.

The above cases suggest that the support of those involved with the implementation process or affected by it is necessary to ensure the successful implementation of public policies and programmes. Though there exist several different routes for improving service delivery, they work only when they find popular acceptance among the major actors and the attractiveness of this further increases when implementing them can be seen to secure some political mileage for those in positions of power. Most certainly, they require wide support from among those who will be affected by their implementation. These cases demonstrate, further, the importance of political leadership in initiating as well as sustaining reforms and the need for wide acceptance among the affected actors. They show that reforms are possible, with positive changes, even in the absence of large systemic changes, if there exists positive support in their favour, as we have discussed in earlier sections of this chapter.

4.8 Conclusion

While Chapter 3 focused on concepts and tools that help us analyse the processes of policy formulation, in this chapter we have looked at how we can approach the analysis of policy implementation processes. We started this chapter by examining why the analysis of implementation of policies is necessary. The case for a strong analysis of policy implementation processes is built on grounds that often the real challenges lie at the implementation stage rather than at the stage of policy formulation. We then looked at the various reasons on account of which policy implementation may not be successful while distinguishing non-implementation from ineffective implementation.

We then went on to examine certain frameworks and concepts that can be employed for the analysis of policy implementation processes. The notion of street level bureaucracy helps us analyse how there can be a gap between the intentions of a policy and its actual outcomes, in that this gap is shaped by the actions of the street level bureaucrats (those engaged directly in the implementation of the policy at the field level). Street level bureaucrats, as Lipsky explained, exercise considerable discretion in the exercise of their responsibilities, and for this reason policies may not be implemented as they are intended to, resulting in what we call an 'implementation gap'.

Legal pluralism perspectives help us analyse how State laws or policies engendered by the institutions of the State can get diluted as they come to the ground and interface with other institutions, laws or practices. Finally, actor-oriented perspectives emphasise that policy intervention extends well beyond the stages of initiation and execution and is shaped by the socially constructed experiences and expectations of both the recipients of change as well as those engaged in the implementation of policies.

Having analyzed different frameworks for the analysis of policy implementation, we turned our attention to the management of the change process itself. We emphasised that the management of change requires as much attention as the formulation of the new policies or programmes. This requires explicit attention to the mobilisation of the necessary resources (financial, technical and managerial). Much depends on identification of and consultation with various stakeholders. Finally, in the management of change at the organisational level, much depends on the forms of exercise of power and influence at that level, through which resistance to change can be overcome and support for change mobilised.

An important factor that can further facilitate the success of policies and gauge the extent to which they have been effectively implemented is periodic monitoring and evaluation of policies. This is the subject of Chapter 5, to which we now turn our attention.

References

Arce, A. and Long, N. eds. 1992. *Anthropology, Development and Modernities: Exploring Discourses, Counter Tendencies and Violence.* London and New York: Routledge.

Benda-Beckmann, F. von. 1988. 'Comment on Merry.' *Law and Society Review* 22(5): 897–901.

Benda-Beckmann, F. von. 1999. 'Between Free Riders and Free Raiders: Property Rights and Soil Degradation in Context (first draft).' Paper presented at the International Workshop on Economic Policy Reforms and Sustainable Land Use in LDCs: Recent Advances in Quantitative Analyse, Wageningen, The Netherlands. 30 June–2 July.

Brinkerhoff, D. W. and Crosby, B. 2002. *Managing Policy Reform: Concepts and Tools for Decision-Makers in Developing and Transitioning Countries.* Bloomfield, CT: Kumarian Press.

Crosby, B. L. 1996. 'Policy Implementation: The Organizational Challenge.' *World Development* 24(9): 1403–1415.

Dunsire, A. 1978. *Implementation in a Bureaucracy.* Oxford: Martin Robertson.

Gerbrandy, G. and Hoogendam, P. 2002. 'Materialising Rights: Hydraulic Property in the Extension and Rehabilitation of Two Irrigation Systems in Bolivia.' In *Water Rights and Empowerment,* edited by R. Boelens and P. Hoogendam, 36–51. Assen: Van Gorcum.

Goel, S. 2016. 'Subtle Sexism in Public Organizations: Understanding Bureaucratic Attitudes and Policy Correlates for Gender Equality at the Work-Place.' Executive Fellow Programme in Management dissertation, Management Development Institute, Gurgaon.

Griffiths, J. 1986. 'What is Legal Pluralism?' *Journal of Legal Pluralism and Unofficial Law* 24(6): 1–56.

Gupta, N. 2005. 'Decentralized Community Managed Water and Sanitation Management in Rural Areas: Role of Women in Pani Samitis in Kutch Region of Gujarat.' MSc project report, TERI School of Advanced Studies, New Delhi.

Hill, M. 2005. *The Public Policy Process*. Fourth edition. Harlow: Pearson Education Limited.

Hogwood, B. A. and Gunn, L. A. 1984. *Policy Analysis for the Real World*. Oxford: Oxford University Press.

Jentoft, S., Bavink, M. and Johnson, D. 2009. 'Fisheries Co-management and Legal Pluralism: How an Analytical Problem Becomes an Institutional One.' *Human Organization* 68(1): 27–38.

Leigh, A. 1988. *Effective Change: Twenty Ways to Make It Happen*. Hyderabad: Universities Press.

Lipsky, M. 1980. *Street Level Bureaucracy: Dilemmas of the Individual in Public Services*. New York: Russell Sage Foundation.

Long, N. ed. 1989. 'Encounters at the Interface: A Perspective on Social Discontinuities in Rural Development.' *Wageningen Studies in Sociology, No. 27*. The Netherlands: Wageningen University.

Long, N. 2002. 'An Actor-oriented Approach to Development Intervention in Rural Life Improvement in Asia', Report of the APO seminar on Rural Life Improvement for Community Development, April 22-26, Japan.

Long, N. and Long, A. eds. 1992. *Battlefields of Knowledge: The Interlocking of Theory and Practice in Social Research and Development*. London and New York: Routledge.

Mathur, K. 1998. 'Introduction: The Emerging Concerns in Public Administration,' In *Development Policy and Administration: Readings in Indian Government and Politics*, edited by K. Mathur, 13–23. New Delhi: Sage Publications.

Meinzen-Dick, R. and Bakker, M. 2001. 'Water Rights and Multiple Water Uses. Framework and Application to Kirindi Oya Irrigation System Sri Lanka.' *Irrigation and Drainage Systems* 15(2): 129–148.

Merry, S. E. 1988. 'Legal Pluralism.' *Law and Society Review* 22(5): 869–896.

Mollinga, P. P. 2003. *On the Waterfront: Water Distribution, Technology and Agrarian Change in a South Indian Canal Irrigation System*. Hyderabad: Orient Longman.

Mooij, J. 2003. 'Smart Governance? Politics in the Policy Process in Andhra Pradesh, India.' Working Paper 228, Overseas Development Institute, U.K.

Moore, E. P. 1993. 'Gender, Power and Legal Pluralism: Rajasthan, India.' *American Ethnologist* 20(3): 522–542.

Narain, V. 2003. *Institutions, Technology and Water Control: Water Users' Associations and Irrigation Management Reform in Two Large-scale Systems in India*. Hyderabad: Orient Longman.

Nuitjen, M. and Anders, Gerhard. eds. 2007. *Corruption and the Secret of Law: A Legal Anthropological Perspective.* Hampshire: Ashgate Publishing.

Pressman, J. I. and Wildavsky, A. 1973. *Implementation.* Berkley: University of California Press.

Rajagopal, B. 2005. 'The Role of Law in Counter Hegemonic Globalization and Global Legal Pluralism: Lessons from the Narmada Valley Story in India.' *Leiden Journal of International Law* 18(3): 345–387.

Reddy, B. S. and Srinivas, T. 2009. 'Energy Use in Indian Household Sector: An Actor Oriented Approach.' *Energy* 34 (8): 992–1002.

Sampford, C., Shacklock, A., Connors, C. and Galtung, F. eds. 2006. *Measuring Corruption. Law, Ethics and Governance Series.* Hampshire: Ashgate.

Spiertz, J. and Wiber, M. 1996. 'The Bull in the China Chop. Regulation, Property Rights and Natural Resource Management: An Introduction.' In *The Role of Law in Natural Resource Management,* edited by J. Spiertz and M. Wiber, 1–23. Gravenhage: Vuga Publications.

Spiertz, H. L. J. and de Jong, I. J. H. 1992. 'Traditional Law and Irrigation Management: The Case of Bethma.' In *Irrigators and Engineers: Essays in Honour of Lucas Horst,* edited by G. Diemer and J. Slabbers, 185–201. Amsterdam: Thesis Publishers.

Sutton, R. 1999. 'The Policy Process: An Overview.' Working Paper 118, Overseas Development Institute, U.K.

Thomas, J. W. and Grindle, M. S. 1990. 'After the Decision: Implementing Policy Reforms in Developing Countries.' *World Development* 18(8): 1163–1181.

Vanderlinden, J. 1989. 'Return to Legal Pluralism: Twenty Years Later.' *Journal of Legal Pluralism and Unofficial Law* (28): 149–159.

Vasan, S. 2002. 'Ethnography of the Forest Guard: Contrasting Discourses, Conflicting Roles and Policy Implementation.' *Economic and Political Weekly* 37(40): 4125–4133.

Vasavada, S., Mishra, A. and Bates, C. 2000. 'How Many Committees Do I Belong To?' In *A New Moral Economy for India's Forests? Discourses of Community and Participation,* edited by R. Jeffrey and N. Sunder. Thousand Oaks: United States. Sage Publications.

Wade, R. 1992. 'How to Make Street Level Bureaucracies Work Better: India and Korea.' *IDS Bulletin* 23(4): 51–54.

World Bank. 2006. *Reforming Public Services in India. Drawing Lesson from Success. A World Bank Report.* New Delhi: Sage Publications.

Znoj, H. 2007. 'Deep Corruption in Indonesia: Discourses, Practices, Histories.'

In *Corruption and the Secret of Law: A Legal Anthropological Perspective*, edited by M. Nuijten and G. Anders, 53–74. Aldershot: Ashgate.

5

Knowing the consequences of public policy

In this chapter, we turn our attention to crucial issues surrounding the evaluation and monitoring of public policy. The chapter is intended not so much to provide prescriptions on how to monitor and evaluate policies; instead to trigger reflection among readers on their experiences with policy monitoring and evaluation, approaches adopted, political motivations and problems encountered.

We start with examining the conceptual connotations of public policy evaluation and distinguish between different types of policy evaluation; particularly, in this context, we emphasise the need to distinguish policy outcomes from policy outputs. We then look at the imperatives and need for policy evaluation. This is followed by a review of different types of evaluation that may be typically carried out as well as the different approaches that may be adopted.

The latter part of this chapter is devoted to an analysis of the politics of public policy evaluation. Policy evaluation is not simply a positivist exercise using scientific tools and techniques, as seen in a linear rational model of the policy process; rather, it is an inherently political activity, shaped by and enmeshed in social relations of power. The linear rational model of policy analysis sees policy monitoring and evaluation as culminating in policy termination and/or continuation. We look at why this may not always be the case and how protecting certain political and legal interests could keep policies in continuation even when analysis has proven that they have not been effective. We conclude the chapter with some discussion on the issues in the monitoring of public policy.

5.1 Public policy evaluation

Policy evaluation could be defined as the process of learning about the consequences of public policy (Dye 2002). Wholey et al. (2004) define policy evaluation to be the assessment of the overall effectiveness of a national programme in meeting its objectives or assessment of the relative effectiveness of two or more programmes in meeting a common objective.

Policy evaluation needs to be distinguished from monitoring. While monitoring provides routine feedback, evaluation offers a more in-depth study of particular issues or concerns at any specific point in time. Public policies, nevertheless, could be evaluated at all phases of policy-making: in the identification and articulation of policy problems, in the formulation of alternative policy options, during the implementation of a particular policy, or at the termination of policy to determine its final impact.

Objectives of public policy evaluation

Morse and Struyk (2006) summarise the many reasons for which policy evaluations might be carried out: to provide a source of feedback and improvement and a mechanism for accountability of policy-makers and implementers, to influence the pattern and direction of government funding, build a sense of ownership among programme staff, and to identify overall policy impacts.

Evaluations enable governments and others to assess policies and programmes (Morse and Struyk 2006). Policy evaluation may provide politicians and citizens with an intelligent basis for discussing and judging conflicting ideas, proposals and outcomes (Fischer 1995). Evaluations can potentially have a significant effect on public policy- either by steering resources away from failed strategies or making the case to expand successful interventions. They could, if harnessed effectively, lead to improvements in ongoing programmes. Policy analysts seeking to develop new policy can learn from the evaluations of similar measures and use this information to understand and estimate costs, impacts and risks of new and proposed interventions.

Types of policy evaluation

It is important, at the very outset, to distinguish between *failures of implementation* (which is the purpose of monitoring to avoid) and *failure of policy*.[1] To evaluate the programme in terms of its original objectives might lead to a conclusion that the policy was a failure; this might, however, be misleading since the policy as originally envisaged might not actually have been put into effect. If it proves impracticable to implement the policy as

---

1 See also the distinction between non-implementation and ineffective implementation in Chapter 4.

originally envisaged, then this too can be considered to be a failure of policy design. In other words, we need to evaluate a policy against what it actually set out to do, that may be different from what may have been initially envisaged or proposed.

Impact evaluation and process evaluation

When talking about policy evaluation, it is important to distinguish between *impact evaluation* and *process evaluation* (Fischer 1995). Designed to supply information about complex social and economic problems and to assess the processes through which their resolution is pursued, evaluations can focus on policy or programme outcomes. This is referred to as *impact evaluation*. The impact of a policy, in turn, could refer to its effects on real-world conditions, including impact on the target situation or group(s), impact on situations or groups other than the target (spillover effects), impact on future as well as immediate conditions, direct costs, in terms of resources devoted to the programme and indirect costs, including loss of opportunities to do other things.

Alternatively, policy evaluation could focus on the processes by which a policy or programme is formulated and evaluated. This is known as *process evaluation* (Fischer 1995). Both impact evaluation and process evaluation are significant in their own right, though impact evaluations tend to be more common than process evaluations, at least so in the Indian context. This point emerged in several discussions with participants in the Post-Graduate Diploma Programme in Public Policy and Management at MDI's School of Public Policy and Governance.

Ex ante and ex post evaluation

When such evaluations focus on the outcomes expected to result from a policy in a foreseeable future, they are said to be *ex ante evaluations*. On the other hand, when they focus on the actual results from their introduction, they are known to constitute *ex post* evaluations.

Some definitions tie evaluation of policy to the stated goals of a programme or policy (Dye 2002). However, we may not always know what these goals really are and because we know that some programmes and policies pursue conflicting goals, Dye argues that it may be appropriate not to limit our notion of policy evaluation to their achievement. Instead, we may concern ourselves with all of the consequences of public policy, that is, with the overall policy impact.

Symbolic and tangible impacts

Further, the impact of a policy includes both its *symbolic* and *tangible* impacts (Dye 2002). It's symbolic impact deals with the perceptions that individuals have of government action and their attitude towards it. In the Indian context, a good illustration of this appears in the work of Arora (2008). In the absence of efforts to limit groundwater withdrawals in the Kurukshetra district of Haryana resulting from the cultivation of a variety of quick maturing paddy called *saathi*, the Agriculture Department responded by burning the crop over large plots of land. Apart from the tangible impact of this measure on the destruction of the crops, this also had a symbolic meaning; it symbolised the complete non-tolerance of this practice by the State government and gave a signal to farmers to simply discontinue this practice. Similarly, austerity measures by governments in power can also be seen to have a symbolic effect. They create an impression of a government that is 'with the masses' in times of a crisis and resource crunch and seek to reinforce signals that similar measures are needed from other sectors of the economy.

Public policy is often judged by citizens, individuals and groups and whole societies in terms of its good intentions rather than tangible accomplishments. In fact, sometimes programmes that may have been very popular may have very little positive tangible impact in practice. Even if government policies do not succeed in eliminating poverty, preventing crime, and so on, the failure of government to try to do these things would prove even worse. Thus, governments seek to implement certain policies in order to reveal their commitment to certain goals and development priorities. It is in this context that we refer to the symbolic effects of certain policies, that is, in terms of the intention or ideologies of the government that they reveal rather than the tangible impacts that are created by their implementation.

5.2 Policy outputs and outcomes

When we talk about the evaluation of public policy, we need to distinguish between the *outputs* and *outcomes* of policy. Grumm (1975) defined outputs as the actual actions of the government while outcomes are the impacts of these.

The *outputs* of policy are essentially the physical results of a delivery process. The *outcomes* of policy, on the other hand, are the impacts of the policy in question. In other words, they are the consequences of the policy outputs. They represent what the physical results of a delivery process translate into. For instance, in a scheme for improving access to safe water, the number of hand-pumps installed are the policy outputs. If, as a result, the incidence of waterborne diseases decreases, that counts as a policy outcome. In a programme on adult education, similarly, adult schools set up are a policy output, while an improvement in the literacy rate could be an outcome of this policy. When we talk of a polio eradication campaign, likewise, the number of polio drops administered would be the policy outputs while the actual reduction in the incidence of polio would be the outcome. The dynamics and processes through which policy outputs get translated into policy outcomes should be a subject of intellectual interest and investigation for students and scholars of public policy.

Studies have shown that simply installing hand-pumps may not be enough to ameliorate the drudgery of women in collecting water (Venkateshwaran 1995). Women may not use the hand-pumps on account of a number of reasons, such as an inconvenient location or perceptions about hand-pump water. Thus, gauging the impacts of drinking water supply interventions simply by counting the number of hand-pumps installed may not be sufficient. It is important to take the next step to understand whether the hand-pumps are used and what kinds of results they have produced on the quality of life of those who use them. It can be limiting to assess the consequences of certain public policy interventions based on the policy outputs alone.

Note that different policy outputs can be used to accomplish policy objectives but with varying policy outcomes. A good example is the recent debate in India on the mid-day meals' scheme, about whether school students should be served biscuits or a conventional balanced meal. Each of these would be different kinds of policy outputs, and with correspondingly different kinds of policy outcomes in terms of the impacts on nutritional status of children. The choice of outputs may further be influenced by the ease of public service delivery. For instance, though the policy outcomes would be different in the case of a cooked meal vis-a-vis a packet of biscuits, in the case of the mid-day meals' scheme discussed above, the latter would be easier to deliver. This may be an important factor influencing the final choice of policy output.

Further, the same policy outputs may affect some outcomes in a favourable way, while others in a non-favourable way. For instance, in a study in a village in Morni block of Haryana in northwest India, I found that while the installation of hand-pumps reduced the drudgery of walking long distances to collect water for women, they were now expected to carry larger volumes of water on their heads, since men who earlier bathed at village ponds now wanted to bathe in the privacy of their own homes (Narain 2003). Thus, while it is more important to evaluate public policy on the basis of outcomes rather than outputs, we need also to look at the wide range of outcomes that policy outputs create.

Governments and politicians draw the attention of public much more to policy outputs, while civil society organisations, academicians and researchers tend to be more interested in the policy outcomes. Policy outputs are a necessary but not sufficient condition for favourable outcomes.

However, unfortunately, monitoring policy outcomes does not usually receive the same attention as does policy outputs. This is for several reasons: first, monitoring policy outcomes can be much more difficult and challenging. Policy outcomes may take longer to emerge and may be less easy to identify and attribute to a specific policy. Policy outputs, on the other hand, tend to be more distinctly visible in physical terms. Besides, policy outputs have a good political appeal and are often used to impress voters and the electorate. Area brought under irrigation, dams built, houses electrified and construction works generated all create a 'feel good' factor and can be used to easily impress the electorate. Policy outcomes are also much more subject to value judgements in the sense of what is good or bad for society (but so is public policy itself!). Measuring policy outcomes may further require specific skill sets that may not easily be available in the government or that could be expensive to obtain.

5.3 Policy evaluation in practice

A number of crucial considerations stand out when it comes to carrying out policy evaluations. Dye (2002) summarises these as follows:

1. *Distinguishing between policy outputs and policy outcomes.* As we noted briefly above, it is important to distinguish between policy outputs and policy outcomes. In describing public policy or even in explaining its determinant measures of policy, outputs are important (they are the tangible products from an intervention). But in assessing policy impact, we must identify changes in society that are associated with measures of government activity.

2. *Identification of target groups.* The target group is that part of the population for whom the programme is intended, such as the poor, the sick, the ill-housed or other, specific marginalised groups in society. Target groups must first be identified and then the intended effect of the programme on the members of these groups must be determined. Is it to change their physical, social or economic conditions? What could be the possible unintended effects on target groups? These are some questions that need to be addressed. Needless to say, careful

identification of target groups from the very outset is essential for effective policy evaluation.[2]

3. *Non-target groups.* Identifying non-target groups for a policy is a difficult process but as important as identifying target groups. These non-target groups may include government bureaucrats, social workers, local political figures, taxpayers and others. Though they are not the main targets or beneficiaries of these programmes, they are affected in the course of their implementation. For example, what is the effect of welfare reform on groups other than the poor, to whom they are targeted? As we saw in Chapter 3, many of them may be adversely affected by these interventions, and to that effect, may oppose them.

4. *Short-term and long-term effects.* Addressing this issue requires attention to the following questions: When will the benefits or the costs of the intervention be felt? Is the programme designed for short-term emergencies? Or, is it a long-term, developmental effort? What are likely to be the short-term effects of a public policy? What are likely to be the long-term effects? Is there a trade-off? If so, is such a trade-off measurable/quantifiable?

5. *Indirect and symbolic costs and benefits.* Programmes are frequently measured by their direct costs. Government agencies may have developed various forms of cost-benefit analysis to identify their direct costs of government programmes. But it is very difficult to identify the indirect and symbolic benefits or costs of public programmes. Rarely can all these factors be included in a formal decision-making model; cost-accounting techniques developed in business were designed around units of production (automobiles, airplanes, tons of steel and so on). But how do we identify and measure units of social well-being? According to Dye, political intuition is often the best guide available to policy-makers in these matters.

6. *Calculating net benefits and costs.* The task of calculating the net impact of a public policy can be quite awesome. This requires taking in to account

---

2 The poor identification of target groups has been an important issue of public policy debate in India. The main issue is that benefits may often not reach the target groups. This has led to some criticisms for instance of the NREGA programme wherein it has been argued by some that it might be more viable to give cash transfers to the participants rather than wages resulting from their employment in asset creation. The current practice results often in pilferage and waste and the creation of assets that may be of little value to the community. Similar issues arise with regard to subsidies. See Gulati and Narayanan (2008).

all the symbolic and tangible benefits, both immediate and long range, minus all the symbolic and tangible losses, both immediate and future. Even if all these benefits and costs are known, it may still be very difficult to come up with a net balance. Some items on both sides of the balance would defy comparison: for instance, subtracting a tangible cost in rupees from a symbolic reward in the sense of well-being felt by individuals and groups.[3]

Approaches to programme evaluation

Notwithstanding the above challenges, most government agencies do make some efforts to review the effectiveness of their own programmes. These reviews may take the form of hearings and reports, site visits, programme measures, (focusing on policy outputs rather than impacts), and evaluation of citizens' complaints (Dye 2002). In this section, we take a look at the different types of evaluation policy-makers could potentially engage with.

Hearings and reports. The most common type of programme review involves hearings and reports. Government administrators may be asked by chief executives or legislators to give testimony (formally or informally) on the accomplishments of their own programmes. Sometimes, written annual reports are provided by programme administrators. It is also common practice to commission consultants, think-tanks or research organisations to carry out evaluations and assessments of specific programmes or interventions. Such evaluations may also be carried out by or at the behest of funding agencies and multilateral organisations, such as the World Bank or others, who are interested in assessing the effectiveness of programmes financially supported by them.

Depending upon the rigor of the assessments as well as the time and resources at the disposal of the evaluators, this method of assessment can provide a detailed evaluation of the programme or policy in question. However, testimonials and reports of administrators may not be very objective, as they may amplify the benefits of the programmes and underscore their negative impacts. The reports are vulnerable to biases in order to protect the position of those associated with the formulation or implementation of these programmes or to justify those who have provided financial support for them.

Site visits. Teams of high-ranking administrators, expert consultants, legislators, funding organisations or some combination of these may decide to visit agencies or conduct inspections in the field. These teams pick up

---

3 See also the discussion on rationalism in Chapter 2.

impressionistic data about how programmes are being run, whether they are following specific guidelines, whether they have competent staff and sometimes whether or not the clients are pleased with the services. An example is teams from funding or donor organisations that visit sites within the purview of specific programmes funded by them.

A limitation of this approach is that these teams may be guided by people at the field level who are engaged in the execution of these programmes to see only selectively those aspects of the programme implementation that present a positive picture. For instance, they may be taken to the best parts of the project or introduced only to those people who have been impacted positively. Besides, these visits tend to be brief and cursory, with only selective impressions and may not allow a comprehensive, in-depth evaluation of the intervention. For this method to be useful, it needs to be supplemented with other approaches as well, such as more detailed written reports or assessments and interviews and meetings with the various stakeholders.

Programme measures. The data developed by government agencies themselves generally cover certain measures of policy output. Examples include the number of recipients in various welfare programmes, the number of persons in work-force training programmes and number of public hospital beds. However, as noted earlier, these programme measures are essentially measures of policy output rather than measures of policy outcome. They rarely indicate what impact these numbers have on society, say, in terms of the conditions of life confronting the poor, their sense of well-being and empowerment, the success of work force trainees in finding and holding skilled jobs, the health of the nation, the cleanliness of cities or the ability of graduates to read and write and function in society.

Many of these measures tend to be purely quantitative and a weakness of that is that they may say little about the quality of impact on the lives of the people that they are intended to benefit. An example in the Indian context is the obsession with quantitative targets in improving access to safe water and sanitation. A commonly used indicator is 'per cent' of habitations covered with a source of drinking water within a certain distance (in India, this is 1.6 km.) This says little about the quality of water service delivery, whether women actually use the hand-pumps or not, the dependability and reliability of water supply or the convenience of location.

Comparison with professional standards. These standards are normally expressed as a desirable level of output: for example, the number of pupils per teacher, the number of hospital beds per one thousand people, the number of cases for each welfare worker. Actual government outputs can then be compared with ideal outputs.

Although such an exercise can be helpful, it still focuses on government outputs rather than the impact of government activities on the conditions of target or non target groups. There is scant evidence that ideal levels of government output have any significant impact on society. Further, these standards may reflect the biases of the professionals arising from their disciplinary training, rather than local contexts and circumstances. Besides, there may be problems arising from applying these standards indiscriminately across different regions or populations.

Evaluation of citizens' complaints. Another common approach to programme evaluation is the analysis of citizens' complaints. Recent efforts in the Indian context are aimed at setting up complaint redressal forums or tribunals. This approach may have certain limitations. Not all citizens voluntarily submit complaints or remarks about government programmes. Occasionally, administrators develop questionnaires for participants in their programmes to learn what their complaints may be and whether they are satisfied or not. But these questionnaires tend to test public opinion towards the programme rather than its real impact on the lives of participants.

While each of these approaches has certain strengths and weaknesses, perhaps the best results can be obtained through a combination of them. This serves the additional function of triangulation and can help in the provision of more objective and unbiased evaluations.

The manner of evaluating public policy

Having looked at the various approaches which government agencies may adopt for the evaluation of public policy, what kinds of techniques are available to governments in order to evaluate public policy? We now look at the various techniques through which evaluation of public policy may be carried out.

Before vs. after comparison. This is considered to be the most common research design in programme evaluation. It compares results in a jurisdiction at two times: before the programme was implemented and after the programme was implemented. This approach focuses mainly on target groups or the people who are intended as beneficiaries. For instance, we may wish to compare school enrolment before the introduction of a mid-day meals' scheme and after the introduction of the mid-day meals' scheme.

While this approach is rather easy to understand and carry out, it is at the same time somewhat simplistic. A major weakness of this approach is that it may be difficult to know whether the changes observed came about as a result exclusively of a specific intervention in question or as a result of other changes that were occurring at the same time. For instance, it may be difficult in the above case, to ascertain whether the increase in enrolment could be ascribed to the introduction of the mid-day meals' scheme alone or whether there were other factors at work such as change in domestic conditions, attitudes among parents and teachers, and so on.

Projected trend line vs. post programme comparisons. In this approach, past (pre-programme trends) are projected into the post-programme time period. These projections can then be compared with what actually happened in society after the programme was implemented.

This approach is perhaps more effective than the previous design, namely, the before vs. after comparison; however, it requires much greater effort methodologically and also needs data for several points of time such that a trend line can be established. Further, here, too, as in the previous approach, it may be difficult to ascertain if certain changes have happened on account of the intervention being evaluated or because of other factors at play.

Compare jurisdictions with and without programmes. In this design, States, union territories or cities that have received a certain intervention are compared with those that have not. For instance, we may wish to compare the incidence of waterborne diseases in a district where drainage facilities have been revamped with one where this has not been done.

In this approach, normally only post intervention periods are considered. It might be more effective if both pre- and post-programme periods are considered. The weaknesses of the previous two approaches can be seen here as well, in terms of the extent to which the difference in the two regions under comparison can be ascribed exclusively to the intervention.

Comparison between control and experimental groups before and after programme implementation. The research design here involves the careful selection of control and experimental groups that are identical in every way, followed by the application of the policy to the experimental group only and the consequent comparison of changes in the experimental group with changes in the control group after the application of the policy. Initially, control and experimental groups must be identical and the pre-programme performance of each group must be measured and found to be the same. The programme must then be applied only to the experimental groups. The post programme differences between the experimental and control groups must be then carefully measured. This research design is often preferred by scientists because it provides the best opportunity of estimating changes that are derived from the effects of specific interventions.

However, as noted by Dye (2002), government sponsored experimental research raises a series of important questions and has several limitations. First, there tends to be a bias towards positivist research. Successful experiments, where the proposed policy achieves positive results, tend to receive more acclaim and produce greater opportunities for advancement for social scientists and administrators than will unsuccessful experiments. The second limitation is in terms of what is called the Hawthorne effect, namely, that people behave differently when they know they are being watched. For example, students generally perform at a higher level when something new is introduced in their classroom routine. Third, there may be problems in generalising results from the specific case or experiment to a larger level, say that of a nation. Results obtained with small-scale experiments may differ substantially from those that would occur if a large-scale, nation-wide programme was adopted. Finally, there are several legal and ethical issues to contend with. For instance, do government researchers have the right to withhold public services from individuals simply to provide a control group for experimentation? Besides, it may also not be politically easy or practical to provide some services to some groups and not to others. For these reasons, this technique may be very difficult to put into practice.

5.4 Problems in analysing the impact of public policy

Needless to say, impact evaluation of public policy is not an easy task, and is confronted with several challenges. Hogwood and Gunn (1984) enlist several problems in the evaluation of public policy. Firstly, if objectives of a policy are not clear or are not specified in any measurable form, the criteria for success remain unclear. For instance, if there has been goal creep or goal shifting, a question that needs to be addressed is whether success be measured against the original objectives or against what now appear to be the real objectives. In fact, even an apparently clearly stated objective may leave open the question of how the success of the programme is to be judged or measured. These criteria need to be operationalised in some objective form at the very outset, at the stage when an intervention is starting to be executed. In some cases, there may be readily available indicators used in previous studies which can be pulled down off the shelf; however, care should be taken to use such indicators only where they are valid indicators of policy objectives.

Second, even when objectives have been specified and priorities among them have been established, the issues remain of what outcomes are seen as relevant to meeting those objectives and what level of achievement in meeting those objectives would constitute success. Hogwood and Gunn argue that it is important to try to establish standards that would be considered to constitute success before the data are collected and analysed.

Third, there can be considerable practical difficulties in attempting to identify and measure side-effects of an intervention but the damage they cause or the spillover benefits they provide may be more significant than the impact in terms of the original objective. There may, therefore, be a problem of how the consequences should be brought into a statement of objectives and how much side effects should be weighted relative to the central objectives.

Fourth, information necessary to assess impact may not be available or may not be available in a suitable from. Fifth, and this is somewhat more complex and challenging than the previous four, while we may have quite a wide range of data about social conditions, it is frequently very difficult to separate out the effect of a particular programme from all other influences on people's lives. For example, improved health indicators can reflect improved living conditions arising from greater affluence and better housing or from improved health education as well as from treatment by doctors and hospitals. Sixth and closely related to the previous point, it is common for a single problem or proportion of the population to be the target of several programmes with the same or related objectives. In such cases, it is impossible or meaningless to assess the impact of a single programme. For example, if traffic rule violation goes down, is this due to improved police methods, better road layout, curbing drunken driving or some other factors, may not be easy to assess.

Problems may also arise when there is a rapid sequence over time of programme directed at a problem and it is difficult to separate out the continuing effects of now withdrawn programmes from the effects of newly introduced ones. What is being considered is the success or failure of a programme to which politicians may have committed their reputations, to which public employees may have made personal commitment as well as have a career stake in them, and from which clients may be receiving benefits even if in terms of evaluation criteria the impact of these benefits does not constitute a success. Evaluation may be seen as threat to the continuation of a programme in which a number of people have an important stake. This will affect how evaluation results are utilised. But it will also affect the ease with which evaluation research can be conducted, since the cooperation of public officials and clients is often required in the evaluation. One paradox of evaluation is that it may only be possible to carry out monitoring or evaluation by promoting to use its results. Finally, systematic evaluation can be very costly. Such costs can be a diversion from substantive policy delivery itself.

Rejection of negative findings of policy evaluations

The linear and rational model of the policy process envisages that consequent upon the evaluation of a policy, a decision is made to continue with or to terminate a policy. That is, if the evaluation of a policy is negative, a decision is taken to terminate it. When the evaluation is positive, a decision is taken to continue with it. In practice, however, even if the evaluation of a policy is negative, we may find that policy-makers may choose to continue with it.

Dye (2002) explains that government administrators and programme supporters are ingenious in devising reasons why negative findings about policy impacts should be rejected. Even in the face of clear evidence that their favourite programmes are useless or even counterproductive, they may argue that

1. the effects of the programme are long range and cannot be measured at the present time, that is, very little time has elapsed since the intervention was executed and that this time is insufficient to evaluate the policy.

2. the effects of the programme are subtle and cannot be identified by crude measures or statistics, that is, they do not lend themselves to easy measurement

3. the effects of the programme are diffused and of a general nature; no single criterion or index adequately measures what is accomplished.

4. experimental research cannot be carried out effectively because to withhold services from some persons to observe the impact of such withholding would be unfair to them, and unethical.

5. the fact that no difference was found between persons receiving the services and those not receiving them means that the programme is not sufficiently intensive and indicates the need to spend more resources on the programme; in this case, absence of resources serves as an escape-hatch for limited or adverse impacts.

6. the failure to identify any positive effects of a programme is attributable to inadequacy or bias in the research itself and not in the programme, that is, the problem is with the manner in which the evaluation of the policy has been carried out rather than with the policy per se.

Dye further goes on to argue that even when evaluative studies produce negative findings, and even when policy-makers themselves are aware of fraud, waste, and inefficiency in the execution of the policy, and even when highly negative benefit cost ratios are reported, government programmes may manage to survive. Once policy is institutionalised within a government, it is difficult to terminate it.

This may be for several reasons. First, policy persistence may be seen as essential for the survival and justification of the bureaucracy and legislative set-up. Among the beneficiaries of any government programme are those who administer and supervise it. Bureaucratic jobs depend on a programme's continuation. Government positions with all of their benefits, pay, perquisites and prestige are at stake. Strong incentives exist, therefore, for bureaucrats to resist or undermine negative evaluations of their programmes or even by claiming that their programmes are failing because not enough is being spent on them. Legislators can likewise use their committee positions to protect failed programmes. The discontinuation of the programme would mean that people who have been associated with its execution lose out their jobs or positions, and of course, the concomitant perks, power and prestige. Secondly, incrementalism might be at work, where policies are introduced with marginal variations over existing ones, rather than being discontinued in totality (as we saw in Chapter 2, while discussing the different models of policy processes). Incrementalism implies that policies put in place are only marginal variations from already existing policies. Thus, previous policies may be modified marginally and reintroduced, if there is found to be some flaw in their execution. This observation reaffirms the political nature of the process of the evaluation of public policy.

5.5 Paradigmatic and philosophical foundation of public policy evaluation: the approach of practical deliberation

The contemporary empirical approach to policy evaluation (as described in the preceding sections) is constructed on the foundations of the scientific method in social research called positivism (Fischer 2005). Positivism is the approach of the natural sciences, and sees social science as an organised method for combining deductive logic with precise empirical observations of individual behaviour in order to discover and confirm a set of probabilistic causal laws that can be used to predict general patterns of human activity (Neuman 1995). A positivist approach implies that a researcher begins with a general cause–effect relationship that he or she logically derives from a possible causal flaw in general theory. A researcher then logically links the abstract ideas of the relationship to precise measurements of the social world. The researcher remains detached, neutral, and objective as he or she measures aspects of social life, examines evidence and replicates the research of others. These processes lead to an empirical test of and confirmation for the laws of social life as outlined in a theory. According to positivism, the ultimate purpose of research is scientific explanation and positivism seeks to develop laws or propositions that explain a social phenomenon such that it can be predicted or controlled.

In the field of policy analysis, positivism is manifested in a collection of empirical-analytic techniques. These include such techniques as cost-benefit analysis, quasi-experimental research designs, multiple regression analyses, survey research, input-output studies, multiple regression analyses, survey research, mathematical simulation models, and systems analysis.

The use of these techniques of policy evaluation is consistent with the rational model of policy decision-making. We reviewed the rational model in Chapter 2, and we briefly recapitulate its basic premises, as done by Fischer (1995).

1. Decision-makers first empirically identify the existence of a problem.
2. They formulate the goals and objectives that would lead to an optimal solution.
3. They determine the relevant consequences and probabilities of alternative means to the solution.
4. They assign a value, that is, a numerical cost or benefit to each consequence.
5. They combine the information about consequences, probabilities, and costs and benefits and select the most effective and efficient alternative.

The positivist perspective on policy evaluation is strongly echoed in some definitions of policy evaluation. One such definition is provided by Nachmias (1979). 'Policy evaluation research could be seen as the objective, systematic, empirical examination of the effects ongoing policies and public programmes have on their targets in terms of the goals they are meant to achieve (Nachmias 1979).' Programme evaluation is the systematic collection of information about the activities, characteristics and outcomes of programmes to make judgments about how well a programme is working and achieving its intended results (Morse and Struyk 2006).

Needless to say, as we discussed in Chapter 2, this approach to the analysis of policy can be seen as being too technocratic, trying to reduce complex social, political and economic phenomena to a set of calculations and models. The same criticism can be seen as applying, in general, to positivist policy evaluation that has been widely criticised as being both a product and agent of the technocratic world view, a pattern of thought that emphasises technical solutions to social and political problems. By viewing society and its problems, and its solutions in technical terms, the technocratic world view seeks to free them from their cultural, psychological and linguistic contexts. Expressed in the precise but abstract symbols of mathematics, the methodologies of positivist policy evaluation are designed to bypass partisan political interests. Their findings are meant to be value free. Positivist evaluation of public policy builds upon the fact-value dichotomy in the social sciences that provides the foundation for a clear-cut partition of scientific and political functions. The positivist evaluation of public policy has been open to wide ranging criticism, on the false separation it creates between logic and practice, facts and values and scientific and political functions.

5.6 Evaluation as a political activity

In contrast to the linear and rational approach to policy analysis that sees evaluation as an objective analytic exercise, Taylor and Bulloch (2005) emphasise the political nature of public policy evaluation. They argue that evaluation itself is socially constructed and politically articulated. It is given meaning within wider social and political relations. While evidence is important in reaching judgements about social policies and programmes, these need to be set within a wider understanding of both the politics of evaluation practice and the political role attributed to evaluation. Evaluation could also be considered as a means of political legitimisation. Evaluation is 'an inherently and inescapably political project imbued with issues of power at every level (Taylor and Bulloch 2005: 3).' Thus, evaluation contributes to political and policy discourses as well at several levels: from formal party politics to local practices; from policy formulation to policy implementation. Dye (2002) notes that politics decide what policies and policy alternatives will be studied in the first place. Politics can also affect findings themselves, and certainly the interpretations and uses of policy research can be politically motivated.

Politics enters evaluation at all levels. To begin with, the social construction of evaluation itself needs to be understood as part of wider social and political relations. First is the framing of the issue to be evaluated, which depends on the dominant policy orientations and the way in which social issues are politically constructed. Defining what is to be evaluated is itself an intensely political act and raises questions about the domination of particular understandings of social problems. It also raises questions about the role and purpose of evaluation. Is it, for example, concerned with legitimisation of a programme based on a particular framing of the issues and policy orientation towards it? Its purposes can also be seen as either instrumental or technical (concerned with the collection of objective evidence, often in easily handled performance data for policy-makers and/or managers) or it can be seen as empowering participants and service users to take control. Also, in evaluations of policy, important is the balance of stakeholder interests and the relative power between them, including service providers and service users; some stakeholders may have more at stake than others and the balance of interests may shift as evaluations unfold.

5.7 Participatory evaluation

One approach to the politics of evaluation that has gained ground is participatory evaluation (Fischer 2005). This comes in different forms, reflecting some of the disagreements between scientific realists and social constructivists. Realists tend towards a view of participation based on the inclusion of participant perspectives by evaluators who still remain firmly in control whereas constructivists see the role of evaluation as giving participants the central voice without privileging the views of the evaluator.

Participatory Rural Appraisals

PRAs (Participatory Rural Appraisals) are widely used in policy evaluation. PRA is essentially a method of enabling communities to share information about their selves using visual techniques and discussions. It evolved from disenchantment with questionnaire surveys founded on a paradigm of positivist research that typically entail high costs, errors, delays and manipulation. A deviation from more positivist approaches, PRAs symbolise a paradigm shift in the social sciences. PRAs are seen essentially as imbibing a question of change in attitude as they involve direct learning from the local people, a principle referred to in the social sciences as 'handing over the stick': those carrying out the PRA exercises become the students and those who are being 'studied' become the masters, people to learn from.

Information is seen as being shared and owned by local people, as against being extracted by outsiders in more positivist, questionnaire based surveys. PRAs employ a plurality of methods. A number of visual techniques are used such as village transects, village maps, venn diagrams, seasonality calendars, wealth-ranking, time lines, trend analysis, focus groups, semi-structured interviews and do-it-yourself exercises. PRA exercises are done by local people, in groups and have typically a strong reliance on visuals. They are interactive and iterative and involve comparisons.

In India, PRAs have found wide ranging applications, in such fields as natural resource management, developing village development plans, and developing programmes for women and the poor and have been applied extensively in sectors such as agriculture and food security. They are widely used by NGOs, students and universities. NGOs such as MYRADA, Action Aid, and Aga Khan Rural Support Programme (AKRSP) have promoted PRAs extensively in India.

There are no strict rules regarding the duration of PRAs; the duration of these exercises depends upon the time available as well as the resources. PRA exercises are normally done in groups of people and through inter-disciplinary teams. Triangulation serves as an important consistency check, in which data obtained from a number of sources is checked against each other.

PRA tools and techniques are understood to have certain advantages over conventional tools. When correctly done, they are useful for rapport building and create an atmosphere of shared learning with those being studied. Often they are more cost-effective and quicker than questionnaires. They are useful in presenting an aggregate picture and are known to engender a sense of fun and interest in these activities.

However, there are important concerns regarding the legitimacy of the use of PRA tools, concerned mainly with questions about how these exercises are conducted. For instance, a fundamental issue is about who participates in these exercises, and whose interests, views and perspectives they come to represent. PRAs may come to represent the views and perceptions of the local elite who are more vocal. PRAs, soon after their popularisation in the 1980s, became what scholars like Robert Chambers came to call an 'instant fashion'; they were done simply to get funding from donors for specific kinds of projects, without truly imbibing the spirit of the philosophy of the PRA.[4] They are often hurriedly done and forced on people; simply using these tools and techniques without the basic spirit underlying PRAs goes counter to the objectives of carrying out these exercises. There is often an emphasis on routinisation, leading to a loss of spontaneity. This has come to be manifest in an emphasis on manuals and procedures for the conduct of PRA exercises.

---

4 See also Chambers (1995).

Practical deliberation

In this section we outline the approach of practical deliberation, which is an approach to public policy evaluation that builds upon but clearly transcends the linear analytic approach to public policy evaluation (Fischer 1995). This approach seeks to move beyond public policy evaluation as a positivist exercise. In this approach, four discourses are distinguished and combined: the technical-analytic discourse, the contextual discourse, the systems discourse and the ideological discourse. Each discourse is built around a basic philosophy that presents an important dimension of the public policy issue to be evaluated and has its set of organising questions. The basic strength of this approach is that it helps view policies in their overall social and political context rather than seeing them narrowly as a means of achieving specific objectives, evaluated through objective approaches, tools and techniques. The approach of practical deliberation is organised as follows:

Level: first-order evaluation

Technical-analytic discourse: programme verification

Verification, the most familiar of four discursive phases, is addressed to the basic technical analytic or methodological questions that have dominated the attention of empirical policy analysis. The methodologies used to pursue questions of verification are the established tools of conventional policy evaluation, such as experimental research and cost-benefit analysis. The basic questions of verification are as follows:

Organising questions: does the programme empirically fulfil its stated objectives? Does the empirical analysis uncover secondary or unanticipated effects that offset the programme objectives? Does the programme fulfil the objectives more efficiently than alternative means available?

Programme evaluation employs such methodologies as experimental research and cost-benefit analysis, in an effort to produce a quantitative assessment of the degree to which a programme fulfils a particular objective (standard or rule) and a determination (in terms of a comparison of inputs and outputs) of how efficiently the objective is fulfilled (typically measured as a ratio of costs to benefits) compared to other possible means.

Contextual discourse: situational validation (objectives)

Validation focuses on whether or not the particular programme objectives are relevant to the situation. Validation is an interpretive process of reasoning that takes place within the frameworks of the normative belief systems brought to bear on the problem situation. It draws in particular on qualitative methods used in sociological or anthropological research.

Organising questions: is the programme objective relevant to the problem situation? Are there circumstances in the situation that require an exception to be made to the objectives? Are two or more criteria equally relevant to the problem situation?

Level: second order evaluation
Systems discourse: societal vindication (goals)

At the second order level, the logic of policy deliberation shifts from first to second order evaluation, that is, from the concrete situational context to the societal system as a whole. In vindication, the basic task is to show that a policy goal from which specific programme objectives were drawn addresses a valuable function for the existing societal arrangements. It is organised around the following questions:

Organising questions: does the policy goal have instrumental or contributing value to the society as a whole? Does the policy goal result in unanticipated problems with important societal consequences (for example, benefits and costs that are judged to be equitably distributed?) Does a commitment to the policy goals lead to consequences (for example, benefits and costs) that are judged to be equitably distributed?

Ideological discourse: social choice (values)
The fourth and final discursive phase of the logic of policy deliberation turns to ideological and value questions. Social choice seeks to establish and examine the selection of a critical basis for making rationally informed choices about societal systems as a whole and their respective ways of life.

Organising question: do the fundamental ideals (or ideology) that organise the accepted social order provide a basis for a legitimate resolution of conflicting judgements?

If the social order is unable to resolve basic value conflicts, do other social orders equitably prescribe for the relevant interests and needs that the conflicts reflect?

Do normative reflection and empirical evidence support the justification and adoption of an alternative ideology and the social order it prescribes?

5.8 Policy monitoring
Before concluding this chapter, we spend some time reflecting on public policy monitoring. Much of the discussion on public policy evaluation

applies as much to monitoring, the only difference being that, as noted earlier in this chapter, policy monitoring is much more of a periodic activity than evaluation.

Monitoring is the routine measurement and reporting of programme operations. There can be many benefits of programme monitoring (Morse and Struyk 2006). These include early detection and correction of performance problems, staff management, identification of more efficient use of resources, securing accountability to external stakeholders, and developing a commitment to improve performance and building confidence among staff. Monitoring serves as some means of securing mid-course corrections.

Successful monitoring follows from a clear understanding of what the policy or programme is trying to accomplish, with what resources, and through which activities. For effective monitoring, it is important that each important programme function be reduced to specific indicators.

Types of policy monitoring

There can be different types of indicators for monitoring programmes. They can be grouped into four basic types, namely, inputs, outputs, outcomes and efficiency. Measuring *inputs* means measuring the quantity of resources used. Measuring *outputs* means measuring the quantity of service provided. Monitoring *outcomes* means measuring the effect and/or result of the programme on its clients or beneficiaries. Measuring *efficiency* means comparing outputs or outcomes produced to inputs used.

Further, monitoring could be done for programme implementation, quality of services delivered, financial management or client and citizen satisfaction. Further, there can be different levels of monitoring: monitoring departmental functions or small programmes, monitoring citywide or regional programmes, or sectoral monitoring, in which we are interested in monitoring the performance of a certain sector.

Designing a monitoring system

Several points need to be borne in mind in designing a monitoring system: First and foremost, what is being monitored should be clearly defined and the measures should be consistent from one period to the next. Second, monitoring is routine. To be useful as a managerial tool, monitoring must be done frequently and at regular intervals. Data and monitoring are not the same; monitoring implies a careful selection and presentation of data that is used to identify problems or success. Presenting monitoring findings to the public and other stakeholders makes the programme more accountable; when the results are positive, this can help build support for programme activities or budget needs.

There are several steps in monitoring a programme: understanding the programme (modelling – model inputs, activities, outputs and outcomes), data collection and reporting, assembling and maintaining data, developing action plans, presenting findings to decision-makers and presenting findings to the public.

Much like the process of public policy evaluation, monitoring is also about control and the exercise of power. It requires not simply data collection but also decisions about what action will be taken if performance deviates from what is desired. Just as we studied the political nature of public policy evaluation, monitoring is also a political activity.

5.9 Conclusion

In this chapter, we have reviewed important issues surrounding the evaluation and monitoring of public policy. We started by reviewing the rationale and objectives of public policy evaluation and distinguished between different types of public policy evaluation. We looked at different approaches that may be adopted for the evaluation of public policies and the problems that policy-makers may encounter in this process. We examined how public policy evaluation is a political activity, rather than an objective, value-neutral activity carried out using a set of tools and techniques to precision. We introduced the approach of practical deliberation that transcends the technical-analytic discourse and facilitates the evaluation of public policy within its wider social and political context.

The important questions that policy-makers need to ask themselves at various stages of the policy process are: first, what is it that we wish to monitor and evaluate and why; and, second, what combination of approaches shall give us the most balanced and objective assessment of what we wish to evaluate. Finally, an important issue is how policy-makers use the results of policy evaluation processes and how effectively they are employed as inputs into the policy-making process. In terms of the analysis in the opening chapter of the book, the issue is: how does analysis 'of' policy become useful as analysis 'for' policy?

References

Arora, R. K. 2008. 'Leadership and collective Action – A case study in common property resources management in Haryana.' P. G. Diploma dissertation, Management Development Institute, Gurgaon.

Dye, T. R. 2002. *Understanding Public Policy*. Tenth edition. Delhi: Pearson Education.

Fischer, F. 1995. *Evaluating Public Policy*. Wadsworth: Thomson.

Grumm, John G. 1975. 'The Analysis of Policy Impact.' In *Handbook of Political Science, Vol. 6*, edited by Greenstein, F. and Polsby, N., 439–473. Reading, Mass.: Addison Wesley.

Hogwood, B. A. and Gunn, L. A. 1984. *Policy Analysis for the Real World*. Oxford: Oxford University Press.

Morse, K. and Struyk, R.J. 2006. *Policy Analysis for Effective Development. Strengthening transition economies*. New Delhi: TERI Press.

Narain, V. 2003. 'Water Scarcity and Institutional Adaptation: Lessons from Four Case Studies.' In *Environmental Threats, Vulnerability and Adaptation: case studies from India*. 107–120. New Delhi: TERI Press.

Neuman, W. L. 1995. *Social Research Methods: Qualitative and Quantitative Approaches*. Third edition. Massachusetts Allyn and Bacon.

Taylor, D. and Bulloch, S. 2005. 'Introduction. The Politics of Evaluation: An Overview.' In *The Politics of Evaluation. Participation and Policy Implementation*, edited by D. Taylor and S. Bulloch, 1–20. Bristol: The Policy Press.

Wholey, J. S., Hattry, H. P., and Newcomer, K. E. eds. 2004. *Handbook of Practical Program Evaluation*. Second edition. San Francisco: John Wiley and Sons.

Index